D1506253

The
Fiery Angel

The
Fiery Angel

*Art, Culture, Sex, Politics, and the
Struggle for the Soul of the West*

Michael Walsh

ENCOUNTER BOOKS
New York • London

First American edition published in 2018 by Encounter Books,
an activity of Encounter for Culture and Education, Inc.,
a nonprofit, tax exempt corporation.
Encounter Books website address: www.encounterbooks.com

Manufactured in the United States and printed on
acid-free paper. The paper used in this publication meets
the minimum requirements of ANSI/NISO Z39.48–1992
(R 1997) (*Permanence of Paper*).

FIRST AMERICAN EDITION

LIBRARY OF CONGRESS CATALOGING-IN-PUBLICATION DATA
Names: Walsh, Michael, 1949– author.
Title: The fiery angel : art, culture, sex, politics,
and the struggle for the soul of the West / by Michael Walsh.
Description: New York : Encounter Books, 2018. |
Includes bibliographical references and index.
Identifiers: LCCN 2017054145 (print) | LCCN 2018007596 (ebook) |
ISBN 9781594039461 (ebook) | ISBN 9781594039454 (hardcover : alk. paper)
Subjects: LCSH: Arts—Political aspects. | Arts and history. |
Civilization, Western.
Classification: LCC NX180.P64 (ebook) | LCC NX180.P64 W45 2018 (print) |
DDC 709—dc23
LC record available at https://lccn.loc.gov/2017054145

Interior page design and composition: BooksByBruce.com

For Julianne Shinto

Contents

INTROIBO

Fire comes and the news is good,
It races through the streets
But is it true? Who knows?
Or just another lie from heaven?
—Aeschylus, *Agamemnon*, from the *Oresteia*, 458 B.C.,
translation by Robert Fagles

In the name of the blessed and Holy Trinity, I do desire thee, strong and mighty angels (*here name the spirits you would have appear*) that if it be the divine will of him who is called Tetragrammaton, &c. the holy God, the Father, that thou take upon thee some shape as best becometh thy celestial nature, and appear to us visibly here in this place, and answer our demands, in as far as we shall not transgress the bounds of the divine mercy and goodness, by requesting unlawful knowledge; but that thou wilt graciously shew us what things are most profitable for us to know and do to the glory and honour of his divine Majesty who liveth and reigneth, world without end. *Amen.*

—Francis Barrett, *The Magus*, 1801

And the voice from above slowly repeated:—Accursed one! Around you the suns shall die out.—And already the sun was nothing but a star.

And everything was slowly disappearing under a veil. The archangel became faint-hearted; Satan shuddered. He sprang towards the star that flickered, pale, on the horizon, Leaping from one peak to another...

He ran, he flew, he cried out:—Golden star! Brother! Wait for me! I am coming! Do not die out yet! Do not leave me alone!—

And the archangel understood that, like a sinking ship's mast, He was drowning in a flood of darkness; He folded his wings with their talons of stone, Wrung his hands, and the star died out.

—Victor Hugo, *La Fin de Satan* (1886), translation by R. G. Skinner

The original bond between the linguistic and mythico-religious consciousness is primarily expressed in the fact that all verbal structures

ix

appear as also mythical entities, endowed with certain mythical powers, that the Word, in fact, becomes a sort of primary force, in which all being and doing originate. In all mythical cosmogonies, as far back as they can be traced, this supreme position of the Word is found.

—Ernst Cassirer, *Sprache und Mythos* (1946), translation by Susanne K. Langer

Where's the Poet? Show him! Show him,
Muses nine! That I may know him!
'Tis the man who with a man
Is an equal, be he King
Or poorest of the beggar-clan
Or any other wondrous thing…

—John Keats, "The Poet" (A Fragment) (1818)

Les pierres du chantier ne sont en vrac qu'en apparence, s'il est, perdu dans le chantier, un homme, serait-il seul, qui pense cathédrale. ("The stones of a construction site are only an apparent jumble, if there is, lost on the site, a man, be he alone, who thinks, Cathedral.")

—Antoine de Saint Exupéry, *Pilote de Guerre* (Flight to Arras, 1942)

Despair I will not, while I yet descry…
That lonely Tree against the western sky…
Let in thy voice a whisper often come,
To chase fatigue and fear:
Why faintest thou? I wander'd till I died.
Roam on! the light we sought is shining still.

—Matthew Arnold, "Thyrsis," (1865), as set to music by Ralph Vaughan Williams in *An Oxford Elegy* (1952)

J'ai seul la clef de cette parade sauvage.

—Rimbaud, "Parade," from *Illuminations* (1886)

Enguerrand de Monstrelet, "The Battle of Agincourt,"
from the *Chronique de France, ca.* 1400–44

Into the West

Once more unto the breach

S ince the publication of *The Devil's Pleasure Palace* in 2015, the
necessity of restoring Western culture to its proper place in our
understanding of ourselves has only become more urgent. The prolonged assault on our common culture—European-American, for want
of a broader, more inclusive description—has intensified, propelled by a
burning hatred for a civilization that extends from the ancient Greeks to
modern Americans and has been responsible for most of the world's artistic, technological, and moral progress for three millennia. Indeed, even to
rise to its defense at this imperiled moment has become controversial—a
measure of just how deep the animosity in civilization's enemies runs.

Whence comes this hatred for the West? The simple but sorry answer is: from ourselves—or at least from a significant segment of the population that has fallen under the spell of what I have termed the "satanic," or cultural-Marxist, Left. Since at least the mid-nineteenth century, Marxists have waged a battle for the soul of the West (for civilizations also have souls, spirits, umbras, penumbras, Zeitgeists) not merely through politics, but through artistic and political philosophy. Sprung from the high brows of Rousseau and Hegel, these demon Athenas were made flesh in the forms of Karl Marx and, later, the Marxist collective known as the Frankfurt School, whose animus toward the West I treated at some length in *Devil*.

In that book, I undertook to show how the Heroic Narrative lies at the heart of Western civilization, antedating even organized religion as a means of explaining ourselves to ourselves, and forming the foundation of the modern nation-state. The eternal battle between good and evil—symbolized by and given both literary and religious form in the figures of "God" and "Satan"—involves all aspects of the human experience, including our laws, mores, sexual relationships, our interactions with one another, and the body politic itself. It's a battle that rages still.

As tools of analysis I chose two principal touchstones of our shared artistic heritage, Milton's *Paradise Lost* and Goethe's *Faust*, and discussed a great many other works (novels, poetry, plays, movies, operas, paintings) along the way in order to illustrate my thesis that the arts most potently embody this struggle, and it is through an understanding of them—an understanding of the human soul—that we can best address the political issues that plague us.

To those who queried whether, in engaging men like Herbert Marcuse, Theodor Adorno, and their colleagues, I was seriously arguing that the writings and teachings of a handful of central-European academics with Dr. Strangelove accents had had a significant effect on both Europe and America, my answer is: yes. *"La plus belle des ruses du diable est de vous persuader qu'il n'existe pas,"* wrote Charles Baudelaire in his prose poem "The Generous Gambler" ("Le joueur généreux," in *Le spleen de Paris* (1862))—a line better known to the general public from the mouth of Verbal Kint (Kevin Spacey) in Christopher McQuarrie's script for the 1995 movie *The Usual Suspects*, when he observes: "The greatest trick the devil ever pulled was convincing the world he didn't exist."

Largely through their creation of "Critical Theory," which posited that everything about Western society must be questioned and, when possible, destroyed, these devils have continued to plague us; their names may be largely unknown, but their influence has been incorporated into just about every "progressive" program, notion, and social-justice act of war against Western civilization and the United States of America we today encounter. Norms are to be overturned, in part because they *are* norms, and in part because they are, to the Left, manifestly the result of some sort of bigoted plot, hatched as early as the dawn of time, and fiendish in its execution—a plot, in their telling, directed against a persecuted minority of misfits and outliers down through the millennia. In other words, themselves.

In fairness, part of the Frankfurters' justifiable and profound animus and anomie (a deadly combination recalling the old saw "an idle mind is the devil's playground") emerged in the aftermath of World War I. This calamity, the greatest in our civilization's history, made all the greater by its stupidity, slaughter, and senselessness, structurally altered almost everything about the West. Although it was not fully recognized at the time, the deaths of millions of young, able-bodied men—often the best and the brightest, the most romantic and most patriotic of their day—robbed Europe not only of their promise, but of their progeny as well.

At a time when abortion was illegal and designer children were unknown, people mourned their dead, said "never again," and got on with their lives. But so many lives that might have been never were. A visit to any World War I cemetery reveals not only a place of peace—the German word, *Friedhof*, is apposite—but a mute reproach to the hordes of childless Europeans who wander through them, searching for some long-lost relative and wondering just what the hell it was he died for.

And yet, this uncertainty about our past, our present, and our future, is the essence of the Western way of life; our notion of "progress" derives from testing and trying often-antithetical propositions and methods, weighing them in theory and in practice, and then deciding which, if any, works. Despite the towering influence of Christianity on post-Roman civilization, it is not, as critics would have it, dogmatic. In other cultures, there are some questions that should not be answered, cannot be answered, must not be answered. Indeed, there are some—many—questions that may not even be asked.

Not in the West—not, at least in the West of freedom of speech, freedom of thought, freedom of inquiry, freedom to give and take offense, freedom to put every civilizational theorem to the test (a freedom exploited by the Frankfurters, who turned that very freedom against the larger culture), a freedom to engage the world and, if and when necessary, challenge God himself on this throne. As John Milton wrote in his *Areopagitica* (1644): "Give me the liberty to know, to utter, and to argue freely according to conscience, above all liberties." Our task is to have the courage to keep asking, even as wisdom sometimes lies in acceptance of an answer we can neither hear nor fully understand. Of such conundrums are religions fashioned, promulgated, and believed.

Today, all of these freedoms, whether constitutional or traditional, are under attack, often in the guise of "real" freedom—freedom from hurt feelings, from a "hostile" environment, or a perceived slight due entirely to the *soi-disant* victim's poor vocabulary, lack of historical knowledge, unfamiliarity with cultural references, or simple stupidity. These attacks generally come from within the Western cultural perimeter, from people who should know better, but who have chosen to align themselves with the West's external enemies—primarily, recrudescent Islam—so as to better function as morale-sapping fifth columnists passing as friends. Wielding the words "bigotry" and "racism" as talismans, they attempt to destroy Western culture by leveraging the American Civil Rights Movement into an all-purpose battering ram against the walls of Athens, Jerusalem, Rome, Paris, London, and New York City.

What do we mean by "the West"? For the purposes of our discussion, let us stipulate that what we call the West today originated with what used to constitute Latin Christendom, which is to say, the western Roman Empire after Constantine at the beginning of the fourth century, which drew upon the classical roots of ancient Greece and the Judeo-Christian principles of the followers of Christ to create something new and vital in world history. It continued with the Holy Roman Empire of Charlemagne and his successors and pretenders through the French Revolution, and comprises modern Europe today from Iceland and Ireland to the Balkans and, to a certain extent, European Russia. Since the eighteenth century, "the West" has also included, in whole or in part, the Western-looking Orthodox countries of Eastern Europe, as well as Europe's principal colonies in the Americas, Australia, New

Zealand, and, formerly, South Africa. It today includes—and this is crucial—non-European and non-Christian countries such as India, postwar
Japan, South Korea, Israel, and once even numbered Iran and Turkey
during their secularized incarnations.

In sum, despite its beginnings on the European continent, the West
and its nation-states share several characteristics, among them political
legitimacy, territorial integrity, language, and, generally, a common religion or faith tradition. Despite the attempts by the cultural Marxists and
radical Islamists to label the West "racist," it is anything but; indeed, not
since the Roman or British Empires at their apexes has there been such
a blend of peoples and places, united through peaceful relations, trade,
the *lingua franca* of English, and the at-least-notional idea of personal
and individual freedom within the framework of a nation-state. There are
differences aplenty, to be sure—Russia's relationship with the West has
always been fraught—but what unites the West today is not only a shared
past but a shared sense of resolve for the future.

If a future there is to be. As Samuel Huntington notes in *The Clash of
Civilizations* (1996):

> The survival of the West depends on Americans reaffirming their
> Western identity and Westerners accepting their civilization as
> unique not universal and uniting to renew and preserve it against
> challenges from non-Western societies. Avoidance of a global war
> of civilizations depends on world leaders accepting and cooperating
> to maintain the multicivilizational character of global politics.... In
> the post–Cold War world, the most important distinctions among
> peoples are not ideological, political, or economic. They are cultural.

This is a hard truth to accept, as well as a truth often denied by those
who persist in peddling the notion of relative worth and cultural inter-
changeability, as if that abstract concept were a) true, b) possible, or c)
desirable. To do so, the cultural Marxists and their fellow-travelers (to
put it in loaded terms they can understand) have adopted a bastardized
form of Judeo-Christianity as a disguise, offering "universality" as the
teleological end of the "arc of history." Don't be fooled.

Anti-religious to a man, the learned doctors of the Goethe University
in Frankfurt could not accept the notion of unanswerability—that some

things were beyond human ken and therefore had to be taken on faith. Their response, therefore, was an anti-philosophy: Critical Theory applied to what these intelligent but profoundly mistaken men thought were the fruits of their own ratiocination—but were in fact their own daemonic, and despotic, emotions. So it is with their philosophy, not their political principles (which are evanescent and changeable, according to their quotidian tactics), that we must deal. And that philosophy was birthed in rage.

Rage is one of the strongest and most destructive of human emotions. We see it in everyone from frustrated toddlers to the window-smashing anarchists and jihadi "lone wolves" now infesting the streets of the West. It is a response to anger and frustration and hostility, but mostly it is a reaction to impotence, the inability to materially change or affect an outcome, and to the enrageds' certain if unexpressed knowledge that their opponents are, to use another of their terms, on the wrong "side of history." This Marxist notion—that history has "sides"—should alone dispel the appeal of the destructive argument, such as it is.

Can a political philosophy be based on rage and destruction? The most famous *enragé* in Western history is Achilles. Indeed, *The Iliad* opens with Homer's invocation of the Muse to begin his epic tale, in the 1990 translation by Robert Fagles:

> *Rage—Goddess, sing the rage of Peleus's son, Achilles,*
> *murderous, doomed, that cost the Achaeans countless losses,*
> *Hurling down to the House of Death so many sturdy souls,*
> *Great fighters' souls, but made their bodies carrion,*
> *Feasts for the dogs and birds,*
> *And the will of Zeus was moving toward its end.*
> *Begin, Muse, when the two first broke and clashed,*
> *Agamemnon lord of men and brilliant Achilles.*
>
> *What god drove them to fight with such a fury?*
> *Apollo the son of Zeus and Leto. Incensed at the king*
> *He swept a fatal plague through the army—men were dying*
> *And all because Agamemnon spurned Apollo's priest.*

It is not the rage of Achilles, however, that wins the Trojan War, but rather the determination of the Greeks and the wiles of Ulysses (whose ulterior motive is, let us keep in mind, his desire to get home to his wife, Penelope—not to save the honor of the House of Atreus) that ultimately collapse the topless towers of Ilium. Achilles' anger avenges the death of Patroclus, but his desecration of Hector's body condemns many more warriors on both sides to prolonged fighting and dying. As I wrote in *Devil:* "Rage is the salient characteristic of Satan and of the satanic in men." Whether you choose to take Satan as a reality, a literary construct, or a bogeyman is up to you, but anyone who has ever watched a fellow human being in the throes of an uncontrollable rage cannot help but feel a supernatural power at work.

Fortunately, defenders of the West and of its prized and precious culture—cherishable all the more in the face of the continuing assault against it by both Marxists and Muslims—are well-equipped to combat the influence of the enraged. Our armory is to be found precisely where contemporary philosophers and politicians are loath to look: in the artistic roots of Western culture and civilization. Thus we turn to them again and again in time of need. Homer has more to teach us about governance than Harvard, and always will.

In an age of categorical specialization, one is tempted to view history as occurring in a vacuum—that is, a succession of geo-political events, some causal, some random, that add up to an imperfect narrative of the human species. A cultural Marxist might go further, and explain history via the means of Hegelian dialectic, the conflict of opposing world-histor-ical forces, and propound its obeisance to certain "scientific" laws in some sort of discernable "arc." A fatalist would say that all is predestination, and any struggle useless.

In none of these worldviews is the place of man paramount, or even particularly significant. Indeed, in each, the human species is reduced, as in Macbeth's celebrated image, to that of mere players, strutting and fretting their way to dusty death, wholly unable to affect the iron laws of destiny. Hence, both Western science and Marxist determinism have turned inward, becoming culturally acceptable forms of navel-gazing, viewing humanity as acted-upon, rather than as actors—pinned butterflies in a lepidopterist's collection rather than free-winged creatures born to fly.

But what evidence do we have that any of this is true? None, except an argument from authority. That basic logical fallacy, however, is obscured by our own reluctance to re-embrace the wellsprings of our culture and to re-connect with its symbols—the arts, which have guided both man and his history since long before the advent of organized religion, scientific principles, or any of the totalitarian heresies in evidence from the seventh to the twenty-first centuries.

The word "norms" has become a much-derided term, as if our culture's traditions and standards were something arbitrarily imposed, rather than having grown organically from history, evolution, and the nature of the people sharing them. The derision originated in the teachings of Herbert Marcuse et al. in American and European universities beginning the 1960s, and was amplified by the coming-of-age of their intellectual charges, the Baby Boomers, who were infused with the revolutionary spirit through appeals to their innate kindness, their youthful desire to right perceived wrongs, and their lack of sophistication and experience in dealing with life as it actually was, rather than as they supposed it should be.

It's no accident that this period in American educational history also saw the first uprising against such concepts as a "core curriculum," reading lists, Western Civ courses, and the notion of the "Great Books," developed and popularized starting in 1952 by the philosopher Mortimer Adler at the University of Chicago in conjunction with the Encyclopedia Britannica. Homer, Plato, Aristotle, the Greek historians Herodotus and Thucydides, Euclid, Archimedes, Virgil, Augustine, Aquinas, Dante, Chaucer, Rabelais, Montaigne, Shakespeare, Cervantes, Bacon, Descartes, Newton—this was the curriculum. Yet no sooner were these collected works, issued first in fifty-four volumes and running through William James and Sigmund Freud, codified in the Western intellectual canon, then they were almost immediately stigmatized by cultural Marxists as a relic of "bourgeois culture."

The modern European (and, by extension, the American) nation-state arose on the basis of a shared culture: language, music and musical style, art, drama. These things were formative, essential—not ornamental. In our time, "the arts" are regarded as something essentially frivolous—a snooty subsection of "entertainment," perhaps, or the playgrounds and playthings of the rich, an innocent way for the elites to pass the time and spend their money, when they're not otherwise further impoverishing the already poor. But that is our time's problem—and the origin of so much spiritual unhappiness in a world whose favorite response to sentiment with which it does not agree is a sneer.

And yet play, players, and playing are essential to any culture: all the world's a stage, and not only to Shakespeare. We cannot understand the nature of a people or a civilization merely by its transient politics; we must also delve into its art, myths, stories, legends, and songs. As the Dutch cultural historian Johan Huizinga (who died in 1945, a prisoner of National Socialist Germany) observed in his seminal work *Homo Ludens* (1938):

> In singular imagery the thought comes back again in the Book of Proverbs, where Wisdom says: "The Lord possessed me in the beginning of his ways, before he made any thing from the beginning. I was set up from eternity, and of old before the earth was made.... I was with him forming all things: and was delighted every day, playing before him at all times; playing in the world. And my delights were to be with the children of men."

Not to understand culture, therefore, is not to understand history, and thus to be disarmed in the greatest fight in which Western culture has ever been collectively engaged: the struggle for its soul. Even in the darkest days of World War II, the question was not whether Western culture, in the corrupted form of the Third Reich, would survive; had the National Socialists won in Europe, there would still have been recognizable works of literature, art galleries, symphony halls, and opera houses, however censored or misappropriated for ideological purposes. That is not obviously true of the utopia envisioned by today's civilizational enemies, whether of the Stalinist or Islamic variety, who pull down monuments, destroy representational art, and outlaw music in the name of "social justice" or Musselman revelation.

That we appear increasingly defenseless against this barbarism is distressing but explicable. One of the West's chief defects is not physical poverty (the focus of so much Marxist thought in the late nineteenth and early twentieth centuries), but spiritual penury (the focus of so much Marxist enterprise today). Forget Christianity: the West no longer even believes in procreation, which is a physical manifestation of its loss of faith in its own cultural ideals and their superiority to all others. Those ideals, however, are still on display and readily available, in the form of what we call today the "fine arts"—which are not the exclusive province of the "elites," but rather of the entire polis, from whom they stemmed in the first place.

Virgil's great epic poem, *The Aeneid*, may have begun as a tribute to the Emperor Augustus, but it quickly became the property of every Roman, as it is today part of the intellectual and spiritual patrimony of every Italian. Far from being un- or anti-democratic, the arts express the nature of the people who gave them birth. To lose them is to lose the "Nation" part of the nation-state and leave only the State. Which is, of course, precisely the goal of the cultural-Marxist project.

Further, while all cultures are worth studying and perhaps, in part, emulating and borrowing from, Western culture has enjoyed its dominance precisely because of its expressive and adaptive superiority. For it alone celebrates the individual over the collective—a radical cultural notion, arising in Greece and gradually expanding via the Roman Empire and Christian Rome into the most important cultural force of the post-Enlightenment world—one that exhibits the superiority of the linguistically and culturally unified nation-state as the foundation of moral, intellectual, and civilizational progress. Will it be superseded by other arrangements—perhaps better, perhaps worse? That is for the future, which is to say, us and the progeny we must have, to decide—if only we have the cultural confidence to do so.

To be sure, culture is not synonymous with high culture; the modern usage of the word is a corruption, not a definition. But what we have come to know as the arts nonetheless form the basis of the larger culture; they are not simply tail fins on the turbocharged chassis of the nation-state. While the arts often have been subsidized and supported by the ruling classes, they spring from the soul of the people—few great artists have emerged from the aristocracy—and have just as often been supported and celebrated by them, which is why they vary in style and substance from nation to nation and from culture to culture. When we speak in general of a "Judeo-Christian" culture, or a "European" culture, what we mean in particular is a Germanic, or Latinate, or British, or American culture, subsumed under the larger umbrellas of ethnicity and geography.

The fact is that the arts and politics, therefore, are not only closely related, but that the one (politics) grows out of the other (the arts). The artistic—moral—ideas of the day quickly find their way into, and often out of, politics, and thus affect the course of history, century by century, era by era, epoch by epoch.

In his scholarly 1987 jeremiad against the state of higher education in America, *The Closing of the American Mind*, Allan Bloom—a translator of both Plato and Rousseau—had this to say:

> The lack of American equivalents to Descartes, Pascal, or, for that matter, Montaigne, Rabelais, Racine, Montesquieu, and Rousseau is not a question of quality, but of whether there are any writers who are necessary to building our spiritual edifice, whom one must have read, or rather lived with, to be called educated, and who are the interpreters and even makers of our national life.... A phenomenon like Wagner's *Gesamtkunstwerk*, a high work of art which is intended to be wholly German, of Germans, for Germans, and by Germans, and is an expression of collective consciousness, is inconceivable to Americans.

This is both criticism and recommendation on Bloom's part. The American sense of culture is not that of nation-state Europe, whose art is inseparable from the languages in which it was conceived and executed. Nobody who did not learn French as a child, in France, is fully capable of speaking French properly—especially to the French, who regard their language and its correct usage and pronunciation as a signifier. Before mass immigration from the *ummah*, particularly North Africa, the French also used it as a way of distinguishing Frenchmen from foreigners; this attitude is now their cultural Achilles' heel. Nevertheless, as Enlightenment Britain's most spectacularly successful colonists, Americans can claim an intellectual patrimony that is not just English in origin, but Continental. We used to partake freely and enthusiastically of it, but the lamentable state of "higher education" today means that, except in the study of the applied sciences, learning is often simply indoctrination in the principles of cultural Marxism, its reading list a chronicle of grievances that puts Martin Luther's ninety-five demands in the shade. Today's college-"educated" radicals are more likely (and sadly only able) to nail a bag of feces than theses to the church door.

Lest the reader think we are now embarking on a *tour d'horizon* of artistic history, he is both right and wrong. Plenty of works of art will make an appearance in these pages. Some will be familiar to any educated reader, others are more obscure; all of them a civilized Westerner should know. And, yes, the list is prescriptive. Yet there is a through-line that connects them all: each, in some way, explicates the human condition through the medium of *storytelling*—and each of the stories resonates across cultures in the human breast, where the heart resides. The worldwide dominance of Western culture, and the widespread adoption of English as a global means of communication, came about precisely because it most ably has told its story, and made available the tangible technological, medical, military, and artistic results to peoples the world over.

You will encounter a lot about music in these pages, more than is usual in a book of this kind, but in such a way that I hope will challenge and stimulate the novice to learn more about it; and to present a new way of encountering the art form to the connoisseur or expert. My own background in classical music is naturally a part of this, as is my wonderment that music, of all the arts, has seen its cultural influence so diminished. Until relatively recently, the great works of musical art—everything from string quartets and piano sonatas to choral symphonies and grand operas—were part of each country's sense of national identity, with the power to provoke discussion, cause riots, and (as Verdi did) unify a nation. It seems amazing today that Mozart's desire to elevate German as a proper language for opera, or the determination of the Czech nationalist composers, such as Antonín Dvořák and Leoš Janáček, to establish the Czech language on an equal footing with German in nineteenth-century Prague, would excite so much controversy. And yet both events had a profound outcome on the political life of the time.

For the squeamish, a brief word about what is meant by the dreaded word, "opera," and what is not. Opera is not about fat people singing, fans hurling bouquets of flowers, gnostic discussions about the relative merits of this or that performer (living or dead), or about which versions of, say, Verdi's *Don Carlos* or Mussorgsky's *Boris Godunov* or Beethoven's *Leonore/Fidelio* are artistically preferable. Rather, I mean the work itself (the word *opera* is simply the plural of *opus*, and means "works"), the highest form of the Western musical theater that began with Claudio Monteverdi in the seventeenth century as a classicizing attempt to reconnect with the theater's Greek roots. Instead of opera, think of it instead as "the works."

An author can generally count on a literate audience to be familiar with the principal cultural totems of the West: the poetry, plays, and novels of Milton and Shakespeare and Dickens and all the other great British writers, and the works of Continental and Latin American authors in translation; with the American authors and poets of the nineteenth and twentieth centuries; with the great works of visual art from the Italian Renaissance through the end of the Romantic Era and into the last century; and with the whole international genre of American, European, Japanese and Indian cinema of the past century or so.

But with music...not so much. There was a time when musical literacy was prized every bit as much as any other kind. There was a time when every American could both whistle "Dixie" and have a pretty good idea of what Beethoven's Fifth Symphony or Liszt's "Hungarian Rhapsody No. 2" sounded like (all you had to do was watch Disney and Warner Bros. cartoons). Once, not very long ago, musical education was the pride of the New York City school system. That time is, alas, gone, Mozart having been replaced by metal detectors. One of my goals in this and the prior volume, has been to encourage the reader to fill in the cultural lacunae in his or her own knowledge and, it is to be hoped, to introduce younger generations not only to the joys of music—deriving joy from musical expression is an essential part of the human experience—but also to its spiritual, emotional, cultural, and political significance.

This, therefore, is a book about finding our way back home, to those first principles, those essentials, which Marcus Aurelius so memorably advocated in Book VIII of the *Meditations* [translation by Maxwell Staniforth]: "Ask yourself, What is this thing in itself, by its own special constitution? What is it in substance, and in form, and in matter? What is its function in the world? For how long does it subsist?"

It is not a book about ephemeral political issues or policy points. Indeed, it is not a book about politics per se, but a book about the arts, and how they adumbrate, influence, and reflect, politics. At the same time, neither is it a book about the arts per se, but a book about politics, and how they are the mirror and instigator and disciple of what is written, printed, sung, filmed, danced, and orchestrated. They are twins—evil twins at times, to be sure—but, in the words of Nietzsche, human, all too human. If Aristotle could write both the *Politics* and the *Poetics* with the same seriousness of intent, and as part of the same world view, maybe we should pay attention.

This volume seeks to illustrate, by means of artistic examples both high and low, an important and rarely remarked-upon truth: that the arts give the lie to the entire cultural Marxist project by recording and revealing timeless—and some particularly timely—truths about human nature.[1] We need not argue that traditional norms, maintained across centuries, are the product of "oppression" or conspiracy: we can experience their fundamental truths in everything from *The Epic of Gilgamesh*, which dates from before 2500 B.C., to the literature, poetry, films, and stage works of our own time. What we find is a remarkable consensus about basic principles of right and wrong; of the proper, if imperfect, relations between the sexes; of the importance of children to the health and future of a culture; of the nature, meaning, and need for heroism. Seen in this light, the entire Marxist-Leftist venture crumbles into dust, in the manner of the Devil's Pleasure Palace at the end of the Franz Schubert opera.

In sum, the arts are not mere reflections of their time, epiphenomena of the economic substructure, as Marx would have it, but hortations and predictions as well. They are vital to our society's health, well-being, and future. With that said, let us now explore their symbiotic correlation, and follow wherever they lead us. For though the path may be at times terrifying, it is the only one open to us if our culture is to survive.

---

[1] I encourage you to read aloud the poetic extracts contained herein. On the tongue, the language will seem more familiar, and the sentiments will be received more directly by the heart.

Caspar David Friedrich, *Wanderer above the Sea of Fog*, 1818

The Unanswered Question

Voices from the past, lessons for the future

When, in the aftermath of World War I, Georg Lukács, one of the fathers of the Frankfurt School, wrote angrily of an *Aufhebung der Kultur*—an overthrowing, or abolition, of Western "*Kultur*" (the word in German has a resonance far beyond its English cognate)—he did so with a bitterness that reflected what any sensible person would have felt contemplating the ruins of empires, and the death of the Romantic dream that had propelled European art, culture, and politics from Goethe on. It was as if all of Germany had turned into a Caspar David Friedrich painting, except that rather than contemplating Nature, or Infinity, or God, the solitary wanderer stares instead into an abyss.

Does he? In the American composer Charles Ives's enigmatic musical essay for strings, woodwind quartet, and solo trumpet *The Unanswered Question*—first paired with *Central Park in the Dark* as *Two Contemplations* (1908)—a lone trumpet insistently poses the "perennial question of

15

existence" in a five-note figuration against a serene string backdrop and an increasingly agitated series of outbursts from the woodwinds, who stand in for us quizzical, quarrelsome mortals. But despite the querulous nature of the woodwinds' chattering argumentation, the chordal strings—the timeless music of the spheres—never waver in whatever cosmic certainty they are expressing, nor does the trumpet cease repeating its relentless *idée fixe*. You can practically hear the piece's three independent strands as background music for the Caspar David Friedrich painting above, but you will listen in vain for an answer.

In one sense, *Der Wanderer über dem Nebelmeer* (The Wanderer above the Sea of Fog) is a static picture: a solitary man, seen from behind, stands high atop a mountain, dressed in early-nineteenth-century hiking garb, walking stick in hand, and gazing out across an Alpine landscape, its peaks partially obscured by clouds. Ah, but what narrative is contained herein? That the artist leaves up to the viewer to supply: who is this man? How did he get there? Was the ascent arduous? Did he come to find solace or release? One step farther and he must certainly plunge to his death—where does his next step take him?

Now the accumulated cultural resonances kick in: what is going through his mind? Is he Goethe's Werther, sorrowing for his lost Lotte and contemplating suicide, as so many fashionable young men of the period did after reading *The Sorrows of Young Werther* (1774)? Is he a young Schubert or a middle-aged Beethoven, devoted to hiking like all Austrians and Germans, and marching up and down hills to bolster his constitution and fire his inspiration?

One thing we do know, however: this man is the hero of this picture, and we have merely briefly intruded upon his moment of introspection in the face of an awesome Nature whose significance only the mind of man can grasp, for Nature is indifferent to itself. Whatever his future may hold for him, however long or short it may be, he is at this moment the only man in the world, caught by the artist in what is the most important moment of his life.

In this he is alone, but not alone. This man is unique, but he is also one of a thousand, a million heroes who populate our culture from Achilles and Aeneas to the Avengers. Though their stories are all different, their stories are also all the same, and in a particular Western way: they are stories of *individuals*, acting at times in concert, but retaining their own identities. Far from being museum pieces, vestal virgins, or hothouse flowers, segregated from the practical world, the arts ought to be seen instead as the wellsprings of our politics, and therefore should help shape our public-policy debates. They are, in fact, the reason we have public and foreign policies in the first place. Just ask Aristotle and Aristophanes; without them, Greek democracy itself is unthinkable, and Alexander the Great's own heroic narrative—to give one of recorded history's first examples—impossible.

In an age that prizes specialization, we think of public and foreign policy as dispassionate disciplines unto themselves, collectively a kind of "political science" derived from Metternich and Talleyrand and filtered through Woodrow Wilson, carving fresh nations from the carcasses of empires in the hopes of achieving a new stability where chaos had previously reigned. Yet both Europeans were aristocrats (Talleyrand was also a bishop), highly educated, steeped in French and German culture, and devoted to both cultural and self-preservation in tumultuous times. There was nothing bloodless or "scientific" about either.

Consider, for example, the following succession of historical events of the eighteenth century, which I will treat in greater depth later in this book:

Beaumarchais–Mozart–The French Revolution–Beethoven–Napoleon.

Or of the nineteenth:

Count Gobineau–Father Jahn–Wagner–World War I–Communism and National Socialism–Hitler.

The progressions are clear: from *Le Marriage de Figaro* the play, to *Le nozze di Figaro* the opera, to the start of the French Revolution and fall of Louis XVI is a span of only five years, and yet in that time the royal edifice was first lampooned, then sexualized, and finally pulled down around the aristocrats' ears. Those with sensitive antennae—among them Louis XVI himself, who initially forbade public performances of Beaumarchais' play—could see what was coming. Most could not.

In the same way, Arthur, Comte de Gobineau's theories of racial superiority were nationalized by Friedrich Ludwig "Father" Jahn (he was not a priest, but the leader of the physical-culture movement—

Turnbewegung—in Germany, nicknamed *Turnvater*, roughly "father of gymnastics"); dramatized by Wagner (most notably in the tetralogy *Der Ring des Nibelungen*); adopted by Wagner's son-in-law, the Englishman Houston Stewart Chamberlain; and put into practice by Adolf Hitler, who said, "Whoever wants to understand National Socialist Germany must know Wagner." Hitler envisioned himself staging *Die Meistersinger* in the real world, a celebration of "holy German art," but brought only the epic destruction of *Götterdämmerung* instead. From the first deep E-flat pedal tone of *Das Rheingold* (1854) the course of the next century was set; and the world of its creator was doomed.

Since the end of World War II, we have ignored the artistic canary in the coal mine at our peril, in part because we no longer take art seriously—certainly, not as seriously as the Western world took it right up to the First World War: a world in which artists could change the course of history, and a mere ballet like Igor Stravinsky's *The Rite of Spring* could set off a riot in the Théâtre des Champs-Élysées, as it did on May 29, 1913. Fourteen months later, that world disappeared. Even closer to our time, can the triumph of the American Civil Rights Movement be separated from the art that gave it birth, from *Uncle Tom's Cabin* to *To Kill a Mockingbird* to *Guess Who's Coming to Dinner*? Lincoln's famous remark to Harriet Beecher Stowe—"So you're the little woman who wrote the book that made this great war!"—may be, alas, apocryphal, but that does not make it any less true.

If mine sounds like a quasi-Marxist, determinist view of history, it's not. Marx's view of history as a kind of progressive deity (something the contemporary Left still shares) could only be a product of the Romantic era, as Marx himself was. Although Western history should not be read as policy but rather as instructive storytelling—*our* story—its connective tissues are unmistakable, its themes and tropes recurring, its moral structure transparent in its tales of heroes and villains. It is easy to see the moral laws of every previous civilization writ large in its deeds and institutions, and their absence's effect on that same culture's degradation and disintegration. It is only when we get closer to our own time that some monsters still appear in disguise.

Such a monster was, and partly still is, Soviet Communism. Hitler, the Austro/German National Socialist, is rightly anathematized, but Stalin, the Georgian/Russian international Socialist, is not. One is hard pressed to stare into the face of the dying Lenin in his wheelchair and not notice the satanic gaze. "He has his father's eyes," says the evil Roman Castevet in *Rosemary's Baby*, and the same could be said of Lenin. And yet for many in the West, it is still an article of faith that Communism "hasn't really been tried yet," and all that's required is the application of a little good will and a lot of blunt force trauma to make it so.

Once economic Marxism failed—everywhere it was attempted—the anti-Western forces had two choices: to give up or to shape-shift, applying their battering-ram of what became Critical Theory in a different arena. The Russians were a great disappointment to the Marxists, who had assumed History's glorious rebellion against a posited authority would come in Britain or Germany, two of the nation-states most dramatically affected by the Industrial Revolution. When, thanks to the Germans, it was delivered instead to the technologically backward empire of the Romanovs, everyone was surprised except Lenin. Despite History's "iron laws" having been proved false, the comrades altered the theory to suit the facts on the ground, and Marxism-Leninism was born.

It is crucial at this point to understand the nature of the Russian mind and the Slavic soul. Russian rulers saw themselves as the inheritors of Greek Orthodox Church and thus the direct descendants of the Byzantine Empire. Byzantium's fall to the Turks in 1453 was one of the signal disasters for Christian civilization. The eastern empire had survived Imperial Rome for nearly a millennium. It had, in part, launched the Crusades, and theoretically stood to benefit from them, although that did not work out in practice as the Byzantines had hoped. It had been a bulwark against complete Islamic conquest of its territories for centuries. The Russians, with their fixation on Crimea, the Black Sea, and the Dardanelles as their egress to the Mediterranean and thus to Western civilization, are essentially defending old Byzantine turf.

At the same time, though, Russia has long been plagued by an inferiority complex regarding the West. The Russians were adept at pushing the eastern boundaries of their enormous land all the way to the Pacific, settling Siberia at strategic points—Spaso House, the residence of the American ambassador to Russia, was built by a textile merchant who made a fortune there—and exploiting the natural resources of the East, including timber and fur. But the educated upper classes nevertheless had to import their high culture from France and Germany, the languages of which are well-represented in Russian loan-words. The young Peter the

Great lived incognito (as "Pyotr Mikhailov") in Zaandam, Holland, in order to learn the trades of carpenter and shipbuilder, and later imported his advisers from Western Europe as he created the Russian navy and expanded the empire.[1]

Similarly, after World War II, the defeated Japanese came to the conclusion that since the West had beaten them in combat, reduced the Emperor from god to man, and destroyed the Empire of Japan, they should adopt the trappings of the West in an effort to understand the Western mind. They adopted cutlery, donned their *waishatsu* (white shirts) and business suits, and enjoyed performances of Beethoven's Ninth Symphony all across the country on New Year's Eve. So enamored of Beethoven's magnum opus were Japanese engineers that the capacity of the standard compact disc was determined by the playing time—about seventy minutes—of the Ninth.

Now, having culturally appropriated some of the West's distinctive characteristics, including the liberal democracy imposed upon them by General MacArthur during the occupation, how have the Japanese changed? In many ways, they remain the same people the West first encountered during the voyages of discovery, the same people whose country was forcibly opened up to trade and commerce by Commodore Perry in the mid-nineteenth century. The same people who have maintained their own outward cultural traditions in their formal modes of dress, and in the kabuki theater and its music.

They are also different, and in two particularly fundamental ways. The cult of the *bushido* warrior, by which they had defined themselves for centuries, was beaten out of them by the American armed forces during the Pacific War; the cult of the emperor was destroyed in the flames of Hiroshima and Nagasaki. A strongly masculine society, whose excesses drove it to commit appalling atrocities during World War II, was essentially feminized in the conflict's aftermath: war was renounced constitutionally as an instrument of national policy, the armed forces were reduced to defensive status, and the status of women was elevated, both socially and in the workplace.

Comes now the uncomfortable question: is Japan now better or worse off? As a nation? As a people? As a culture?

---

1 This event was commemorated not only by the twin statues in St. Petersburg and Zaandam, but in Albert Lortzing's 1837 comic opera Zar und Zimmerman (Czar and Carpenter).

Consider Japan's current estate. Its young men, avid consumers of the output of the world's most inventive porn industry, have become seemingly uninterested in actual sex; as a result, Japan has entered a demographic death spiral as it becomes a land of asexual old people. Normally, when a culture's young men can't fornicate, they fight. Testosterone has to go somewhere. But Japanese men can neither fight nor, it seems, fuck, and a result the *Nihon-jin* and their country are fated to disappear, like Hemingway's character Mike going bankrupt in *The Sun Also Rises*: gradually and then suddenly.

It's worse than that, however. Unlike Western Europeans, the Japanese allow almost no immigration, and thus they seem perfectly willing to die out, like the samurai at Shiroyama, rather than populate their country with aliens and foreigners and still have it be called "Japan." There's something admirable in that, something self-sacrificial and noble, but it's also utterly baffling. Japanese women are among the most sexually alluring on earth, and Japan's Shinto-based culture does not regard sex in the same restrictive way that the Christian West used to. And yet we are witnessing an historic first: ritual *seppuku* on a national scale. In Western Europe, others will soon follow in Italy, Spain, and Germany, and the smaller countries along Russia's western border, such as Moldova and the Baltic states.

In our politically correct culture—the terminology is a legacy of Trotsky and the Frankfurt School—it is inadvisable to argue in favor of both lethal belligerence and essentially unrestricted heterosexual intercourse. And yet, what other solution is there for Japan? Its constitutional proscription against offensive warfare (which can easily be redefined as defensive warfare—which is how the Japanese justified their surprise attack on Pearl Harbor in 1941) can disappear the minute Japan is assaulted; since 2015, the Japan Self-Defense Forces can assist allies with "material support." At the same time, its birth rate could be elevated by the abolition of abortion, and its sexual dysfunction could be cured by the diminution or eradication of pornography, and the consequent reconnecting of the sex act to certain masculine virtues—such as, well, virility. That such virility was always inherent in Japanese culture should make its restoration feasible.

Russia is in a similar bind, but with an even greater task before it. The Russians were always outmanned in their successful efforts to extend their empire from St. Petersburg to Vladivostok. The United States fits a

population of more than three hundred million quite easily into a country
of 3.8 million square miles; Russia, by contrast, is attempting to control
an area of 6.6 million square miles with a population of less than half of
America's. That something is a near-impossible task has never deterred
the Russians before, in part because their reputation for ferocity—as the
Germans experienced first-hand—cowed their enemies, even as their faith
and historic mission—conservators of Hellenistic Christian culture via the
Orthodox Church—animated their courage. The neo-pagan Germans,
laboring under the National Socialist delusion, were no match from them,
from Stalingrad to Berlin.

Nations that lose their wills soon enough lose their ways. Just ask the
remains of the British Empire, which wavered with the passage of the 1933
Oxford resolution "that this House will in no circumstances fight for its
King and Country" (carried 275–153), and was finally put to rest by Chur-
chill's defeat by Clement Attlee in 1945. Similarly, nations that never, for
various reasons, had much of a will, abandon it quickly enough in the face
of political correctness or the Zeitgeist, whichever comes first. Ireland is
a good example: one of the most oppressed nations on earth enjoyed less
than a century of independence and freedom from the Easter Rising of
1916 to its joining of the European Union in 2009. An enforced history of
forelock-tugging has reduced the Republic to a colony of Brussels, instead
of London.

What's needed now is a new *Gradus ad Parnassum*, a rediscovery of
what got us here in the first place: the way forward. Without an understanding and appreciation of the culture we seek to defend in both domestic and foreign policy, the entire enterprise is fundamentally futile. A
culture that believes in nothing cannot defend itself, for it has nothing to
defend. Not to understand our culture—or, worse, to reject it out of hand
in a rebelliously juvenile manner—is not to understand history, and is not
to understand politics. Which is to say, is not to understand ourselves.

We proceed, then, from the premise that the past not only still has
something to tell us, but it also has something that it *must* tell us, if only
we will listen. That while we stare intently toward the future (the will-o-
the-wisp of the Left), it is to the past to which we should be listening—for
it alone holds the sum total of the human experience in its dusty, bony
hands. "The past is a foreign country; they do things differently there,"
wrote the British author L. P. Hartley in the opening words of his novel

The Go-Between (1953), made into a memorable 1971 movie by the play-wright/screenwriter Harold Pinter and the director Joseph Losey at the peak of their collaboration.

But is it really? True, it wears funny clothes and ofttimes speaks in deceased cant or embarrassing jargon, spouting long-forgotten catch phrases with little or no meaning in the present. Then again, so did our younger selves. And how foreign do we consider those dapper young fellows and radiant girls to be, even as we age? The past is, as the saying goes, the thing what brung us.

The future is unknown, and always must be, in this temporal sphere. It is also as silent as the tomb—even more silent, in fact, since if we read, and listen to, and observe the artifacts of the past, we can hear them speaking to us. The future has no artifacts: no poems, no symphonies, no paintings, no films, no soaring architecture to both house and inspire. It may have them, someday—but then again, it may not. "Predictions are tough," as Yogi Berra—or maybe Niels Bohr (strange linguistic bedfellows indeed)—famously said, "especially about the future."

Ask the residents of Berlin in 1933 how they imagined their city would look in 1945. Actually, we don't have to ask, because Adolf Hitler and his favorite architect, Albert Speer, provided us with blueprints for the glorious capital of the Thousand-Year Reich, anchored by a great *Volkshalle* without which no self-respecting socialist state would have been complete. By 1986, P. J. O'Rourke would describe it as "a pretty good imitation of Minneapolis." No one would have or could have expected that at the time.

That's the future for you. And yet we choose to woo it, and spurn the centuries gone by to propitiate a fickle, inconstant, and ultimately unknowable lover, when the past, in the form of Calliope, one of the Muses and the goddess of music and dance, is lying seductively right beside us, whispering in our ears, if only we will listen.

Let us listen, then, to the angels of our nature, for better and worse. They have much to tell us.

CHAPTER ONE

The Fiery Angel: Guardian, Herald, Phoenix

The Fiery Angel
From Death, Life—and Vice Versa

In the great Narrative of our existence, angels have been with us as long as the recorded history of humanity. Call them what you will: divine spirits, ghosts, the unseen, celestial creatures who worship at the throne of God, boon companions to various Biblical figures, and even, in the form of the Angel Gabriel, the being who helped Daniel interpret his dreams, the harbinger of both the coming of John the Baptist and the birth of Christ, and who delivered a verse of the Koran to Muhammad.

Angels are both guardians and heralds, connecting us imperfectly in the realm of fantasy or revelation or hallucination to our futures and our fates; the Greek αγγελος and Hebrew *ma'lāk* both literally mean "messenger," delivering dispatches, or warnings, from God. More seen than heard, angels sometimes whisper in our ears at moments of crisis or peril. In his first inaugural address, Abraham Lincoln memorably evoked them at a time of national crisis:

> Though passion may have strained it must not break our bonds
> of affection. The mystic chords of memory, stretching from every
> battlefield and patriot grave to every living heart and hearthstone
> all over this broad land, will yet swell the chorus of the Union, when
> again touched, as surely they will be, by the better angels of our
> nature.

"Better angels," of course, is comparative: better than what? So there must be worse angels as well, cosmologically speaking; fallen angels, if you will. One need not believe, literally, in angels in order to grasp the metaphor, but without a knowledge of them, and their role throughout human history in literature, myth, legend, and scripture, one is hard-pressed to understand or appreciate much of the art of the Christian era.

Angels may be good or bad, then, but almost never are they anything less than dramatic; how could they be otherwise, given their primordial role in the Battle in Heaven (described in *Revelation*), the titanic struggle between the forces of Lucifer, the Light-bringer, and of God, led by his champion, the Archangel Michael? It was Michael who confronted Lucifer and his host—a full third of all the angels in Heaven, according to lore—and sent them hurtling into the Lake of Fire, which is where we find them at the opening of Milton's *Paradise Lost*. At the end of the poem, it is Michael of the flaming sword who banishes Adam and Eve and bars them from re-entering Paradise until their original sin—of wanting to be like God (so very much like Lucifer's sin) by knowing both good and evil—is expiated and expunged by the coming of the Redeemer.

Asexual, angels nonetheless contain erotic theological qualities, if only implicitly. That Gabriel announces two significant pregnancies is in itself fraught with subtext; Raphael is a patron of Christian marriage; and Michael, the hyper-masculine commander of the Heavenly Host, is the archetype for every fearless warrior who's ever lived. But let them fall, as Lucifer fell, and the contained and repressed eroticism bursts forth. Concupiscent demons abound in our literature, from the nocturnal demon lovers, the incubus and succubus, to seductive devils of all descriptions. In fact, they are central to the dark side of the Western narrative, in part because they make such compelling characters and in part because they force us, through art, to face up to our worst impulses and our darkest desires.

One of the most vivid angels in the literature is to be found in Sergei Prokofiev's challenging and chilling opera *The Fiery Angel*, written between 1920 and 1926, but unproduced until 1955, two years after the composer's death.[1] Its raw intensity, its obsessive reliance on a handful of themes (one of them—the first notes of the opera and thus the most important—derives from the opening ostinato of Stravinsky's seminal ballet *The Firebird*, thus instantly linking its never-glimpsed title character with the mythological phoenix), vividly reflects the characters' own sexual obsessions.

And what obsessions they are. Set in the sixteenth-century Rhineland, with a libretto by the composer based on the 1908 novel by the Russian Symbolist poet and author Valery Bryusov, the opera tackles sexual hysteria, conventional morality, black magic, the Inquisition, overwhelming lust, and blind love in the face of constant rejection; along the way, both Faust and Mephistopheles make cameo appearances. Indeed, the full title of Bryusov's novel—based on his own sobering and frustrating experience as a member of a love triangle involving a *femme fatale* named Nina Petrovskaya—is:

> *The Fiery Angel*, or a True Story of the Devil who at Various Times Appeared to an Innocent Virgin in the Shape of a Holy Angel, Luring her to Sinful Actions; of the Ungodly Practices of Magic, Alchemy, Astrology, Cabalistic Art, and Necromancy; of the Trial of the Aforesaid Virgin under the Presidency of his Reverence, the Bishop of Trier; and also of Meetings and Conversations with the Knight and Thrice Doctor Agrippa of Nettesheim, and Doctor Faust, Written by an Eyewitness.

In other words, expect from both novel and opera a symphony of cultural references. In this, we come to one of the strengths of Western culture: its accretionary and syncretic approach to its own existence. Few

---

1 Prokofiev died the same day as Stalin, March 5, 1953, but his passing went unannounced for a time so as not to interfere with the national mourning for the Leader and Teacher.

works of art—just as few political developments—come about or exist in
a vacuum, although the increasingly sterile manner of their study at the
university level would lead an unwary student to think otherwise. One
might object that, at its worst, this is the portmanteau school of artistic
creation, to cram as many references into the chosen form as possible
until it bulges and explodes. But just as Puccini in his mature works often
foreshadowed the musical material of his next opera in the one he was
currently writing, so also do artists from Euripides to the present adumbrate each other. "You have no idea how it feels to hear behind you the
tramp of a giant like Beethoven," complained Brahms, struggling to write
his C minor symphony. But he managed.

This is also, as the reader may have already noticed, my approach in
both this book and its predecessor: by tracing artistic themes and connec-
tions backward through the ages we can, like Hänsel and Gretel, eventually
find our way home—deep in our past, near the origin of species, to coin a
phrase. If Bryusov's novel fired the imagination of an artist of Prokofiev's
stature, it not only must have had some larger cultural resonance but
also have had, inherent in the material, the potential for enlargement and
expansion—another series of signposts on the way into our future, which
is to say, back to our past.

The story involves a knight named Ruprecht, who returns to Germany
from a trip to the Americas and takes temporary lodgings at an inn on the
outskirts of Cologne. The only available room, in the attic, is rude and din-
gy, but Ruprecht has no choice. Curiously, inside the room a connecting
door is nailed tightly shut. To an eerie, trilling orchestral accompaniment
reminiscent of Salome's erotic fixation on the head of John the Baptist in
Richard Strauss's *Salome*, a woman's piteous cries and alarums coming
from behind it cause Ruprecht to break it down—and there stands Renata,
in dishabille and cringing in terror from invisible threat. She immediately
rushes into his arms.

His response: "*Libera me, Domine, de morte aeterna.*" ("Save me, Lord,
from Death eternal," a responsory from the Catholic Office of the Dead).
If you think this all will end badly, you're right.

In a kind of grotesque parody of the first act of Puccini's *La bohème*,
Renata—addressing Ruprecht by name, to his wonderment—immediately pours out her life story: how she was visited as a girl by a fiery angel
named Madiel who protected and nurtured her until the time she turned

sixteen; when she begged the angel to become her lover, he suddenly vanished. Later, she met Count Heinrich, whom she believed to be the living incarnation of her angel Madiel, and they lived together in his castle for one magical year, until he, too, abandoned her. Ever since, she's been tortured by demons.

When Ruprecht makes a romantic overture, the formerly pliant girl suddenly turns cold and spurns him. But he's already lost; even the landlady's insinuation that Renata is a prostitute cannot dissuade him from his physical passion for her. So when Renata suggests they flee the accursed inn and seek the mysterious Heinrich in the city, the suddenly bewitched hero immediately agrees. And demons and spirits and black magic are set loose in the land.

Of course, she won't let him have her; as Ruprecht's sexual frustration mounts, a soothsayer predicts Renata's life will end bloodily. To assist in their quest for Heinrich, Ruprecht and Renata consult a bookseller named Yakov Glock in order to study the black arts, including the kabbalah. Glock leads them to the *magister* magician Agrippa, who informs Ruprecht that true magic lies in the study of science and philosophy. (We can practically smell Faust and Mephisto coming.) But three skeletons in the corner rattle their bones and shout, "You lie!"

In Cologne, where the great cathedral is under construction in the background, Ruprecht and Renata find Heinrich's townhouse and even encounter Heinrich himself, who immediately recoils from the girl in horror, blaming her for seducing him and wishing nothing more to do with her. A vengeful Renata demands that Ruprecht defend her honor by challenging the cad Heinrich to a duel—but then, when he does, she insists that he not injure her fiery angel. Disarmed, Ruprecht is severely wounded and, reverting to her seductive nature, Renata finally tells him she loves him. But when he asks her to marry him, she decides that their relationship is a sin and he a tool of the Devil. Cutting herself with a knife, she bleeds and flees.

Ruprecht is counseled by Faust and Mephistopheles, who have been watching the entire charade. They lead him to a nunnery, in which Renata has taken refuge to seek divine forgiveness. But she's brought her hyper-sexuality with her, and has infected the nuns with it; the cloister is being plagued by supernatural occurrences. An Inquisitor is summoned to effect an exorcism in the dark and dank cellar, but it goes badly. As

Ruprecht, Faust, and Mephisto watch unseen from a hidden gallery above, Renata and the nuns attack the Inquisitor. One of the Inquisitor's men throws open the cellar door, allowing piercing daylight to stream into the room. As the nuns scream in terror, the Inquisitor pinions Renata, declares her guilty of carnal intercourse with Satan, and condemns her to torture and death at the stake.

Wow. It's almost no wonder the opera never got a performance during the composer's lifetime, although that had more to do with Prokofiev's residence in the Soviet Union and the exigencies of production elsewhere in Europe at the time. Still, the opera's extravagant subject matter, its frank depiction of sexuality, its blending of the realistic and the supernatural—as if there were no material difference between them—and its stark musical language (its principal themes are driven by rhythmic ostinatos that ape the characters' psychological obsessions), pretty much ensured that, even in a time when modern opera was being born—Alban Berg's seminal *Wozzeck* was premiered in 1925—*The Fiery Angel* would have a tough time coming into the world.

But, as noted, even something as starkly original as *The Fiery Angel* is not, and could not be, *sui generis.* Its panoply of references and allusions extends in every direction, from its spooky German setting to its Symbolist literary origins, to its early-twentieth-century avant-garde musical language. Unlike Béla Bartók's one-act opera *Bluebeard's Castle, The Fiery Angel* is not a work that seduces and astonishes as it draws the listener into its supernatural environment; rather, it bludgeons its audience into submission with a relentless assault on both the senses and the soul.

This is meant as both a compliment and a recommendation for further study, for this recondite work is a symbol—an *optimistic* symbol—of Western culture. For only in depicting the terrors and wonders of many of our greatest cultural pathologies in our art, are we able to face up to them, and thus face them down.

To begin: this is very much Renata's story. While the elusive Angel Madiel is the title character, and while Ruprecht is the nominal hero, at the end of the opera he can only watch helplessly—unheroically—from the wings for the entire last act (depending on how you count, there are five), while Renata battles her satanic nature and her fate. Defiant to the end, like a female Don Giovanni, she is essentially dragged down to Hell, kicking every cloven-hoofed step of the way. As the Inquisitor pronounces his sentence, the music climaxes on a rising brass fanfare, and then simply stops. We have reached the end of our story, and there is nothing more for anybody to say. Ruprecht's ineffectuality—his *impotence*—one of the opera's subtexts, could hardly be more intensely illustrated; his powerlessness in the face of demon woman is also ours. Camille Paglia, whose understanding of and appreciation for the chthonic is unsurpassed, would have a black-leather-clad field day with Renata.[2]

Who, exactly, is Renata? When we first meet her, she is the crazy lady in the attic, who once met a man…and thought he was an angel. She is possibly a hooker. She is almost certainly possessed by the Devil. She, like Rosemary in Roman Polanski's 1968 film *Rosemary's Baby*, may have had sexual intercourse with Satan. She may be a witch. She is manifestly dangerous, both to herself and any man she encounters. She begins and ends the opera in some form of captivity. She certainly deserves to be locked up, if not tortured and burned alive.

Further: is her story real? Is, in fact, the story we are watching unfold on stage, or reading in Bryusov's novel, even supposed to be real? Are we to believe in its admixture of realism (duels, bloodshed) and the supernatural (talking skeletons, Mephisto)? Of course, it's a fable and an allegory—but what sort of fable? A cautionary tale that violates—or in Ruprecht's case, tries to violate—the third and most important of Nelson Algren's three rules: "Never sleep with a woman whose troubles are worse than your own"? For that matter, is Ruprecht's story real, or simply a gigantic hallucination? A literal-minded age that has lost its capacity for credulous wonder wants to know.

The answer is that it does not matter. The purpose of narrative art is not just to tell a story but also to illuminate the human condition by means of storytelling. Prokofiev and Bryusov have not so much written a story but composed a symphony of allusions; our job as audience members is to decode them, and then decide for ourselves what they mean.

This should also be our approach to our own history, which is not a dusty mausoleum of facts, periodically exhibited for our decreasing edification upon a mortuary slab, but is instead a ripping yarn that, in teaching us about the past, is also instructing us about the present and the future.

---

2 As the author of *Sexual Personae* observed in a 2017 interview in the online magazine *Tablet*: "Too much familiarity may undercut sexual passion. When mystery goes, so does the sizzle."

No wonder the Marxist historians of the Frankfurt School and their descendants made the study of history one of their prime targets, framing
the events of the past within a bastardized Hegelian dialectic in order
to shape or stifle the future, and to impart the propaganda necessary to
bring their glorious, atheistic, and fundamentally anti-human new world
into being—ironically, in the guise of humanism. That it cannot—can
never—come into being except at the price of millions of lives, matters to
them not one whit; that is, in fact, its satanic point.

In short, they wish to steal our history from us—the primary purpose
of Critical Theory—and replace the same set of facts with a different,
comprehensive interpretation. This they do in the most intellectually
dishonest way possible, by reducing complex tales to a simple anti-narra-
tive, in which our heroes are their villains, in which our accomplishments
are history's *schandes*, and in which our future is headed for the dustbin.
Stripping away nuance, subplots, character development, and anything
else that does not immediately serve their political purposes, they would
present us with the Worst Story Ever Told.

So, as an exercise in cultural analysis that will serve as a template for
this book's thesis, let us briefly dissect *The Fiery Angel* and once again
observe how, in culture and thus in history, phylogeny recapitulates
ontogeny; the reverse of the scientific principle, now largely discredited
but once widely accepted, and first articulated by Ernst Haeckel in 1866.

As we have seen, the setting is Germany in the sixteenth century—
1534, to be exact—a time of enormous religious and social turmoil. In
1517, Martin Luther had promulgated his ninety-five theses, setting off the
Reformation and eventually provoking the Thirty Years War (1618–48),
one of the bloodiest conflicts in European history. The historical Faust
may have also lived around this time, dying *ca.* 1540. Simultaneously,
the Renaissance, imported from Italy, was infusing medieval Germany
with the humanistic values of the South, a collusion between the gothic
and classical humanism—given literary immortality by Thomas Mann in
the characters of Naphta and Settembrini in *The Magic Mountain*—that
would resonate for the next half-millennium and more.

It's no accident, then, that there are so many echoes of the Faust
legend—the indispensable founding myth of both Romantic and modern Germany—to be found in *The Fiery Angel*. Count Heinrich, the
incarnation of mad Renata's angel Madiel, shares a Christian name with

Faust. The frenzied sisters of *Angel*'s finale mirror a similar scene in the third act of Meyerbeer's Paris grand opera *Robert le diable,* in which dead nuns rise from their graves and stage a bacchanal; the opera itself tells the tale of a medieval Norman knight whose barren mother had sex with the Devil and thus bore a son.

The name of the mysterious, flaming angel, Madiel, contains echoes of the demonic Samiel, the Black Huntsman, in Carl Maria von Weber's *Der Freischütz* (1821), an opera that also includes a wager with the forfeiture of the soul as the stakes. The angel Madiel is referenced in in Francis Barrett's bible of occult magic, *The Magus* (1801), and is also mentioned in other esoteric books from the Middle Ages and the Renaissance.[3] Madiel may be only a figment of Renata's fevered imagination, but he is a historical figment—as is, by the way, another character in the opera, Heinrich Cornelius Agrippa of Nettesheim, who lived from 1486–1535.

Consider also the name of the hero, Ruprecht, which has a special resonance: in German legend, *Knecht Ruprecht* is the boon companion and attendant of St. Nicholas, whose feast day in Germany, December 6, is when good children get their presents and bad children get a visit from the terrifying Krampus the night before. The composer Robert Schumann, drew a small musical portrait of *Knecht Ruprecht* in his *Album for the Young,* and a slippery fellow he is.

Ruprecht of *The Fiery Angel* is a *Landsknecht*—a mercenary, a soldier of fortune—and not a *Ritter* (knight), and thus a commoner, which is why when we first meet him he is putting up for the night in a seedy inn, and not a castle. As his relationship with Renata evolves, it becomes clear that his namesake's association with Nicholas, however, is chiefly on the dark side: not jolly St. Nick, but Old Nick, i.e. the Devil. (When Wotan, in Wagner's *Die Walküre* kills Hunding, he dispatches him with the contemptuous words, *"Geh' hin, Knecht!"*—begone, miserable servant.)

Of particular interest to us at this juncture—besides the obvious fact that Renata is at least metaphorically a female vampire who sucks the life out of every man she meets in service to her demon lover, Madiel—is the sunlight trope first established by Bram Stoker in his 1897 novel, *Dracula,* and forming the climax of films from F. W. Murnau's *Nosferatu* (1922) to Francis Ford Coppola's *Bram Stoker's Dracula* (1992). Our first glimpse

---

3 Cited as well in other grimoires, including the apocryphal *Sixth and Seventh books of Moses.*

of Renata as she is released from her walled-up tomb establishes her as a
creature of the night, while at the opera's climax, it is the sunlight streaming through the opened cellar door that neutralizes her power over the
nuns, allowing the Inquisitor to condemn her to death.

It's not necessary to know any of these references in order to enjoy, if
that is the right word, the opera or the novel; yet how much richer and
fulfilling is the experience when you do. To know these things—to be able
to encounter a work of art (any art, whether visual, aural, or plastic) is,
in fact, to be *civilized* in one of the principal senses of the word. And it is
precisely this civilizational literacy that we are in such danger of losing,
perhaps have already lost, today.

Just a few years after Prokofiev's attempt to breach the forbidden wall of
powerful female sexuality, his fellow Soviet composer Dmitri Shostakovich
tried to do the same thing in his masterpiece *Lady Macbeth of the Mtsensk
District*, which got its first performance in 1934. Two years later, it after
considerable international success, was denounced in *Pravda* as "Muddle
instead of Music" in an editorial that may well have been written by Stalin
himself, and certainly published at his behest. A representative sample:

> From the first minute, the listener is shocked by deliberate dis-
> sonance, by a confused stream of sound. Snatches of melody, the
> beginnings of a musical phrase, are drowned, emerge again, and
> disappear in a grinding and squealing roar. To follow this "music" is
> most difficult; to remember it, impossible....
>
> Passion is here supposed to be expressed by noise. All this is not
> due to lack of talent, or lack of ability to depict strong and simple
> emotions in music. Here is music turned deliberately inside out in
> order that nothing will be reminiscent of classical opera, or have
> anything in common with symphonic music or with simple and
> popular musical language accessible to all. This music is built on
> the basis of rejecting opera - the same basis on which "Leftist" Art
> rejects in the theatre simplicity, realism, clarity of image, and the
> unaffected spoken word.... Here we have "Leftist" confusion instead
> of natural human music. The power of good music to infect the
> masses has been sacrificed to a petty-bourgeois, "formalist" attempt
> to create originality through cheap clowning. It is a game of clever
> ingenuity that may end very badly.

The danger of this trend to Soviet music is clear. Leftist distortion in opera stems from the same source as Leftist distortion in painting, poetry, teaching, and science. Petty-bourgeois "innovations" lead to a break with real art, real science and real literature.

Lady Macbeth is having great success with bourgeois audiences abroad. Is it not because the opera is non-political and confusing that they praise it? Is it not explained by the fact that it tickles the perverted taste of the bourgeois with its fidgety, neurotic music?

The bit about "Leftist confusion" is a nice touch, coming from the very *Rodina* of Marxism-Leninism. Still, Shostakovich—in fear of his life—withdrew the opera under an official ban, and it did not appear again on the world's stages until 1962, when—stripped of its frank "pornophony"—it appeared in a bowdlerized version as *Katerina Ismailova*. Today it is performed as the composer intended—and remains no less startling and stunning.

To take just one example: at the beginning of Act Three, Katerina and her lover Sergei, having earlier murdered her husband, Zinovy, are heading to the church to get married. Katerina shudders as she glances at the entrance to the cellar, in which they have concealed Zinovy's body.

KATERINA: I feel afraid, Seryozha!
SERGEI: Don't be afraid of the dead. It's the living you should fear.
KATERINA: I know that.
SERGEI: Then if you know it, what's the point of standing there? People will notice.

They leave, whereupon a member of the living promptly shows up: the Shabby Peasant, a drunk, a stock figure of Russian drama, who's seen Katerina staring (guiltily) at the cellar door and assumes that's where she keeps the good stuff. He decides to head down to investigate.

What happens next we might plainly and pedestrianly summarize as follows: the Peasant breaks into the cellar on his quest for hidden booze. He is overwhelmed by a noxious stench; "Has all the food gone bad?" he cries. He discovers Zinovy's moldering corpse and runs off to call the cops. Cut to the police station.

Not so fast. For now the real drama begins—entirely in the orchestra.

The music has been building in agitation as the Peasant's *delirium tremens* mounts, then surges as the frightened man flees in horror and the curtain briefly closes. To say it explodes would be an understatement. A frothing fit of musical madness, part comic, part lunatic, it is the aural embodiment of Katerina's unleashed and unpunished sexual passion, a circus-march nightmare of hacking strings, prattling woodwinds, blaring military trumpets, racketing snares and rumbling bass drums. It's one of the most startling and frightening examples of madness in all dramatic music.

Not even Renata in *The Fiery Angel* can achieve this level of red-zone crazy—all the more remarkable considering that it happens off-stage. Even film cannot plumb the depths of this madness, since film cannot show us what is going on inside a character's head, only his outward expression and body language. (Shostakovich and Prokofiev were both expert film scorers.) Music, however, has no such limitations. Combine this passage with the plaintively detumescing trombones that underscore the end of the Sergei–Katerina sex scene, and it's no wonder Stalin banished the opera.

Shostakovich discussed this period in his 1979 memoir, *Testimony*, "as related to" and edited by Solomon Volkov. While there remain those who consider the book more invented by Volkov than actually dictated by the composer—mostly Leftists who resent Shostakovich's frank mockery of Stalin and other Soviet leaders, as well as his sardonic and dyspeptic tone regarding the society in which he lived—it has a ring of emotional truth about it that is hard to gainsay, especially since it so dramatically contradicts the composer's official image during his lifetime. While his music was always popular in United States, Shostakovich was widely viewed at his first American appearance, at the Cultural and Scientific Conference for World Peace in New York City in March 1949, as a dull, dutiful, Communist propagandist. The self-portrait in *Testimony* (or the portrait Volkov painted of him) was considerably at odds with that.

Others, such as the composer's son, Maxim, have endorsed its authenticity, as did many of the famous Russian performers who had known Shostakovich personally and had performed his music. The British director Tony Palmer made a sterling cinematic version, released in 1988, starring Ben Kingsley as the composer and Terence Rigby as Stalin. The reader may decide for himself:

On January 28, 1936, we went to the railroad station [in Arkhan-
gelsk] to buy a new *Pravda*. I opened it up and leafed through it—
and found the article "Muddle Instead of Music." I'll never forget
that day, it's probably the most memorable in my life. That article
on the third page of *Pravda* changed my entire existence. I was
printed without a signature, like an editorial—that is, it expressed
the opinion of the Party. But it actually expressed the opinion of
Stalin, and that was much more important.... From that moment on
I was stuck with the label "enemy of the people," and I don't need to
explain what the label meant in those days. Everybody still remem-
bers that. I was called an enemy of the people quietly and out loud
and from podiums.

Prokofiev could perhaps be thankful that *The Fiery Angel* did not bring
down the wrath of Stalin on his head. Despite the fact that the opera had
to wait until 1955 to get its first staging, its creative process did not stop
in the early 1920s. The composer took the musical material a step further
in 1928 when he reworked its principal themes into his Third Symphony, whose thematic sequencing closely tracks the structure of the opera
throughout its first three movements, with the finale summing up all of
the macabre elements with typically Prokofievian flair. Shorn of its theatrical elements, this strangely neglected symphony emerges as one of the
composer's most striking instrumental essays, dazzlingly orchestrated
and allowing concert audiences to experience the essence of Renata and
Ruprecht without the distractions of plot or stagecraft.

Perhaps it's fitting, then, that we conclude on a final resonance: the
reactionary power of "progressivism." Had Stalin or any of the other
nomenklatura been seated in the royal box at the Bolshoi in Moscow
or the Maly Theatre in then-Leningrad, *The Fiery Angel* might well
have met a fate similar to *Lady Macbeth*. To paraphrase the American
author Tom Wolfe's astringent observation, "The dark night of fascism
is always descending in the United States and yet lands only in Europe,"
the dark night of censorship is always descending on the avant-garde
from the Right and yet strikes almost exclusively from the Left. Marxist
ideology, like the God of Abraham, can brook no other gods before it.
It must be alone, exclusive, supersessive of all other deities, including
Yahweh and Allah.

Guided by the spirit of our succubus, Renata, let us now meet the demons who, real or fantasized, continue to haunt the Western imagination and challenge our civilization to this day—and face them down.

CHAPTER TWO

Albert Besnard, *Le Pendu*, 1873

Gaspard de la Nuit

The God we mistrust, the Devil we desire, the Fates we deserve

How wonderful the scene, how telling, how apposite. The year is 1842, the crest of the wave of literary Romanticism which has flooded across Europe since the end of the eighteenth century. Revolution is in the air, and will arrive within six years; and after it, the flood tide of Darwinism, Marxism, and Wagnerism that would finally overwhelm the old Continent and wash it toward the shores of the First World War.

The poet Aloysius Bertrand takes a seat on a park bench in a quiet garden in Dijon; next to him is an old man, unkempt and likely *verklempt*, paging through a manuscript whose subject is the search for meaning in Art. What is sentiment in Art? And what is meaning? Does Art derive from love (and thus God), or it is fueled by reason, devoid of *Dieu et Amour*, and thus possibly satanic? The old man—"Gaspard" himself, as

39

it turns out—tells Bertrand that art itself needs not the satanic notion of ideas: "*L'art est la science du poète*." That Art is merely sentiment writ large. But Satan would say that, wouldn't he?

The strange man thrusts the book upon Bertrand, telling him he will reclaim it on the morrow. The book's title: *Gaspard de la Nuit* (Gaspard of the Night).

Of course, he never comes. When Bertrand returns the next day, he finds himself saddled with the manuscript. Helpful but fearful villagers tell him that M. "Gaspard" is either in Hell or on the prowl, for everyone knows him to be Satan himself: the Father of Lies, the Illusionist, the Antithesis made flesh and dwelling among us. Following the only course available to the true artist, the poet shudders, embraces evil, and vows to see the book published. The result, allowing for its fictive genesis, was Bertrand's short but influential volume of prose poetry, one that changed not only the course of French verse—Baudelaire's *Les Fleurs du mal* could not have been written without it—but of French music and thus of French civilization as well. Poetically, it was only published in 1842, the year after Bertrand's death.

Thesis, antithesis. Hegel sought to fashion a synthesis; Marx deluded himself into thinking he had, using the gears of what he called dialectical materialism to grind humanity into powder. But Europe in the nineteenth century contained its own, real-life thesis and antithesis in the forms of the nation-states of Germany and France. The former was the rump remains of the Holy Roman Empire (the First Reich), once barbarian, now ruled by dukes and princelings, and speaking various dialects of German; France could trace its lineage back to Caesar's Gallic Wars, which brought the Celts into a real empire, bequeathed it the most literary of the Romance languages, and grounded it in the rule of law. One had *civilisation*, the other *Kultur*.

With the defeat of Napoleon, France and England had finally sorted out their rivalries and destinies, which had been firmly intertwined since the middle of the twelfth century, when Eleanor of Aquitaine gave birth to Richard the Lionheart, and not only affected the future courses of both England and France, but of the Crusades as well. France's new mortal enemy was the emerging German state, being welded together by Prussia under Otto von Bismarck; the 1870 Franco-Prussian War, lost by France, directly resulted in the birth of the Second Reich the following January: the Reich of the German *Kaiser* (Caesar).

One is tempted to observe that the political enmity was mirrored by the cultural conflict between the two countries, but that would be getting it wrong way 'round. The deep cultural and historical differences between France and Germany *created* the political conflict; the differences in languages were also differences in the very manner of thought—the modes of expression, not only in poetry, but in the subjects of the literature; the radical differences in the sounds of their music put not only the leading artists of the day at odds with each other, but royal houses and creeds as well.

Wagner sought to find musical and commercial success in Paris in the mid-nineteenth century, and so brought with him his opera *Tannhäuser* for special performance in 1861. But the French premiere was a failure; the lack of a ballet in the second act—a longstanding Parisian tradition—condemned it to the derision of the Jockey Club swells in attendance mostly to ogle their dancer mistresses, so that even a passionate public defense of Wagner and an attack on the Jockey Club by Baudelaire couldn't salvage Wagner's French career:

"Gardez votre harem et conservez-en religieusement les traditions; mais faites-nous donner un théâtre où ceux qui ne pensent pas comme vous pourront trouver d'autres plaisirs mieux accommodés à leur goût. Ainsi nous serrons débarrassés de vous et vous de nous, et chacun sera content." ["Keep your harem and conserve your traditions religiously; but give us a theater in which those who do not think like you find other pleasures better suited to their taste. In this way, we would be rid of you and you of us, and everyone would be happy."]

Typically, Wagner blamed his failure on the French and the Jews (in the form of the king of the Paris Opera, the German-born Jewish composer Giacomo Meyerbeer), and returned home to Germany to graciously accept the patronage of King Ludwig II of Bavaria and construct his own monument to himself and his music at Bayreuth. He never forgave France.

Later, Claude Debussy explicitly rejected Wagner, Wagnerism, and the whole notion of the *Gesamtkunstwerk*, the unified work of art that, in a deliberate echo of the theater's Greek roots, combined music, poetry, and stagecraft; the crowning example of which was Wagner's *Ring* cycle. Debussy, the quintessential Frenchman, rejected Wagner's grandiosity of aim and extravagance of expression in favor of what became known as Impressionism: the personal instead of the political, the carefully observed, shimmering tone painting (*The Afternoon of a Faun*,

Three Nocturnes) instead of the world-historical canvas. And yet, when it came time for Debussy to write his lone opera, *Pelléas et Mélisande* (1898), he wound up adhering more strictly to the rules Wagner had laid down in his long monograph *Oper und Drama* back in 1851 than Wagner himself ever did: no arias, no choruses and, one might venture to observe, almost no fun.

This is not to say that there was no crossover; there were plenty of French Wagnerites and German anti-Wagnerites, prominent among them the composer Brahms and the philosopher Friedrich Nietzsche, a former disciple who turned on the Master (as Wagner was called by his acolytes) in both *The Case of Wagner* and *Nietzsche contra Wagner*. But music was international; any educated European musician spoke, read, and wrote in multiple languages. Wagner's father-in-law, the great pianist Franz Liszt, was born in Hungary, spoke German, wrote his letters in French, and fluently seduced (and was seduced by) women all over the Continent in the universal language of love.

Today, the Left has deemed inter-cultural exchanges as inappropriate "appropriation," thus demonizing a Western syncretism that has served the culture spectacularly well since the Romans supplanted the Greeks but adopted their gods and legends. Debussy himself was greatly influenced by the novel sounds of the Balinese *gamelan*, and worked their tonal structures and instrumental sheen into his own music and orchestration. Like Bertrand contemplating the manuscript of "Gaspard," the poet—the *Western* poet—must actively appropriate the work of another, an alien. That the music, art, and artifacts of the Third World—the "developing" nations—whose culture is, after all, only given universal meaning by its adoption by the West (who, otherwise, would ever have heard of the Balinese *gamelan* beyond Bali?) is now considered so sacrosanct as to be untouchable is simply another sign of *Der Untergang des Abendlandes*, as Oswald Spengler wrote in 1926: the decline of the West.

Spengler was viewing the West through the same prism Georg Lukács was, during the interregnum between the two halves of the same European conflict that was mostly resolved in 1945. His pessimism can be forgiven. The protection of civilization, it seems, is a rear-guard action, effected only after the forces of darkness—called today "Progressivism" (as the same movement was during the Woodrow Wilson administration; every-thing that was old is new again)—have essentially won. During a time of cultural muscularity there is no need for it; just ask Sir Richard Burton, John Hanning Speke, David Livingston, or any of the other great British explorers of the nineteenth century, who sought to expand the science and knowledge of the West, and bring it to other lands; today, this is derisively called "colonialism."

For what, in the end is a "civilization" if not the sum total of its science, art, and literature, which together have partially dictated its language, customs, and ways of thought? The library at Alexandria, the crowning glory of Hellenistic Egyptian civilization, may have been destroyed in successive waves of barbarism, first Roman and then Christian, culminating in the Muslim Arab conquest in the seventh century, but it is not for its physical attributes that it was prized, but rather for what it contained—which is *why* it was destroyed and why it is still mourned today.

It's easy for us, at such great temporal remove, to forget what was lost. We may read about the vanished Library, but what possible meaning can it have for us today? In the age of Google and the iPhone, do we even need a "library" for anything other than to allow the homeless to easily access their constitutional right to free pornography on the computers?

And yet...it is not just the actual Library we today mourn, but also the very *concept* of such a library. Hellenistic Egypt (founded by Alexander, and hence neither ancient Egyptian nor Arab Muslim), the interstice between ancient Greece and republican/imperial Rome, was a critical link between Ulysses and Aeneas. Indeed, Imperial Rome is unthinkable without it—few remember today that the Civil War waged between Pompey and Caesar was largely fought in Greece, and finally settled in Egypt; whence otherwise comes Shakespeare's *Antony and Cleopatra*? (Cleopatra was Ptolemaic Greek.)

So what happened to it? What happened to the greatest repository of knowledge in the ancient world, an institution that connects us to our Greek patrimony—and via, the Christianized Mediterranean world that arose around the tomb of Alexander himself, the first planned *polis*, laid out rationally, as later the Paris of Baron Haussmann and the Washington, D.C., of Major L'Enfant would be? "For the ancients," writes Thomas Cahill in *Mysteries of the Middle Ages; the Rise of Feminism, Science, and Art from the Cults of Catholic Europe*: "Alexandria, cultural successor to war-devastated Athens, became in the third century B.C. the great City of the Mind; and for all the untroubled urbanity of its polished surfaces, it buzzed, it buzzed noon and night with theory, disputation, and intellectual engagement."

What could be more Western than that? Disputation, argument, theory, intellectual engagement—these are the very hallmarks of Western civilization, as opposed to the static nature of Islam, whose only proper theological study is itself, and which can only erupt in rage (and rarely if ever in disputation) over fundamental tenets. Build it up, tear it down—it does not always take war to do that, but is inherent in our nature. Call it what you will: the "creative destruction" of capitalism, "urban renewal" (what an Orwellian term for the bulldozing of once-stable, now-derelict American neighborhoods), or simply "progress." Alexandria, a city firmly grounded in Aristotelian logic and yet a hotbed of conflicting political and religious principles, was, even more than Athens, the first great urban center of Western learning.

Naturally, the Library had to be destroyed. First by Caesar during the endgame of his civil war against Pompey in 48–47 B.C., when the *Mouseion* (Museum) built by Ptolemy I Soter or Ptolemy II Philadelphus accidentally caught fire; then damaged by the Roman emperor Aurelian in the third century; later burned as a temple of paganism by the order of the Monophysite Christian emperor Theodosius in 391; and finally razed during the Muslim conquest of Egypt in 642 A.D. Half a million texts vanished in the flames. The conflict between religion and reason, in other words, has been with Western civilization from the beginning. Something burns, something is created anew—and nothing is destroyed that cannot be born again. It is no wonder that the fiery phoenix, rising from its own ashes, has become a symbol of Western culture.

The phoenix, Stravinsky's firebird, Prokofiev's Madiel, burning but never consumed by the flames—the symbol of the Library at Alexandria has come down to us through the centuries, perhaps illuminated by one of the seven wonders of the ancient world, the nearby Lighthouse. The fact that most of the city is now under water only adds to vanished Alexandria's poignancy.

This may read like an epitaph, but it can just as easily be interpreted as an encouragement. If mighty Ozymandias's empire can vanish beneath the sands, so can the even mightier Alexander's great city sink, like Atlantis, beneath the waves of the Mediterranean Sea. And then, like the phoenix, rise again—in Rome, Paris, London, Berlin, New York, Singapore, New

Delhi, Sydney, and Christchurch. Madiel always reappears, to tempt us and guide us, if only we will swallow our fear, open ourselves to wonder, and follow.

In sum, the West's fascination with evil and its willingness to accommodate it up to a point—and sometimes beyond that point—is both its Achilles' heel and its unique cultural strength, the quality that sets it apart from the hierarchical societies of the Middle East and Asia. The cultural-Marxist Left has sought to tar the Christian and post-Christian West with the very sin it so admires in other cultures, and has created a fantasy history in which a hapless proletariat had an arbitrary dogma imposed upon it by popes and potentates, and from which it has been crying out ever since for "liberation." That Marxism is the very definition of an imposition seems not to occur to some, while for others is the very feature of the system they wish to impose.

Little wonder: Marxism seeks to replace pluralistic discourse with its own form of coercive totalitarianism—socialism "with a human face." That the face is not human at all, but satanic, needs constantly to be pointed out, as does Marxism's claim that the thing it wishes to replace—Judeo-Christian morality or even its Settembrinian stepchild, secular humanism—is actually the thing it wishes to replace it with: a form of Judeo-Christianity with the God of Abraham replaced by the Arc of History. Meet the new boss, not quite the same as the old boss...

Like Islam, Marxism posits a moral universe of good and evil, but seeks to eradicate what it defines as evil without ever coming to terms with it, or indeed questioning whether it is, in fact, evil. Part of this sleight-of-hand is accomplished linguistically, by adopting Christian terms such as "peace" "spiritual enlightenment," "tolerance," and "fairness," but meaning something very different by them—often, in fact, the opposite. To a Western Christian, for example, "peace" means the absence of war; there can be such a thing as "peaceful coexistence," on the theory that good international boundaries make for good neighbors. That was the theory behind the post–World War II spheres of influence that evolved in the wake of the Allied triumphs in Europe and Asia. The shadow war between the West and the Soviet Union that followed was waged at the margins, in the streets of South America, in the chaos of Africa, and in the back alleys of Berlin.

Radical Islam rejects that notion of "peace," which is why its borders are, in Huntington's inflammatory description, bloody:

> In Eurasia the great historic fault lines between civilizations are once more aflame. This is particularly true along the boundaries of the crescent-shaped Islamic bloc of nations, from the bulge of Africa to central Asia. Violence also occurs between Muslims, on the one hand, and Orthodox Serbs in the Balkans, Jews in Israel, Hindus in India, Buddhists in Burma and Catholics in the Philippines. Islam has bloody borders.

The word "peace," to a fundamentalist Muslim does not mean the absence of war (which in any case is constantly being waged in the *Dar-al-Harb*) but the final triumph of the *Dar-al-Islam* when "peace" is achieved by everyone becoming either Muslim, a slave, or dead. The Islamic notion of "peace," therefore, should be termed more aptly "total victory."

The triumph of Islam would necessarily mean the disappearance of borders, beginning with the concept of nation-states. The fifty or so Islamic "countries" around the world wield a disproportionate influence in the United Nations; but were they to be honest, and represent only the single *ummah* of Islamic aspiration, the anti-American and anti-Israel bias of that organization would be greatly lessened.

The unholy alliance between the cultural Marxists and Islam is evident in the Marxists' desire to do away with borders as well. (That they find useful-idiot fellow travelers among the open-borders crowd on the capitalist side is simply the happenstance of temporarily aligning interests.) Hence the Left's wholehearted endorsement of illegal immigration into the United States, largely across the Mexican border, and its support of the waves of Muslim and African "refugees" that have washed across Europe over the past few years. The death of the nation-state—begun by the hollowing out of its native population via birth control, abortion, and other extensions of "women's rights," and their replacement by cultural aliens (mockingly dubbed "enrichers")—has long been a goal of Marxism, whether economic or cultural. To that end, then, the desire for European countries to preserve their peoples and their cultures is now attacked as "racism" or "white supremacy"—the evocation of the bugbears of the American Civil Rights Movement is entirely intentional—the unspoken premise being that every African and Asian has a right to live in Paris (but no Christian has a right to practice his faith in Riyadh), and that any opposition to "immigration" can only be based on bigotry and "hate." That the Europeans might have a right to their own territory is now rejected out of hand as a cultural anachronism.

A word about "hate," a useful term much demonized by the cultural-Marxist Left, which is itself both hateful and hate-filled. There is nothing wrong with hate. The Christian is taught to hate—*hate*—sin; members of all faiths are instructed to hate Satan, however defined. We are commanded to abhor and abjure Evil. Properly applied to the correct targets, "hate" is a protective emotion and a valuable weapon. Critical Theory, however, even has been applied to "hate," which has been rendered indefensible in the service of any cause the radical Left hates.

The fight for the nation-state, then, must begin with a defense of its right to existence and self-determination. This was formerly a right that all acknowledged, a potent weapon to wield against real racism and exploitative colonialism. But, like so many other things, it has now outlived its usefulness to the Left, and can be dispensed with—in fact, transformed into a crime against humanity instead of a human right.

Since the nation-states under attack are European and American, where does the politically incorrect pushback begin? How can it begin? With precisely the subject under discussion here: with the knowledge of good and evil. As Milton notes in his great essay on freedom of expression: "It was from out the rind of one apple tasted that the knowledge of good and evil, as two twins cleaving together, leaped forth into the world. And perhaps this is that doom which Adam fell into of knowing good and evil, that is to say of knowing good by evil."

Knowing good by evil is the most fundamental concept of the Western way of life. It is the basis for all legislated morality—contrary to the Leftist bromide, we can and very much do legislate morality; what they are referring to is legislating specifically *sexual* morality, which obsesses them. Knowing good by evil is how we discriminate (in the neutral, indeed positive sense of the word) between competing choices. It is how we define ourselves as a people. Is good better than evil? Plainly so, or else the words have no meaning. Absent evil, can there be any good? Were Adam and Eve in the Garden good? Without a choice, how? When Eve made her choice, it was not to become bad—rather, it was to

"become as God" and know both good *and* evil—a distinction hitherto
denied her and Adam.

Milton called his essay, which was occasioned by a personal crisis
regarding his wife, the *Areopagitica* for a specific, culturally resonant
reason. In ancient Athens, the *Areopagus* was a rocky place near the
Acropolis, whereupon cases of homicide were tried. Although a real location, its most famous case was Orestes' trial for the murder of his mother,
Clytemnestra, dramatized by Aeschylus in the third of the *Oresteia* plays,
The Eumenides. The Furies demand vengeance upon Orestes for the crime
of matricide, one of the gravest human transgressions; Orestes pleads
mitigating circumstances—he was avenging the death of his father, Agamemnon—and calls the god Apollo as a character witness. The goddess
Pallas Athena presides:

> ORESTES: Apollo, give your testimony now. Explain, on my behalf,
> whether I was justified in killing her. For I do not deny that I did it,
> as it is done. But decide whether this bloodshed was, to your mind,
> just or not, so that I may inform the court.
> APOLLO:...She received him [Agamemnon] from the expedition..,
> then, as he was stepping from the bath, on its very edge, she threw
> a cloak like a tent over it, fettered her husband in an embroidered
> robe, and cut him down. This was his death, as I have told it to
> you—the death of a man wholly majestic, commander of the fleet.
> —Translation by Herbert Weir Smyth

In the end the vote is tied. Athena herself casts the tie-breaker in
favor of Orestes, and transforms the raging Furies, the *Erinyes,* into the
Eumenides, the Kindly Ones.

To read the *Oresteia* today is to be reminded of several things. First,
how good a playwright Aeschylus was, how sharply drawn the play's
principal characters are (especially poor doomed Cassandra, brought
back from Troy by Agamemnon as his mistress), and what a compelling
story the only surviving Greek trilogy makes. The first scene of *Agamemnon,* as a watchman sees the signal fires in the distance, approaching
the House of Atreus, is as dramatic an opening as you will see in any
movie. And the slow build to the victorious warrior-king's inevitable
doom is gripping.

The second reminder is how, at the dawn of Western civilization, the *Oresteia* so clearly articulates the moral issues that continue to occupy our society. In *The Eumenides*, it allows both sides to state their cases, which are of near-equal weight; it establishes the number of jurors at twelve; it even provides for a divine tie-breaker in Athena, who soothes the passions of the losing side by transforming their natures.

Third is the resonance (there's that word again) the cycle continues to have. As noted above, Strauss's opera *Elektra* is based on the story; in the twentieth century, the German composer Carl Orff (of *Carmina Burana* fame) adapted two of Sophocles' Theban plays: *Antigonae* and *Oedipus der Tyrann*, in the German versions by Friedrich Hölderlin. In an attempt to recreate the spirit of the times, Orff's text is chanted more than sung, with the orchestra confined to a percussion battery, periodically exploding into paroxysms of lust, anger, and rage. One doesn't attend a performance of any of Orff's *Theatrum Mundi* (World Theater) works expecting to be enchanted by the *melos* but rather to have one's ears pinned back by the fierce, urgent retelling of the tragedies. His approach was effectively the opposite of Wagner's at Bayreuth, where again the spirit of Greek drama was invoked, even as it turned into Norse (the *Ring*), Celtic (*Tristan und Isolde*), or German (*Lohengrin*) myths instead.

Clearly, Greek drama has never been very far from Western stages, or movie theaters for that matter—*O Brother Where Art Thou?* (2000), *Troy* (2004), *Chi-Raq* (2015), are but a few examples. Not only are classical Greek stories timeless, but they can be told and retold and never lose any of their moral and emotional impact. Why? Because they connect us directly, through the medium of storytelling, with the wellsprings of our culture—our *Ur*-Culture. We feel it, even if we don't think about it.

To reduce the stories—call them exemplars—to the status of mere myths or fairy tales, however, is to rob them of their moral component. Which is precisely the aim of those who would separate Western civilization from its origins; the Greek and Roman myths, along with the epic poetry and drama of the period, can be negated if they can be made to seem manifestations of, say, the "patriarchy," or clear evidence of a conspiracy against women, homosexuals, and people of color. This is the essence of cultural Marxism, the Left's answer to Lukács's famous question, "Who will save us from Western culture?"

Crucially, the Greek myths limn moral situations for which there is no clear prescription. Is Orestes guilty of murder? Does Achilles' rage at Hector justify his sacrilegious treatment of the Trojan hero's body? Is Ulysses' habitual trickery, most especially the brazen deceit of the Trojan Horse, whose entry into Ilium sets off the final, appalling wave of murder and destruction, in any sense justifiable? Every one of these is an evil deed, and yet in each case we are asked to celebrate it.

Behold, then the Western dilemma—the embrace of Evil for a greater good—a conundrum that has occupied soldiers, statesmen, creative artists, and theologians for three millennia. Not for us is the passive serenity of Buddhism and Shintoism, nor the often-homicidal certainty of Islam. Instead the West embraces a constant questioning, a constant desiring, a constant impulse to give the Devil his due while besting him on the field of battle, in imitation of St. Michael, who never made the mistake of underestimating his opponent. As with Adam and Eve, it seems, it is impossible for the men of the West to know good without also knowing evil.

Contained within Western civilization from the time of Plato and Aristotle, like the confused seeds of Psyche, is the concept—the *necessary rivalry*—of good and evil. Not as antithetical but unequal forces—in which Satan is symbolically cast out by ritual and rote, by self-flagellation and exorcism, and whose final defeat is never seriously in doubt—but as equals on the field of battle, which is men's souls. God may not be able to lose to Lucifer, but we can.

Out of the rind of one apple . . . The poet Milton certainly commanded a veritable Creation of imagery, which he put to the service of Christian allegory and theology in *Paradise Lost* (1667), and which was almost immediately complemented by Bunyan's *The Pilgrim's Progress* (1678). That Milton and Bunyan were two of the most influential non-conformists of the Christian seventeenth century is neither accidental nor unremarkable. From the very beginning of Christianity, there was dissension.

Was there an original Eve who did not resemble, in outward appearance, a chimp? And if so, therefore what? Was the year 1859: in which Darwin published *The Origin of Species*, charting our rise from the planet of the apes; Marx emerged with *A Contribution to the Critique of Political Economy*; and Wagner annihilated three centuries of stable tonality with *Tristan*—the three great transformative events of the Romantic era, as Jacques Barzun showed in *Darwin, Marx, Wagner*—an anomaly or all too typical of the Western striving for self-contradiction and (it must be admitted) self-abnegation?

But, oh, that gibbet; oh, that noose. How attractive, how seductive, how sexy they can be.

"Gaspard has been a devil in coming, but that is only logical since it was he who is the author of the poems," wrote the French composer Maurice Ravel in 1908. "My ambition is to say with notes what a poet expresses with words." He thus at one stroke created one of the masterpieces of the piano literature—after the finale of the triptych, the daemonic *Scarbo*, nothing could be more difficult—and demolished the notion that art merely apes existence, when in fact art *is* existence.

The two virtuosic movements, *Ondine* and *Scarbo*, present the greatest pianistic challenges in the three-movement suite, but it is with the macabre middle movement, *Le Gibet*, written in the dark key of E-flat minor, with which we are here concerned. Ravel introduces the music on the printed page with a quote from Goethe's *Faust*, in French: "*Que vois-je remuer autour de ce Gibet?*" ("*Was weben die dort um den Rabenstein?*," which is to say, "What are they weaving round and round the gallows-tree?"), setting the scene before the pianist sounds the first note.

Eugène Delacroix, who at age thirty so strikingly illustrated an 1828 edition of *Faust*, chose this short scene of the *Gespenster unter dem Galgen* ("Spooks under the gallows") for one of his eighteen lithographs (literally, "engraved in stone"). The picture is murky, the focus on Faust and Mephisto aboard their fleet steeds, the *Gespenster* and the dead man in the background, in shadows—*im Schatten*. But its power comes through. The flight, the corpse, the witches—here is Western European history of the eighteenth and nineteenth centuries summed up in a single picture: no matter how swift our rides, the Devil (as Schubert so vividly illustrated in his song *Erlkönig*) is always at our side.[1]

We no longer see hanged men these days, but the sight was common enough throughout history, until relatively recently in fact, that it was often the subject of paintings, poems, tone poems, and, later, photographs. Some public executions were akin to sporting events; others took place along the sides of the road, or in a field. The writer Victor Hugo, exiled to the Channel Island of Guernsey (where he wrote *Les Misérables*), encountered and sketched a hanged man swinging from a gibbet, his body surrounded by pecking birds; Hugo also protested and commemorated the

---

1 Musically, both Liszt and Wagner depicted the Faust legend abstractly in their "*Faust*" Symphony and "*Faust*" Overture, respectively, while on the operatic stage, we have both Gounod's *Faust* and Ferruccio Busoni's *Doktor Faust*.

death of the American abolitionist John Brown in another drawing—this one more detailed, made in 1859—entitled simply *Ecce* (Behold).

The brief episode from *Faust*, which occurs near the very end of Part One, just before the final scene, is transitional, just a few lines of dialogue: Faust and Mephistopheles, dashing through an open field aboard black stallions as they abandon the *Walpurgisnacht* revels for Gretchen's dungeon. But what freight it carries! Faust sees a group of people weaving something around the Ravenstone—a hanging place—and asks Mephisto what they're doing. The devil says he doesn't know. Faust exclaims that they're hovering, rising and falling, consecrating something. With a shout of *"Vorbei!"* Mephisto urges him onward. That's all there is to it. But its impact on Ravel was remarkable. Why?

In a word, Fate. The weaving is, of course, a dead giveaway; weaving is what the Norns do in the Eddic sagas of Scandinavia, determining the individual destinies of all of us. Goethe transforms them explicitly into witches, fluttering like the crows around a hanged man, *schweben auf, schweben ab*, in eager anticipation of sending another soul—Faust's? Gretchen's?—to hell.

Ravel, the master scene-painter, chooses not to depict the kinetic energy of the soaring and swooping witches, but concentrates instead on the implacability of the nameless victim's fate, the B-flat octave the tolling of a supernatural, dispassionate, disinterested bell—John Donne's bell, perhaps. "Any man's death diminishes me/ because I am involved in mankind./ And therefore never send to know for whom/ the bells tolls; it tolls for thee." It's an accomplishment of perverse genius, worthy of the impish devil Scarbo himself, who promptly appears in the next movement to wrap things up in a blaze of daemonic, pianistic glory.

So what can we learn from *Gaspard de la Nuit*, beyond the sheer musical enjoyment of listening to a master pianist perform the entire suite? The answer is, in a word, cultural linkage. The artists of our mature Western culture—we may date it roughly from the Renaissance—have always been closely in tune with the spirit of their times, and have left to us its expression in words, music, and deeds. We read about Henry II, Queen Elizabeth, Talleyrand, and Czar Nicholas—but what we largely remember about them is their offices, and their influence on the military and passing political issues of the day. But we accord them entirely too much honor and influence, as if Elizabeth Regina's wars against her enemies in

France and at home were all that mattered about the sixteenth and early seventeenth centuries—a period that also gave us Shakespeare. Elizabeth's judgments about human beings were expressed in their elevation or execution, and teach us little or nothing; the Bard's instruct us yet.

Ravel's insight into the dark side of the human soul, delivered at the end of the Romantic era, premiered just five years before the cataclysm of World War I, and disarmingly expressed via a pianistic showpiece that puts even Liszt's *Transcendental Études* to shame, was not simply a one-off. If you look and listen closely to the art of the period—Paul Fussell covers it brilliantly in his cultural history of World War I and its effect on the present, *The Great War and Modern Memory* (1975)—you can hear the artists talking to us, warning us, like some shades from the future although still living here on earth.

Fussell, for example, opens his great meditation on the signal calamity of Western culture, with a discussion of a piece of journalism written by Lytton Strachey (of *Eminent Victorians* fame) and published on December 19, 1914, when the war was still in its infancy, and everybody assumed that everybody else would be home by Christmas.

> His language was dark. He spoke of events *remorseless, terrible, gruesome*. He noted that "the desolation is complete" and recalled a phrase of Gibbon's appropriate to the kind of irony he was contemplating: "the abridgment of hope...." But actually Strachey was not writing about the war at all. In his 2,000 words he doesn't mention it. Instead, he is reviewing Thomas Hardy's most recent volume of poems, *Satires of Circumstance*, published in November, 1914, but containing—with the exception of the patriotic and unironic "Men Who March Away," hastily added as a "Postscript"—only poems written before the war. Many emanate from Hardy's personal experience as far back as 1870. As if by uncanny foresight, Hardy's volume offers a medium for perceiving the events of the war just beginning...

One of the Hardy poems under review is "Ah, Are You Digging on My Grave" from 1913, written in the voice of a dead woman, who hears a scratching in the earth above her coffin. Who could it be? She runs through the possibilities: Her lover? Her family? Some enemy? In the end,

it turns out to be the dog, which delights her: "Why flashed it not on me/
That one true heart was left behind!" Then the dog delivers the bad news:
he was simply burying a bone, and had totally forgotten that his former
mistress lay entombed just below.

But it wasn't just the writers, poets, and musicians who could hear
the message; it was the common soldier as well, whose entry under arms
coincided with perhaps the last great period of literacy in the Western
world. As Fussell notes:

> By 1914, it was possible for soldiers to be not merely literate but
> vigorously literary, for the Great War occurred at a special histor-
> ical moment when two "liberal" forces were powerfully coinciding
> in England. On the one hand, the belief in the educative powers of
> classical and English literature was still extremely strong. On the
> other, the appeal of popular education and "self-improvement"
> was at its peak, and such education was still conceived largely in
> humanistic terms ... If not everyone went so far as to agree with
> Samuel Johnson that "the chief glory of every people arises from its
> authors," an astonishing number took literature seriously.

Soldiers referenced lines from *Richard III* in letters home. Generals in
despair riffed freely on Keats's *Ode to a Nightingale*. The British television
show *Blackadder*, in its final, devastating season devoted to the Great War,
may have lampooned "the endless poetry" of the conflict, but poetry there
was—before, during, and after the war—and would that Douglas Haig
and the German general staff had heeded the poets more and Clausewitz
less. Home by Christmas? For Tommy and Brother Boche, in the grave by
Christmas was more like it, buried alive in a trench or in the mud, with
not so much as a dog to mourn them. And the Christmas after that, and
the Christmas after that.

It took the epic disaster of Flanders' fields to finally force Europe to
face the consequences of its folly. And did it listen? Of course not. The
inter-war period, which lasted a mere generation, twenty-one years, saw
the depths of cultural defeatism (the Oxford resolution of 1933) and the
rise of the Frankfurt School, which launched its attack on Western culture
precisely in the arena of cultural literacy, irate that it had not spared the
world from a fate forced upon it by "reasonable" politicians, treaties, and

military men. "The sleep of reason produces monsters," as the famous Goya drawing has it; but Europe would have done better to listen to its monsters while they were still speaking through its artists, rather than unleashing their full fury as the limitations of Reason were encountered at the Somme, Vimy Ridge, and Passchendaele, the message delivered by Big Bertha and her unholy Valkyrie sisters.

Naturally, the artists had—briefly, temporarily—the last word, and not just in the poetry of Siegfried Sassoon and Robert Graves. In music alone, the Great War produced three of the most poignant laments for a vanishing civilization in history. As the Zeitgeist would have it, they were all composed and premiered nearly simultaneously: Gustav Holst's *The Planets* (and in particular the opening "Mars, the Bringer of War" movement 1918); Sir Edward Elgar's Cello Concerto, Op. 85 (1919); and Ravel's "Poème chorégraphique pour orchestra": his orchestral masterpiece *La valse* (1919–20).

Instructively, two of them—Ravel and Holst—later denied that the war had anything to do with their music. That is Reason talking again—the part of the composer's brain that must concentrate on formal structure, harmony, orchestration, and the like: the many technical details of transferring what it is in the heart and on the lips to the head. Still, it's impossible to listen to any of these three works and not hear, as Elgar unquestionably did, the sound of the guns firing just across the English Channel during the last year of the war. We accept the composer's technical mastery as a given, and neither hear it, nor see it, nor notice it. The music, however, goes straight to our emotions, and to our hearts.

Everyone who's ever darkened a concert hall, or even watched a television commercial, is familiar with Holst's "Mars." Written in 5/4 time—the same time signature later made famous in jazz by Dave Brubeck in "Take Five"—the music begins as an ominous rumbling, slowly building into a macabre march, always one beat off but ever forward, as implacable as the Greek god for whom the angry Red Planet is named. Like the doomed men on both sides of the trenches, ordered over the top and into the teeth of the machine guns and the batteries, it has no choice but to advance—until it finally ends, crashing, against its last, dying but defiant chords.

Elgar's concerto was his last major work. Its failure at its premiere—it didn't really shoulder its way into the standard repertory until a twenty-year-old Jacqueline du Pré electrified audiences in the mid-1960s with

her passionate interpretation—wounded the composer, who was aware
his music was already going out of fashion in the aftermath of the Great
War's carnage. When his wife, Lady Alice, died the following year (she
was eight years his senior), her death sent the composer into a creative
tailspin from which he never recovered. Although he lived until 1934, and
found some important champions in his later years, he was at the time of
his death regarded as an embarrassing relic of Edwardian England, walrus
mustache and all.

Elgar's music always had a noble, confident air about it—*nobilmente* is
one of his favorite tempo markings—but not until the Cello Concerto did
it plumb the tragic depths that had been lurking behind the Col. Blimp
exterior all along. From its dramatic opening, chordal recitative for the
soloist, it is at once both virtuosic and elegiac—less a concerto in the
manner of, say, Dvořák's, than a requiem for a world that had committed
suicide. The trappings of pomp and circumstance remained for a time—
but the spirit had gone out of the Empire. The confident zeal and lust for
discovery that had animated Burton and Speke, Stanley and Livingstone,
had died face down in the mud and blood of Ypres. All that was left was
for Elgar to compose its swan song.

Ravel's *La valse* began life as early as 1906, when the composer had
bruited the idea of writing an homage to Johann Strauss, Jr., the Waltz
King. That came to naught, but he returned to the notion in 1911's *Valses
nobles et sentimentales*, written originally for piano and orchestrated the
following year. Still, it wasn't right. Something more, something deeper,
was necessary.

What was it about the waltz, which had reached its apogee in mid- and
late-nineteenth-century Vienna, that suddenly caused it to speak, from
the grave, to composers on both sides of the disputed Alsace-Lorraine
territories? Although waltzes had long since gone out of fashion, Richard
Strauss employed them to great effect in his 1911 operatic masterpiece *Der
Rosenkavalier* as a deliberate anachronism. As the musical representation
of the peak of the Austro-Hungarian Empire of the Habsburgs—the same
royal house that brought down most of Europe with it at Sarajevo—the
waltz, with its barely repressed sexuality, the anxious, anticipated, accent-
ed second beat that in proper Viennese performance gives it its forward
propulsion, had come to symbolize a vanishing Central Europe: the world
of the spas at Marienbad and Karlsbad, the summer pleasures of the

Prater, the Vienna Woods, and the Bohemian forests. Germany, in other words, with the Germanness rubbed away, leaving only the *Schlagobers*.

There it was: Ravel dove into the heart of the waltz and found not the whipped cream, but its Teutonic heart. What Mars had been for Holst—militarism with a military face—and what the War had been for Elgar—an unmitigated tragedy—*La valse* would now reveal the immediate past for what it truly was: the Grand Illusion. The moralists had been right; having sex standing up and whirling about a dance floor would inevitably lead to waltzing. Phylogeny recapitulates ontogeny.

And so *La valse* tears into the waltz with a ferocity that knows few equals in the artistic canon, musical or otherwise. The lilting one-TWO-three of Austrian Strauss becomes the threatening, demanding ONE-two-three of Germans on a wrong-footed march—surely Ravel was inspired in this regard by the waltz movement of Berlioz's *Symphonie fantastique*, its predecessor in sinister, Francophone viciousness, with or without the optional cornet *obbligato*: an advance on Paris in three-quarter time. This time, it's personal.

To spare you the suspense: *La valse* doesn't so much end as self-destruct. Whirling itself into a sexual frenzy, it finally collapses on the metaphysical dance floor—they shoot horses, don't they?—with nothing left to give or say. Musically, it's the last word on the subject—literarily, that would be Thomas Mann's *Der Zauberberg* (The Magic Mountain), begun in 1912 and published in 1924, and Erich Maria Remarque's *Im Westen nichts neues* (All Quiet on the Western Front), published five years later—and perhaps it's fitting that it came from a Frenchman, whose country bore the brunt of the conflict. Its relative brevity is not the soul of wit, but of the soul leaving the body, which is still swaying on *Le Gibet*, while the *Hexenzunft* gathers round, brewing up a new, incoming storm, and cackling madly away.

Taken collectively, then—and remember that these are just three of the many artistic responses to the gathering storm both before and after the First World War[2]—what can we learn from these masterpieces? If art could be explained rationally, or even descriptively, it might be political commentary. But it's not. Instead, it's an emotional reaction to, or warning about, the human condition that cannot be reduced to a newspaper edi-

---

2 Ravel's dark, brooding *Piano Concerto for the Left Hand* (1932) was commissioned by Paul Wittgenstein, who had lost his right arm in the war.

torial, television commentary, or social-media post. It is not a slogan, no matter how hard the unholy Left has tried to make it so. It is not "Muddle Instead of Music" in *Pravda*. Neither is it "the people, united, shall never be defeated," even though the American composer, Frederic Rzewski, turned that radical catch phrase into the subject of an hour-long theme and variations for piano in 1975.

More: what can we learn from Bertrand and his "Gaspard"? What can we learn from our cultural fascination with evil, with Satan, with the dark side, while we simultaneously—in matters of public policy and politically correct groupthink and righthink—do our best to stamp out evil (restrictively defined) while denying its very existence? It's all very well to wish away evil, or to try and legislate against it—but the fact that it persists ought to give us a clue that such a task is not only impossible, but undesirable. Our knowledge of good and evil—Eve's gift to humanity—is what makes us like God: postlapsarian pilgrims who are sadder but wiser in the wide world outside the Garden as we take our halting, imperfect steps on the long journey home.

It classical times, the way was called the *Gradus ad Parnassum*—the steps to Parnassus, the highest peak of a Greek mountain range, where Apollo and the Muses disported themselves, and a goal toward which all educated men aspired. The phrase has come to denote the path to enlightenment and achievement that is celebrated in most if not all human societies, with the goal being wisdom and mastery. They are, in fact, the steps to civilization itself.

The problem is, today we define "civilization"—when we define it at all, or define it invidiously as a form of "racism"—almost exclusively in terms of politics and political programs. Where the men of ancient Greece and Rome prided themselves on their *virtue*—their inherently manly qualities, their virility—today we present a list of our *values* or, worse, our *principles*, immediately recalling Marx's famous riposte: "Those are my principles, and if you don't like them ... well, I have others." (Groucho, not Karl.)

"Preenciples" is more like it. For what good are "principles" in the absence of a test? Merely Milton's "fugitive and cloistered virtue, unexercised and unbreathed." What good are they in the face of monstrous evil? What use are "values" in the face of an opponent who prizes them not, and rejects them utterly? They collapse in the face of conflict, turn to ashes, and wash away like tears in the rain. History is replete with civilizations and cultures that stopped believing in their own basic tenets, turned certainties to questions, morals to "values," and vanished. Livy's warning to the Augustan Romans in the Preface to the first five volumes of his *History of Early Rome* ultimately went unheeded:

> I hope my passion for Rome's past has not impaired my judgement; for I do honestly believe that no country has ever been greater or purer than ours or richer in good citizens and noble deeds; none has been free for so many generations from the vices of avarice and luxury; nowhere have thrift and plain living been for so long held in such esteem. Indeed, poverty, with us, went hand in hand with contentment. Of late years wealth has made us greedy, and self-indulgence has brought us, through every form of sensual excess, to be, if I may so put it, in love with death both individual and collective.
>
> [translation by Aubrey de Selincourt]

By the same token, contemporary Europe, playing out the anti-religious skein that began with the French Revolution and which has continued in force during the postwar de-Christianization of the Continent, seems destined for the same fate.

Therefore, we must always seek to confront evil directly in our art, in part because it is so dramatic.[3] The confrontation is not merely symbolic. Every sentient reader or viewer regards the malevolent presence of the villain and asks himself: could that be me? We try on the evil we observe for size, wondering if the shoe might fit and, if so, how snugly. We understand, if only intuitively, that the Bad Guy is the hero of his own story, and that the Good Guy is the fiend trying to prevent him from realizing his desire.

Thus, Satan wants Heaven, or at least a Heaven of his own; Mephisto wants Faust's soul; Mordred wants Arthur's royal seat; Iago wants to destroy the Moor of Venice; Hans Landa, the charming Nazi devil of Quentin Tarantino's *Inglourious Basterds*, wants to catch and kill the Jewess, Shoshanna, while Ernst Stavro Blofeld defies James Bond to achieve world domination, and the Joker just wants to watch the world burn. That they

---

3 "Imaginary evil is romantic and varied; real evil is gloomy, monotonous, barren, boring. Imaginary good is boring; real good is always new, marvelous, intoxicating."—Simone Weil, *Gravity & Grace* (1947)

are all frustrated and defeated is part of the fun—we want the real heroes to win, even if in real life they don't always—but a great story always contains at least the plausible possibility that evil can triumph. And then what do we do?

CHAPTER THREE

Théodore Géricault, *Le Radeau de la Méduse*, 1819

The Raft of the *Medusa*
Politicized art or art as politics?

Quick: would you rather read a think-tank white paper from around the time of the Reagan–Gorbachev Reykjavik summit in 1986, assuring the Boston–Washington corridor that the Soviet Union would remain the only other superpower indefinitely, and that its stability was vital to the balance of power, or watch *Rocky IV*, released in 1985? Which better predicted the events of November 1989?

Consider, for example, this review of Strobe Talbott's 1984 book on arms control, *Deadly Gambits*. Talbott, then a writer for *Time* Magazine—he later left to join the Clinton administration as Deputy Secretary of State, and parlayed that into becoming president of the Brookings Institution— undertook in a widely unread book to contrast the arms-control policies of the Jimmy Carter and Ronald Reagan administrations, to the latter's detriment, of course. This concluding passage from the contemporaneous *New York Times* review provides a flavor [emphasis mine]:

> Mr. Talbott, who is diplomatic correspondent at *Time*, had previously written "Endgame: The Inside Story of SALT II." What is striking about the two books is that "Endgame" was about how President Carter and his top aides—Zbigniew Brzezinski, Secretary of State Cyrus R. Vance, and Defense Secretary Harold Brown—were directly in charge of the arms control process. "Deadly Gambits" shows how President Reagan, Secretary of State George P. Shultz, Mr. Weinberger, and the three different national security advisers, had little to do with making arms control policy because they **lacked the intellectual tools or interest** in the subject.
>
> He is particularly mocking of Mr. Reagan, who, Mr. Talbott writes, liked to give speeches on arms control, "but behind the scenes, where decisions were made and policy was set, he was to remain a **detached, sometimes befuddled character.**" Mr. Talbott says that even though Mr. Reagan presided at 16 meetings of the National Security Council on strategic arms talks, "there was ample evidence, during those meetings and on other occasions as well, that he frequently did not understand basic aspects of the nuclear weapons issue and of policies being promulgated in his name."

The Soviet Union's collapse began five years later with the fall of the Berlin Wall, and the Cold War ended two years after that. There was no nuclear exchange between the Russians and the Americans. Containment, technological superiority, and firmness of purpose at the highest levels of American and Western foreign policy for forty-five years had worked—and the end came just after Reagan left office.

Talbott's career checked all the boxes of the American foreign-policy establishment, including education (Hotchkiss, Yale, Oxford, where he was Bill Clinton's roommate); youthful attention as translator of Nikita Khrushchev's memoirs; top-tier American journalistic experience (*Time*); service in government and at a prestigious Beltway think tank. And yet his record on all the major foreign-policy events of the past several decades was dismal, mirroring that of most of his conventionally thinking colleagues in both journalism and academe. If this is what specialization achieves, then let us have less of it.

A far more significant international event in the history of the Cold War end game took place over two weeks in April 1986, when the great Russian-born virtuoso Vladimir Horowitz made his first and only return to the land of his birth. The pianist's visit was skillfully negotiated by Peter Gelb, a grand-nephew of the violinist Jascha Heifetz, who was then with Columbia Artists Management Inc., the leading music-management agency in the country; Gelb later became the general director of the Metropolitan Opera in New York City.

The opening was provided by a cultural-exchange agreement that had been concluded between Reagan and the Soviet premier, Mikhail Gorbachev, at their Geneva summit on November 21, 1985. Gelb contacted Bernard Kalb, a former journalist who was Assistant Secretary of State for public affairs in the Reagan administration, and suggested that a Horowitz visit be the first of the exchanges. The trip was jeopardized several times, particularly in the wake of an incident at Spaso House in which the piano in the residence had its strings slashed by someone on the household staff after the ambassador, Arthur Hartman, had hosted an informal concert by a leading *refusenik* pianist, Vladimir Feltsman. (Feltsman emigrated to the United States in 1987.) It took a personal letter from President Reagan, hand-delivered to Horowitz's residence on East 94th Street in Manhattan, and guaranteeing both the pianist's safety in Russia and that of his custom-shipped personal Steinway piano—without which he never performed—for the exchange to be solidified.

As it happened, the visit was bookended by two major news events. The first was the American air assault on Muammar Gaddafi's Libya on April 15, 1986, in retaliation for the terrorist bombing ten days earlier of the La Belle discothèque in West Berlin, in which two American servicemen were killed. The second was the nuclear meltdown at Chernobyl on April 26. Their noses out of joint over Reagan's actions against a then-Soviet ally, the Russians gave the pianist and his entourage a chilly reception at the airport and boycotted a dinner in his honor at the Italian embassy in Moscow. The Chernobyl accident, meanwhile, took place on the Saturday before Horowitz's final U.S.S.R. concert, but word of the disaster did not leak out until the visitors had decamped.

I was privileged to witness the entire Russian trip. This is what I wrote in *Time* Magazine of the concert's significance at the time (issue of May 5, 1986):

The first recital provoked an unprecedented near riot. As the security gates in front of the Moscow Conservatory swung open to admit the pianist's chauffeured Chaika, hundreds of young people burst through the police lines and stormed the Conservatory's Great Hall. Plainclothes and uniformed guards managed to grab a few of them, sending several sprawling. But many, perhaps most, raced past astonished ticket takers and run upstairs to the balcony, where they crouched in the aisles and stood shoulder to shoulder against the walls. In a country that takes special pride in preserving public order, romantic exuberance rarely overwhelms regimentation so publicly. It was fitting for the occasion.[1]

In an unconscious echo of Rocky's "If I can change and you can change, everybody can change" speech at the end of his winning bout against the Russian champion, Ivan Drago, Horowitz had this to say about the Soviet Union and the Russians:

> Before leaving New York City, the pianist had been sanguine about his chances of success, both as a musician and as a cultural ambassador. "I am not a Communist, but I can understand their way of thinking better than most Americans," he declared. "We all know there is good and evil everywhere. I was brought up to seek the good. In the Soviet Union today, the good is the music they produce. I hope that by playing in the Soviet Union, I will make the good better. Music inspires. It does not destroy and kill."

The sentiment may have seemed naïve at the time, but in retrospect, how right Horowitz was. Despite being completely apolitical—Horowitz was sometimes childlike in his appetites and pleasures, a man whose often puckish exterior masked the barely controlled, and sometimes uncontrolled, fury of his playing—he was correct in several of assessments. For one thing, he did understand the Russians better than most Americans; he certainly understood them better than Talbott, and better than most members of the State Department and the Central Intelligence Agency,

---

1 When I reached my balcony seat, I found three students occupying it, one in the chair and two on the floor.

who consistently viewed the Soviet Union through prisms of their own self-advancement and continued employment.

Horowitz's recitals in the Soviet Union (there were two in Moscow, one private, one public), and one in Leningrad—not to mention the disaster at Chernobyl—were followed eight months later by a political event that should have vastly outweighed the concerts in diplomatic importance: the summit between U.S. president Reagan and Soviet premier Gorbachev in Reykjavik, Iceland. It ended in what appeared to be apparent failure, when Reagan walked away from the meeting after Gorbachev demanded that, in addition to both sides destroying their nuclear arsenals, Reagan give up the so-called "Star Wars" anti-missile defense system, known officially as the Strategic Defense Initiative (SDI). The president refused—but it was clear that SDI was causing the Warsaw Pact a great deal of worry.

Once again, if the diplomats had been paying attention to *artistic* events, this would have come as no surprise either to Reagan or Gorbachev or their fleets of advisers. Just fourteen months previously, I had been standing in biting cold outside the Semper Opera House in Dresden, East Germany, listening to the GDR's leader, Erich Honecker, denounce the nascent "Star Wars" program in terms that clearly communicated the Communist world's fear of American technological superiority.

It was in part a propaganda event: the great opera house was reopening on February 13, 1985, exactly forty years to the day after it and most of Dresden had been destroyed *"durch anglo-amerikaner Bomber"* near the end of World War II. The purpose was to show off East German infrastructural advancement to an international audience, and even if much of the restoration work had been done by non-German artisans, and the town's best hotels had been built by capitalists, the regime was determined to open up a new *Schaufenster*—a "picture window"—through which others could gaze upon its accomplishments. The two works chosen to rechristen the house were the ones that had been playing its stage during the Allied air attacks: Weber's eerie *Der Freischütz* and Richard Strauss's nostalgic *Der Rosenkavalier*.

But it was Honecker's hour-long stemwinder in the *Theaterplatz* in the bitterest cold, with the noble *Frauenkirche* still lying in ruins nearby (it's since been restored and reconsecrated) that resonated. Honecker could remind his audience of the perfidy of the West—look what they did to us—denounce American militarism, and yet still point hopefully to a missile-free future if only Soviet diplomacy were given a chance to work.

This, then, was the context in which Reagan and Gorbachev met, although few understood it at the time. The Communists' inferiority complex regarding the West, which had always been fueled by fear, jealousy, and resentment, was becoming uncontrollable. Chernobyl had made the U.S.S.R. a laughingstock in the world's eyes. Reagan, the poker player, was pushing new chips into the pot, seeing whatever the Russians had and raising them an SDI. When the president refused to abandon "Star Wars"—whether it would even work was then very much in doubt—he bankrupted the Russian chess players. Seeing no way out of the financial and military checkmate, and knowing the extreme limitations of the Soviet command economy, Gorbachev tipped over his king and resigned. Three years later, the Wall came down.

Did Horowitz effect all this himself? Of course not. Each event was a piece in the mosaic. But his was more catalytic than most: what the Horowitz concerts demonstrated to the Communists was that they could not succeed even in something as simple as controlling the entrances to the Tchaikovsky Hall in the heart of Moscow. Yes, the security men counter-attacked during the battle on the stairway, pushing and shoving a few students down the stairs and into the surging crowd. But the students were not to be denied, and in the end, neither were the East Germans, the Poles, the Czechs, the Hungarians, and finally even the Russians.

Therefore, the argument must be made, and taken seriously, that the study of the arts belongs every bit as much in the realm of public policy as, say, the study of political "science" (a term that reeks of Marxism, since there is no more that is "scientific" about politics than there is about history) and arguably more so. For one thing, storytelling has been around a lot longer than the Kennedy School of Government; for another, its track record in predicting and ameliorating various catastrophes throughout history has been much better. Certainly better than all the wise men whose gaze floated from their navels to the Kremlin and back again, and yet never saw the end of the Soviet Union coming.

As things turned out, Horowitz's return to the Soviet Union was a trip that presaged the end of the Soviet Union, the irony being that this most apolitical of artists contributed to one of the greatest political earthquakes in history. Had he been acting politically, however, things might have been very different. The recitals would have been seen as a provocation, an insult; they would never have occurred. The Soviets were masters of politicized art and music, which is why they were blindsided, and reduced to tears, by the very purity of Horowitz's artistry.

Indeed, what are we to make of politicized art, which flourished in the U.S.S.R. and the other Communist bloc countries throughout much of the twentieth century, only to leave behind the residue of a failed politics and nothing worthwhile in the way of art? To take just the Soviet Union, the composers we best remember from the Stalinist period are Prokofiev and Shostakovich—not Tikhon Khrennikov, the longtime head of the Union of Soviet Composers and a member of the Central Committee of the Communist Party. Perhaps significantly, Khrennikov was closely associated with the infamous "Resolution of 1948" from the Committee for Artistic Affairs, which specifically singled out Shostakovich for abuse, accused him of "decadent Formalism," and officially banned some of his works, including his sixth, eighth and ninth symphonies.

Always the wily apparatchik, Khrennikov pushed to have the resolution rescinded ten years later, after Stalin was safely dead. And, thanks to his bureaucratic savvy, his career flourished—operas, symphonies, piano works, chamber music, and film scores just poured from his pen. And yet you've never heard a single note of any of them.[2]

One composer who wrote frankly political art was the West German Hans Werner Henze, once a critical darling, now neglected since his death in 2012. A flamboyant homosexual, Marxist Communist, and a limousine liberal who enjoyed the finest things in life, Henze made his mark in 1961 with his opera *Elegy for Young Lovers*, to a libretto by W. H. Auden and Chester Kallman, about the monstrous but necessary selfishness of the artist (in this case, a poet[3]), who uses the lives of others as raw material for his work including, at the end, their deaths. Henze followed that up four

---

2 During a formal interview with Khrennikov at the Composers Union, I asked him how he could sit in a room with pictures of Shostakovich et al. on the walls with a clear conscience, knowing that he had almost gotten them killed. He went instantly nuclear, pounding the table and demanding to know how I had the effrontery to ask such a thing. I replied that I was doing him a favor, as a question about the Resolution of 1948 would be one of the first queries he got upon his arrival in the United States. for a musical event. He thought about my answer for a moment, broke into a big smile, invited me to attend a performance of one of his operas that evening, and hosted a formal lunch for me at the Union shortly thereafter. The trip to America was, however, canceled.

3 After the fashion of Byron, as we shall see.

years later with *Der junge Lord* (The Young Lord), about a trained ape who is taken for a nobleman by the foolish residents of a small German town in the early nineteenth century. Both are strong works that hold the stage well, and some of Henze's music has an even larger place in the history of twentieth-century music, especially his 1968 oratorio *Das Floß der Medusa* (The Raft of the Medusa), after the famous picture by Géricault—his public coming-out as a radical Leftist, which cemented his career even as it diminished him as an artist.

Henze saw the great painting as an opportunity to deplore the evils of militarism and capitalism: the *Méduse* (filled with snakes) was a French naval frigate that ran aground near Mauritania *en route* to Senegal in West Africa in 1816. After the captain, the government officials, and the priests had escaped in the lifeboats, one hundred and forty-seven lesser souls went into the water aboard a makeshift raft; at their chance rescue by the *Argus* (of the all-seeing eyes) after two weeks at sea, only fifteen were left. Henze dubbed his work a "documentary oratorio," and intended it as a requiem for Che Guevara, who had been "killed in action in Bolivia in October 1967," during the writing of the piece.

Say this about Henze, though: he was fully committed to socialism, as long as his luxurious lifestyle near Rome didn't count against him. Fluent in several languages, an engaging, witty conversationalist, a connoisseur of Calvados, an elegant dresser, Henze was the very picture of a sophisticated, educated European of his time. He was also an indefatigable essayist, who eventually published a selection of his collected writings from 1953 to 1981 as *Music and Politics*, in which he argues explicitly in favor of politicized art, of the non-Soviet variety, to be sure.

> The bourgeois artist, or one who feels himself to be socially secure, tends to disintegrate the material at his disposal while he is creating, whereas the alienated one, the outlaw, puts all his energy into achieving the opposite with the same material, namely to try to integrate himself at all costs.... he looks for understanding not among *nouveau-riche*, middle-class consumers, but among individuals or minorities with whom he believes he can communicate. Thus both his behavior and the form of his works are implicitly provocative, and more or less consciously he makes this provocation his goal.

He was, of course, describing himself here.

The English translation of this essay, first published in 1964, is "The Bourgeois Artist," but the German title is better: *"Künstler als Außenseiter"* or "The Artist as Outsider." And yet Henze made the same mistake so many others on the Left continue to make to this day, which is to regard their form of rebellion—socialism—as something transgressive when in fact it is a commonplace. The really transgressive thing would have been to be an unabashed capitalist, but that might have had a negative impact on his quality of life. Blame Hitler:

> I came to the Left just like anybody else, I imagine. People of my generation [Henze was born in 1926], after all, are bound to have a very clear recollection of fascism. To have seen that Hitlerism lived on after the fall of Hitler, that fascism had put on a different mask, has left many people, including myself, with a fascism-trauma...
>
> I can conceive of utopian possibilities only in socialism. Utopia is defined by the absence of capitalism, the absence of the dominance of men over men, the liberation of art from its commercialization. I visualize the disappearance of the musical elite and of globe-trotting virtuosi; the overcoming of all this ideology of stardom in music, which I regard as a relic from the previous century and as a *maladie de notre temps.* It would mean that the composer is no longer a star, as today, but an *uomo sociale,* someone who learns and teaches. He would be someone who shows other people how to compose; I could envisage composing become something that all people can do, simply by taking away their inhibitions. I think there is no such thing as an unmusical person.
>
> —"Must Music be Political?" 1969 interview in the *zürcher student*

The bits of French and Italian are a nice touch, as is the lower-case "z" in the title of the Zurich student newspaper, to which Henze gave the interview. Viewed across the span of five decades, the sentiments are both trite and inaccurate. Hitlerism died with Hitler in 1945; it was ruthlessly expunged in West Germany and to this day you will find no serious person who advocates a restoration of the *Führerprinzip* or the reconquest of Poland. The "fascism" that sensitive souls like Henze detected was largely imaginary; but leftism was a safe harbor for a would-be *Außenseiter* like him, someone who wished to *épater le bourgeoisie,* but still live like one of them as they cheered his music.

Further, the "utopian possibilities" Henze gleaned in socialism are invisible to anyone with any experience of actual socialism; too many bodies have floated down the river and over the dam. And yet, because it "hasn't really been tried yet," Communism's allure continues among the young, who don't know any better, and the cynical, who know it's doomed to failure but, like good Communists everywhere, see a chance to make a buck.

Like the desperate survivors aboard the raft of the *Medusa*, the Left has turned into a tribe of cannibals, devouring its own in pursuit of what it hopes will be salvation. Henze wished his oratorio to be apprehended as an allegory of the struggle against death and the "comfortable temptation to despair." Once perceived as revolutionary, *The Raft of the Medusa* could be staged again today without changing a word of the text, an element of the staging, or a note of the music; and a sizable crowd would show up to listen, nod … and never seem to notice that in their minds the year is still 1968, and always will be. Like Henze, who saw Nazis under the bed everywhere in rubble-strewn Germany after the war, they believe that the barricades of 1968 are still the place to be. Just as long as nobody actually gets hurt.

Here we arrive at the salient difference between art and propaganda. Géricault's masterpiece captures the horror and despair of the raft's victims just as the *Argus* heaves into view on the distant horizon. Will the ship see them? Will it arrive in time? Or will it simply sail past, oblivious? The eye is immediately drawn to the black youth at the apex of the triangle of human figures on the right (the precariously tilting mast to the left forms the other), waving a red shirt—the bloody shirt of revolution—as the possibility of rescue spreads among those passengers still well enough to stand, and care. We need not know a thing about the historical back story; Géricault doesn't ask us to. Our sympathies are instantly with the human wretches, some dead, others dying, which is exactly as it should be. The work speaks for itself, and in purely human terms.

Khrennikov, Henze, and countless other now-forgotten purveyors of politicized art do precisely the opposite: they make the backstory defiantly political, and put it in the foreground. We will be made to understand that the death agonies of innocents are not the focus of the piece; rather, *the political point that can be made out of them* is. This is, in essence, the fundamentally heartless approach of the Left to art, and the chief reason why such art does not survive the death of either the artist or, more important, his state patron. To them, a piece of art under consideration or in perfor-mance functions not as a unique work in itself, but as a commentary—a political commentary—upon an historical event. Like the hero of Henze's *Elegy*, it uses people as fodder, employs corpses as homages to Che, and implicitly calls out for more violence to avenge the violence it portrays.

And then the artists go home to their comfortable villas in Italy, their apartments on the Upper West Side of Manhattan, their homes in Beverly Hills, crack open the Calvados, and toast themselves for a job well done.

CHAPTER FOUR

Jacques Daret, *The Visitation*, from the Arras *Altarpiece of the Virgin, ca.* 1435

The Woman Without a Shadow
How a culture dies, one child at a time

T he Visitation, the second of Catholicism's Joyful Mysteries, is one of the most important events in the Christian Bible. The Angel Gabriel has announced both to Zacharias—husband to Elizabeth, beyond her childbearing years—and Mary, the Virgin, as yet sexually unknown by her espoused Joseph, that both women will soon bear sons: John the Baptist and Jesus the Christ.

Despite its very ordinariness—women have been getting pregnant since the dawn of human history—it's an iconographic moment with considerable resonance for today. After all, it's only in the past half-century or so that we have managed to separate sex from conception (and thus from morality) and, more recently, sex from sex. Pregnant women, once a routine sight in America and the West, are today a relative rarity. Large families, once the norm, are remarkable and, to some environmentalists, reprehensible—an unconscionable demand on the allegedly finite resources of the planet and affront to all right-thinking people.

To radical feminists, of course, the scene is equally abhorrent. Neither Elizabeth nor Mary is shown working at a trade, such as carpentry, or commanding a Roman legion. Both, in the eyes of the cultural-Marxist Left, have been reduced to their physical properties—brood mares—and, worse, seem to be enjoying the experience, sharing a sisterly embrace of wonder and joy in their moment of self-actualization as not only mature females, but fully realized *women.* Throw in the religious/historical element, that the two cousins are about to give birth to two of the most consequential men in history, and you have a prescription for quivering outrage.

More: both are unusual pregnancies; neither woman should have been, at that moment, with child. Of the childless, older Elizabeth, Luke 1:36 tells us: *"And, behold, thy cousin Elisabeth, she hath also conceived a son in her old age: and this is the sixth month with her, who was called barren."* And to the virgin, Mary, the Angel Gabriel speaks some of the most famous words in scripture:

> *1:26 And in the sixth month the angel Gabriel was sent from God unto a city of Galilee, named Nazareth,*
> *27 To a virgin espoused to a man whose name was Joseph, of the house of David; and the virgin's name was Mary.*
> *28 And the angel came in unto her, and said, Hail, thou that art highly favoured, the Lord is with thee: blessed art thou among women.*
> *29 And when she saw him, she was troubled at his saying, and cast in her mind what manner of salutation this should be.*
> *30 And the angel said unto her, Fear not, Mary: for thou hast found favour with God.*

31 And, behold, thou shalt conceive in thy womb, and bring forth a
son, and shalt call his name Jesus ...
34 Then said Mary unto the angel, How shall this be, seeing I know
not a man?
35 And the angel answered and said unto her, The Holy Ghost shall
come upon thee, and the power of the Highest shall overshadow thee:
therefore also that holy thing which shall be born of thee shall be
called the Son of God ...
37 For with God nothing shall be impossible. (Luke 1:26–37)

Behold the paradox at the heart of Christian morality. For a betrothed virgin to become with child, a sin must have been committed—and yet we know from Gabriel's words to her that she is sinless, favored of the Lord. And the fruit of this sin-that-is-not-a-sin will be Messiah, the conqueror of Sin's offspring, Death.

Here we have, in one of the Christian West's *Ur*-myths, two miracles: Divine intervention (proof, to believers, of the Deity) in order to change the course of history (proof, to most historians, who accept the historical Jesus). Whether one accepts Jesus as the Christ matters not: the fact remains that history was changed. And not only history, but the course of Western thought, Western art, and Western culture. It is possible to mourn the vigorous paganism of the Roman Republic and early Empire, but it is impossible to deny that Constantine's embrace of previously persecuted Christianity in 312 Anno Domini changed the world.

One of the most significant ways in which Christianity did just that was in its elevation of women from chattel to equal partners with men. Not "equal" in the sense demanded today, which is to say proportionally represented in the upper echelons of government, corporate governance, and the professions, but equal in their intrinsic worth as human beings. This may come as a surprise to the militantly anti-Christian "feminists" of the movement's latter stages, many of them radical lesbians and "transgender" advocates whose bitterness toward both God and Nature is manifest, and who have hijacked the cause of the Suffragettes of the turn of the last century and the bra-burners of the Sixties, and turned it into a revenge drama. But it is a fact.

As Thomas Cahill observes, it was figures such as the anchorite Hildegard von Bingen, Eleanor of Aquitaine, Francis of Assisi, and Thomas

Aquinas who introduced the notion of an equal status for women into the European consciousness.

> Hildegard is mindful that Heaven is the final goal of everyman and presses ordinary people to life and live that will make them welcome there. But above all she attacks the clergy for the enervated presentations of Christian truth and the scandal of their compromised lives.... In her day, the courage of "poor little" Hildegard's attack would have been thrilling enough to make the hairs on a listener's neck stand up.

The idea of the equality of the sexes in God's eyes is a fundamentally Christian concept. Today, when the meaning of the word "equality" has been enlarged and expanded in the wake of the French Revolution, and then constricted and diminished again in turn by the reductive Marxist revolution, this may not seem like much. But to the women—and men—of the time, it was everything.

And why not? From the start, Christianity gave an honored place to women in its pantheon: not just to Elizabeth and Mary but, during the life of Christ, to Martha and the Magdalene. Who, after all, rushed to the Tomb on Easter morn to discover it empty, as empty as a woman's womb after giving birth? Women. From Mark 16:

> 1 And when the sabbath was past, Mary Magdalene, and Mary the mother of James, and Salome, had bought sweet spices, that they might come and anoint him.
> 2 And very early in the morning the first day of the week, they came unto the sepulchre at the rising of the sun.
> 3 And they said among themselves, Who shall roll us away the stone from the door of the sepulchre?
> 4 And when they looked, they saw that the stone was rolled away: for it was very great.
> 5 And entering into the sepulchre, they saw a young man sitting on the right side, clothed in a long white garment; and they were affrighted.
> 6 And he saith unto them, Be not affrighted: Ye seek Jesus of Nazareth, which was crucified: he is risen; he is not here: behold the place where they laid him.

*7 But go your way, tell his disciples and Peter that he goeth before you
into Galilee: there shall ye see him, as he said unto you.*
*8 And they went out quickly, and fled from the sepulchre; for they
trembled and were amazed: neither said they any thing to any man;
for they were afraid.*
*9 Now when Jesus was risen early the first day of the week, he
appeared first to Mary Magdalene, out of whom he had cast seven
devils.*
*10 And she went and told them that had been with him, as they
mourned and wept. 11 And they, when they had heard that he was
alive, and had been seen of her, believed not.* (Mark 16:1–10)

Christianity transformed women from chattel and helpless rape victims into human beings (a trick of cultural prestidigitation that Islam has not managed to accomplish in well over a millennium) who may not have had the *political* rights of men but who had the *human* rights of men. Christianity elevated women from generative to venerative, building on the pagan goddess cults of Greece and Rome, whose literature featured countless examples of the feminist ideal—the "strong woman." Christianity turned marriage from the transfer of sexualized property into what today we would call a "relationship," one of equals, not of master–slave. Christianity insisted upon the legitimacy of children, the proper transfer of wealth and, to a certain extent, of status. It may have weakened the Empire, in Gibbon's insistence, but it immeasurably enriched the culture of Christian Europe that superseded it. Scribble, scribble, scribble indeed.

By contrast, Islam still constrains women, largely out of fear of their potent sexual allure, which is deemed to make the Islamic male lose control of his senses: bewitched by the power of pussy. Pious Muslims regard the uncovered Western woman as a whore, whose exposed hair alone is a satanic temptation. They understand, correctly, that the free deployment of women's sexuality has destabilizing social consequences (something the Western male has, imperfectly, learned to deal with) and, with their advocacy of *sharia* law, seek to put the Christian genie back into Aladdin's lamp. Where Christianity, through its liberation of women, forces men to improve themselves morally, imparting the virtue of self-restraint, Islam seeks to protect the weaker sex—men—from the stronger, and so allows them to beat and even murder the females in their orbits.

What's wrong with misogynist Islam? Its literature suggests an answer.

In 1885, the celebrated British explorer, linguist, adventurer—one of the few infidels ever to penetrate the "holy city" of Mecca—and connoisseur of exotic sexual practices, Sir Richard Burton, published his multi-volume, unexpurgated translation of *The Book of a Thousand Nights and a Night*, a collection of fables from across the Muslim world dating from the eighth to the thirteenth centuries. The tales of Scheherazade have come down to us in sanitized form, from Ali Baba and the Forty Thieves to Disney's *Aladdin*, but in the original they reflect the Arab world's obsession with genitals, body fluids, lust, purity, faithfulness, and its fear of unbridled female sexuality and the magical powers of women's bodies, which demands they be kept hidden, all tied up with honor.

A couple of choice, rather tame, examples from Burton's Volume Five:

The Caliph Harun Al-Rashid and Queen Zubaydah in the Bath.

THE Caliph Harun al-Rashid loved the Lady Zubaydah with exceeding love and laid out for her a pleasaunce, wherein he made a great tank and set thereabouts a screen of trees and led thither water from all sides ; hence the trees grew and interlaced over the basin so densely, that one could go in and wash, without being seen of any, for the thickness of the leafage. It chanced, one day, that Queen Zubaydah entered the garden and, coming to the swimming-bath, And Shahrazad perceived the dawn of day and ceased to say her permitted say.

Now when it was the Three Hundred and Eighty-sixth Night

She said, It hath reached me, O auspicious King, that Queen Zubaydah entered the garden one day and, coming to the swimming-bath, gazed upon its goodliness; and the sheen of the water and the overshading of the trees pleased her. Now it was a day of exceeding heat; so she doffed her clothes and, entering the tank, which was not deep enough to cover the whole person, fell to pouring the water over herself from an ewer of silver. It also happened that the Caliph heard she was in the pool; so he left his palace and came down to spy upon her through the screen of the foliage. He stood behind the trees and espied her mothernude, showing everything that is kept hidden. Presently, she became aware of him and turning, saw him behind the trees and was ashamed that he should see her naked. So she laid her hands

on her parts, but the Mount of Venus escaped from between them,
by reason of its greatness and plumpness; and the Caliph at once
turned and went away, wondering and reciting this couplet:
   I looked on her with loving eyne o And grew anew my old repine:

A second episode deals with precious bodily fluids, and the ever-present possibility that some other man will attempt to climb the Mount, perhaps inadvertently leaving behind his spoor:

THE Caliph Harun al-Rashid went up one noon-tide to his couch, to
lie down; and mounting, found upon the bed-clothes semen freshly
emitted; whereat he was startled and troubled with sore' trouble.
So he called the Lady Zubaydah and said to her, "What is that spilt
on the bed?" She looked at it and replied, "O Commander of the
Faithful, it is semen." Quoth he, "Tell me truly what this meaneth or
I will lay violent hands on thee forthright." Quoth she, "By Allah, O
Commander of the Faithful, indeed I know not how it came there and
I am guiltless of that whereof thou suspectest me." So he sent for the
Kazi Abu Yusuf and acquainted him of the case. The Judge raised
his eyes to the ceiling and, seeing a crack therein, said to the Caliph,
"O Commander of the Faithful, in very sooth the bat hath seed like
that of a man, and this is bat's semen." Then he called for a spear and
thrust it into the crevice, whereupon down fell the bat. In this man-
ner the Caliph's suspicions were dispelled—And Shahrazad perceived
the dawn of day and ceased saying her permitted say."

"This is the popular prejudice," notes Burton in a footnote, "and it has doubtless saved many a reputation." Not to mention many a life. Yet somehow it is always Christianity that it is accused of having a sexual fixation. In fact, the *Arabian Nights* are a cornucopia of pornography; no need to hunt for the juicy bits, just open an unbowdlerized version at random and your reader's eye will espy the wonders of the harem. If you seek the source of much of the Muslim world's pathology today you need look no further than the *Arabian Nights* and the tales of Scheherazade—a woman, of course.

Just three years after Burton's publication of the *Tales*, the Russian composer Nikolai Rimsky-Korsakov presented the world with his orches-

tral suite *Scheherazade*, one of the most striking and original examples
of so-called "program music" (that is, music that explicitly tells a story in
sound pictures). The piece, which is really a symphony, is in four movements: "The Sea and Sinbad's Ship," "The Tale of the Kalendar Prince," "The
Young Prince and the Young Princess," and the big finale: "The Festival
at Baghdad—the Sea—Shipwreck on a Rock Surmounted by a Bronze
Warrior—Conclusion." From its premiere in 1888, it has remained solidly
in the standard repertory.

It's unlikely that Rimsky was familiar with Burton's explicit and ribald
translations of the Arabic originals and he certainly would have made
no public acknowledgement of it in any case; Victorian pornography,
however scholarly, tended to be a private, *samizdat* affair. Of the period,
the closest thing to the frank, explicit eroticism of Burton's translations
of the *Arabian Nights* is the oeuvre of Aubrey Beardsley, particularly his
obscene drawings for *Lysistrata*, with their exaggerated, swollen genitalia
symbolizing the play's overall tone of sexual frustration; in the illustration
"The Examination of the Herald," the Spartan messenger's engorged prick
is as thick as a tree branch and extends the length of his torso, a sign of
the acute pangs of heterosexual inactivity felt by the Greek men in Aristophanes' play.

Still, the music exudes sensuality (especially in the third movement),
and is tinged throughout with an orientalism that never descends into
parody or pastiche. Linking the movements is the Sultan's peremptory
theme, which is answered by Scheherazade's seductive solo violin as she
spins out her tales, hoping to live just one more day before her sanguinary
lord and master has her executed for the crime of…what, exactly?

> The Sultan Schariar, convinced that all women are false and faith-
> less, vowed to put to death each of his wives after the first nuptial
> night. But the Sultana Scheherazade saved her life by entertaining
> her lord with fascinating tales, told seriatim, for a thousand and one
> nights. The Sultan, consumed with curiosity, postponed from day to
> day the execution of his wife, and finally repudiated his bloody vow
> entirely.

Even in the bloodthirsty world of Islamic sexual dysfunction, true love
can win out.

That Christianity is Public Enemy No. 1 in the minds of today's "feminists" speaks to their lack of historical knowledge or their resentful malevolence, or both. For them, as for the Left in general, sexual license is the only real "freedom" worth enjoying, or fighting for. Never mind that—as was utterly predictable[1]—it has resulted in the diminution of marriage (one of the Frankfurt School's goals, to be sure), the rise of out-of-wedlock births, the fetishization and indeed sacramentalization of abortion. Having staked out their territory—moving swiftly from equal rights to equal pay to superior rights to the conscientious-objector refusal to obey the laws of God and (until recently, man), to triumphing over a weak and arbitrary Supreme Court in *Roe v. Wade*, and to commandeering a major political party in the furtherance of its malign and literally anti-human political program—the "feminists" now seek to destroy their primary biological target: men.

Any rational—which is to say, historically literate human being, whether male or female—understands the necessity, and the troubling and challenging complications, of the male–female relationship. Indeed, those complications are the fun of it. The "War between the Sexes" may be a joke, but it is an earnest one: part of defining oneself as human involves solving the conundrum. "Women," goes the old joke, "can't live with them, can't kill 'em." And vice versa, however much either sex wishes it could. Or, should we say, "gender"?

Observe the Left in action: "gender" is a grammatical term, having nothing to do with biological sex. That it has become a synonym for sex—and as, *mutatis mutandis*, "sex" is now a synonym for sexual intercourse—is precisely the point. The command of the high ground of the language has always been, for the Left, of paramount importance. Relying on the snowballing ignorance of their youthful target voters, the cultural Marxists have insisted upon conflating the words "sex" and "gender," to the point at which "gender" (a linguistic term, remember, and thus in essence a "construct") is not only descriptive when they want it to be, but also literary, in the sense that is "assignable" and thus discardable, like a moth-riven suit of clothes.

But it's not. What's between your legs may be surgically excised or appended, but it remains what you were born with—and thus, in essence,

1 And as forecast by Pope Paul VI in *Humanae Vitae*.

who you are. Nota bene that word: *essence*. That is a word the Left emphatically rejects when it comes to actual essentials, and instead prefers to describe as "essential" things like Marxist "group identity." For just as Yahweh or Allah cannot have false gods before him, so neither can the Left have alternative interpretations of "facts" or "essences" even suggested, lest some unwary innocent fall into the right-wing trap of…accurate historical analysis.

The key to understanding the Left—"feminist" or otherwise—is that it (along with Marx and his successors), utterly rejects *all previous historical facts and interpretations of history* in order to proclaim its New World Order. In order to make that case, the unholy Left must needs overthrow and consign history itself to the ash heap of history.

The culturally suicidal nature of this impulse ought to be easily recognized. A culture without pregnant women, and lots of them, is doomed to extinction in as little as a few generations. Aristophanes' *Lysistrata* is usually considered a comedy about the withholding of sex by the Greek women to bring the Peloponnesian War to an end: no peace, no nookie. It's a message that began to resonate with the proto-feminists of the 1960s, who merged with the anti-war Left to combine agendas and associate sexual relations (then rapidly becoming liberalized, although even something as innocuous today as cohabitation was still tinged with transgression) with the war in Vietnam.

Certainly the text supports that—indeed, throughout the play the Greek women are portrayed as every bit concupiscent as their men:

LYSISTRATA: *Oh, Cleonice, my heart is on fire; I blush for our sex.*
Men say that we are tricky and sly.…
CLEONICE: *And they are quite right, upon my word!*

The memorable scene between Myrrhine and Kinesias, in which the cunning wife tortures the sexually desperate husband by constantly delaying her preparations for bed and then abandoning him for the safety of the Acropolis, wherein the other women have barred themselves, makes the point quite clear.

But there's an important subtext to *Lysistrata*, something perhaps forgotten in the era of the Pill and *Roe v. Wade*: to withhold sex until the warring males come to their senses and exchange their metal swords for more fleshly foils doesn't simply deprive the men of transitory sexual release but—if continued indefinitely—of their offspring as well; principally, their sons. Think about it in historical context: the constant bloodshed of the wars between the Greek city-states demanded a continuous supply of new helots, ready to move from the plow to the battlefield on a moment's notice. Soldiers were vital to the survival of the *polis*. Additionally, a man's worth was expressed in part through his sons, young men who would carry on the father's seed with their own, and keep the family name resounding unto the generations.

If this all seems quite primitive today, it's not, no matter how the feminists rail against the "patriarchy," and seek to permanently sever the relations between the sexes from any emotional symbiosis or cooperation. Sex has been reduced to dispassionate, meaningless coupling (something Aldous Huxley predicted in *Brave New World*) and now, in some quarters, not even that: sex between the opposite sexes has become politically incorrect. It's easy to laugh at this, but if recent history is any guide—and it should be—these people are deadly serious, waging their war on human nature with grim determination and utter humorlessness. There is literally no idea too stupid for the Left to conceive and believe, if not quite achieve, in its war against God, and against us.

Barrenness, however, used to be one of the worst things that could happen to a couple. The inability to produce a child was seen by some as a social humiliation, a sign of God's disfavor, or a tragedy, and certainly something to be countered via medical science when that became possible. So it's ironic that, just as we have succeeded in facilitating the conception and birth of children, including implanting fertilized embryos and so-called fetal adoption, in which a viable fetus is surgically transplanted into another woman's uterus and then carried to term, the West has decided to stop having babies, particularly in Europe.

Which brings us to *Die Frau ohne Schatten* (The Woman Without a Shadow), an opera by Richard Strauss with an original libretto by Hugo von Hofmannsthal. Begun in 1911 and composed largely during the First World War, the work got its premiere in 1919 at the Vienna State Opera. Coming on the heels of the powerful *Elektra*, the beguiling *Der Rosenkavalier*, and the curiously charming experiment of *Ariadne auf Naxos* (in which a Wagnerian Heldentenor suddenly shows up near the end of a semi-comic opera, and it almost makes sense), *Die Frau ohne Schatten* puzzled audiences at its premiere, and in fact didn't really find its place in the repertoire until the Metropolitan Opera mounted a spectacular production in the mid-sixties at its new home in Lincoln Center that took full advantage of the revolving stage's then-revolutionary technology. *Frau* was the thing to see, as well as hear.

The opera relates the tale of a semi-divine Emperor who has taken to wife the daughter of the mighty but unseen god, Keikobad (whose ominous leitmotiv is the first music we hear, in much the same way that the murdered Agamemnon's thunderous theme opens *Elektra*), and a mortal woman. The catch is that the Empress cannot cast a shadow—a symbol of her inability to bear a child—and if she doesn't acquire one before the first year of their marriage is up (in three days), she will return to the spirit world and the Emperor will be turned to stone ("*Er wird zu stein*," as the music constantly reminds us). The Empress and her Nurse descend into the world of human beings where, the Nurse assures her mistress, a "shadow" is to be found.

And it is found—in the home of Barak the Dyer and his wife. (This woman, the most important character in the opera, has no name; she is always referred to as the Dyer's Wife.) Barak, it seems, desperately wants a child, but his Wife is not interested. When she gets an offer for her "shadow" from the Empress, she's tempted to take it, but as the first act closes she suddenly hears reproachful children's voices emerging from the fishes she is frying in a skillet—the singing voices of her unborn children:

> CHILDRENS' VOICES: Mother, Mother, please let us in the house!
> The door is bolted, and we can't get in. We're in the dark, and very afraid. Mother, Mother—oh, woe! Woe!...Let us in, or call our beloved Father, so that he can open the door for us!

Even a symbol can't get much more specific than that.

Luckily, this fairy tale has a fairy-tale ending: the Empress, facing both her own and her husband's mortality, is touched by Barak and the Wife's moral dilemma and refuses to destroy their potential for happiness by taking the shadow. She thus embraces her own fate, but in so doing, through self-sacrifice, saves herself, her husband, and her marriage, while also rekindling the Wife's passion for her spouse. The unborn children will finally be allowed, literally, to come inside, and thus come to life.

Here is the childlessness/sexual license argument, put on a Viennese stage a century ago, and even more potent and poignant now than it was then. For audiences of the day, the idea that a woman could be tempted to give up her womanhood—her womb—was inconceivable; the Dyer's Wife is portrayed throughout much of the opera as cold, heartless, and calculating, in addition to being easily tempted to stray sexually (with no consequences of pregnancy) with the apparition of a Young Man that the wicked Nurse conjures up.

And yet at the same time, this is the Vienna of Arthur Schnitzler's *La Ronde* and Freud, a hothouse of sexuality that, almost a century later, turned up again in Stanley Kubrick's last movie, *Eyes Wide Shut*. Sex without consequences—the "punishment" of a baby—was as desirable then as now, even more so, since it was far more difficult. Repressed female sexuality was being analyzed by Dr. Freud over at Berggasse 19, while Klimt, wearing only a robe and no underwear, was painting the clothing over his anatomically correct female nudes, the better to communicate the hidden, inherent eroticism of their bodies, disguised only by a veneer of paint.

So *Frau* is not an anomaly, but an artifact of its time and place. That it is also universal in its themes—eternal, one might almost say—despite its somewhat forbidding musical exterior makes it an important work, although more from the perspective of Hofmannsthal's libretto than Strauss's music. That it also marks the beginning of Strauss's musical decline seems inarguable (his great symphonic tone poems were already mostly behind him), and none of the stage works that followed—*The Egyptian Helen, Arabella, Daphne, Die Liebe der Danae*—measure up to the achievements of the period 1903–19. Only *Capriccio*, written during World War II, near the end of the composer's long life, recaptures some of the old magic.

We don't, however, go the musical theater so much for the theater as for the music, which is why operas can be listened to and enjoyed in recording, whereas the librettos are almost never produced as straight plays. The music not only offers up the tunes we enjoy but, more important, provides the subtext of the words and the stage action, imparting a deeper, sometimes hidden, meaning to the experience.

How, then, does this all relate? What do the Visitation, *Lysistrata*, and *The Woman Without a Shadow* have in common?

As we've seen, they all have sex and pregnancy (or lack of it) at their hearts. The reason Bible stories—or any stories, for that matter—have been with us for so long, and resonate so strongly, is not that they have great plots. Once we learn which of the Ten Little Indians killed Roger Ackroyd aboard the Orient Express, we've solved the mystery of the plot. We can no longer be surprised by the rabbit that Agatha Christie just pulled out of her hat. But in a work of art, what matters are the life lessons we learn from it, and continue to learn each time we re-encounter it.

There's a common misconception that the moral precepts in the Bible are prescriptive, which is to say laid down by God and engraved in stone. And certainly that is true of the Ten Commandments as they have come down to us. But the commandments themselves are pointless without the illustrative morality plays that make up scriptures to give them meaning.

The Ten Commandments are a dramatic moment in *Exodus*, the high point of the Pentateuch, and the foundation not only of Judaism but of Christianity as well. But the Commandments themselves simply codify, in prescriptive form, the lessons illustrated throughout the Torah and the Christian Bible. That is to say, they are a response—divine, literary, mythological—to the natural condition of Man, *which antedates them.*

Storytelling, then—whether sacred or profane—is a culturally inter-locking set of variations on a near-eternal thematic thread: Man's Fate. It's no accident that in *The Ring of the Nibelung*, the Three Norns (Fates) are always seen at work, weaving the rope of Destiny. (When the rope breaks in *Götterdämmerung* we know the end is near.) They are, in the Norse my-thology upon which Wagner based his great tetralogy, the *Ur*-storytellers, envisioning and then recording the fate of every human being, even the unborn. And we are all simply characters in the drama.

Thus, the meeting of Mary and Elizabeth, each joyously celebrating the separate miracles of their impossible pregnancies, establishes the icon on which subsequent generations of artists have worked their changes. For the Greeks, the withdrawal of sex and the possibility of the end of the patrilineal line were, even in a comic play, enough to bring warring Athens and Sparta to the bargaining table, and to force the men to choose between two essential aspects of their innate nature: the desire to im-pregnate and the lust to take a life that some other woman has carried to term. For the *fin de siècle* Viennese, indolently sipping their Turkish coffee while opening an invitation to a secret sex party or a session with

Freud—the name means "joy" in German—the decision whether to even bother procreating as they hurtled toward a world war that would destroy nineteenth-century European civilization would soon be taken out of their hands and put into the hands of Keikobad. Across the centuries, therefore, are these human stories related, not only to one another, but woven by our own Norns into our future.

All three of these seminal stories, it should be noted, are about women. There is nothing either hysterical nor overtly sexually alluring about either Elizabeth or Mary. Unlike the bawdy Lysistrata, the pitiful Empress, the scheming Nurse, or the frigid Dyer's Wife, the biblical women are serene, almost unearthly. Both their sons will meet gruesome deaths: John the Baptist will be beheaded and his dead lips kissed by Salome in a fit of erotic passion (the subject of the first Strauss opera, to a libretto based on the play *Salome* by Oscar Wilde). Jesus will die the world's most iconic death, nailed to a Roman cross after prolonged torture, and left to die in front of his mother, and who is thus lowered from Godhood to dark, chthonic earth[2] as Jesus ascends not to Heaven, but descends instead on his three-day journey into the underworld before the glory of the Resurrection.

Is Jesus unique in undertaking such a journey? No. Orpheus, in Greek myth, descends to Hades to reclaim his lost love, Eurydice, and fails, later to be torn apart by the Thracian women. In Book Six of Virgil's *Aeneid*, written just a few years before the historical Jesus, the Trojan hero Aeneas ventures into the spirit world as well; accompanied by the Sibyl and ferried across the river by Charon, he eventually encounters his father, Anchises, in Elysium, where he is given a vision of his fate as the founder of Rome.

Although women are not plentiful in the *Aeneid*, the poem does contain two striking female characters: Dido, queen of Carthage, who kills herself after her abandonment by Aeneas; and fleet Camilla, the Amazonian warrior-princess who dies defending her homeland against the invading Trojans. Unlike Dido—about whom Henry Purcell wrote one of the earliest operas in the repertory, *Dido and Aeneas* (1688–89)—Camilla is a minor figure. But what an entrance she makes, and how powerfully the poet draws her, in some of the most beautiful and descriptive verses in any literature. In an epic that features the lives and deaths of countless

---

2 Mary herself, according to Christian theology, never suffers the corruption of the flesh, but was assumed bodily into Heaven, to sit eternally at the side of her Son.

warriors, Camilla stands out for her beauty, her bravery—and her femininity. She is, in fact, the original wonder woman:

> *Last, from the Volscians fair Camilla came,*
> *And led her warlike troops, a warrior dame;*
> *Unbred to spinning, in the loom unskill'd,*
> *She chose the nobler Pallas of the field.*
> *Mix'd with the first, the fierce virago fought,*
> *Sustain'd the toils of arms, the danger sought,*
> *Outstripp'd the winds in speed upon the plain,*
> *Flew o'er the fields, nor hurt the bearded grain:*
> *She swept the seas, and, as she skimm'd along,*
> *Her flying feet unbath'd on billows hung.*
> *Men, boys, and women, stupid with surprise,*
> *Where'er she passes, fix their wond'ring eyes:*
> *Longing they look, and, gaping at the sight,*
> *Devour her o'er and o'er with vast delight;*
> *Her purple habit sits with such a grace*
> *On her smooth shoulders, and so suits her face;*
> *Her head with ringlets of her hair is crown'd,*
> *And in a golden caul the curls are bound.*
> *She shakes her myrtle jav'lin; and, behind,*
> *Her Lycian quiver dances in the wind.*
>
> [translation by John Dryden]

So it is not true, as contemporary "feminists" and cultural Marxists like to argue, that women were of a status inferior until the arrival of Betty Friedan and Gloria Steinem. As usual, the radical Left's arguments are not factual but definitional. Having hijacked the specific goals of the Civil Rights Movement, with its focus on the free and unfettered exercise of the franchise, the feminists define everything subsequent in terms of a chimerical political "equality" made all the more gossamer by the fact that a far more important equality already exists—one dictated by a Supreme Being and not the Supreme Court.

Enraged by the fact that women are not men, their argument all along has been with God. Sex-reassignment surgery—stop and savor the Marxist flavor of that word, "assignment"—may be able to create the temporary illusion of essential transference, and there may well be a few instances of genuine sexual dysmorphia that are biological and not mental. In any case, sex-switching has a long history, replete with real-life *Hosenrolle*, transvestite roles in which men passed as women (think of David Henry Hwang's play, *M. Butterfly*, based on a true story) and women, binding their breasts, have often passed as men: Ludwig van Beethoven's lone opera, *Fidelio*, is about exactly that, until the youth "Fidelio" removes his disguise and stands revealed as the beautiful Leonore, come to rescue her husband, Florestan. And where would film comedy be without Billy Wilder's *Some Like It Hot*, starring Jack Lemmon and Tony Curtis in the drag show to end all drag shows—so convincing that they both compete ably with and for Marilyn Monroe.

Still, the attempt to move from suffragism to fatherhood—and thus, in a symbolic way that only Dr. Freud is equipped to analyze, to equate the franchise with the tumescent, potent penis—will prove too heavy a lift. End-stage feminism cannot get past its nineteenth-century Marxist-Romantic roots, viewing life exclusively as a struggle against occult masculine powers combined in conspiracy—for some unknown reason!—against the female. Which is to say, against their own mothers, wives, and daughters.

Previous generations embraced the acceptance of reality as a virtue, something to which even a proto-feminist like Hildegard von Bingen acquiesced, even as, in her cloister, she wrote her poetry, drew her pictures, composed her music, and lectured the male bishops about their wicked ways. But not today's feminists. Once they transform themselves into men, what is left? No wonder a minority of them, the hatchet-faced descendants of Carrie Nation and the Suffragettes, are rushing toward the burqa and the niqab, and the harem of Harun al-Rashid as re-envisaged by Osama bin Laden. The end-stage of feminism is the abolition of women.

As Mary and Elizabeth and Lysistrata and Dido and Camilla and the Empress, the Dyer's Wife, the Lady Zubaydah, and poor mad Renata know, the joke's on them.

CHAPTER FIVE

Edward Elgar's "Dorabella" cipher

The Mystery of Dorabella

In matters of art, politics, love, and war, naked is the best disguise

There's a Hollywood screenwriting term that well characterizes the current age: "on the nose." Not as in, "You hit it right on the nose," meaning that you correctly guessed an answer, analyzed a situation, or placed your bet exactly right. This would be a compliment.

The Hollywood term is not. In constructing a motion-picture script, the last thing a screenwriter wants to do is hit the dramatic or emotional situation "on the nose," meaning that he has written the scene to say and mean exactly what is on the page, and nothing more. No nuance, no hidden signifiers, no uncertainty, no ambiguity—no subtext. No one will buy or make a script that is on the nose. When the Boy finally screws up his courage enough to ask the Girl, "do you love me?" her reply should not be yes or no, but something more along the lines of, "would you like a biscuit?" A direct question should only rarely be answered directly; better to answer it with another, apparently irrelevant, non sequitur of a question. Or, at the end of a scene, leave the question in the air and cut away.

The mark of the amateur screenplay is that no question goes unanswered, and the answer is always exactly what you might expect it to be. In real life, we generally respond to interrogatories; in movies, we have no time for such mundanities; the subtext—the subterfuge—is not answering a direct question, but instead answering it with another, apparently irrelevant, question or statement. Even today, the country Irish tend to answer a question—"Is this the way to Dublin?"—with another, legally unassailable, non-responsive question: "Sure, and why wouldn't it be?" or "Who says it is?" The idea then, was not to get them into trouble with the English authorities; the idea, today in Movieland, is not to get in trouble with your audience.

In John Frankenheimer's great thriller *The Manchurian Candidate*, the hero Bennett Marco, played by Frank Sinatra, is smoothly picked up aboard a train by the beautiful Eugenie, played by Janet Leigh. Now, the appearance of a train in any good film is always a harbinger of sexual activity and/or violence: think of Cary Grant and Eva Marie Saint aboard the train at the end of *North by Northwest*, or Sean Connery, Robert Shaw, and Daniela Bianchi riding the Orient Express in *From Russia with Love*. Put Sinatra and Leigh on the train and you just know sparks are going to fly. And they do, but in an entirely unexpected way. In one of the greatest falling-in-love scenes ever written (taken from the Richard Condon novel by screenwriter George Axelrod), the two appear to be talking directly past each other as they share a cigarette break. But, of course, they're doing anything but.

The sequence opens with Sinatra sitting at a table in the café car, brooding and trying to light a cigarette, another cinematic signifier of sexual activity. As the camera pulls back, we see that Leigh is sitting right nearby, at a small table of her own: "Mind if I smoke?" he asks her; "Not at all, please do," she replies. When a breeze blows out the match, he rises angrily, knocks over the table and storms out of the cafe and into the space connecting two cars.

Leigh suddenly appears, successfully lights her own cigarette with a lighter instead of a match, takes a drag, hands it to Sinatra, and prepares to strike up a conversation. Without a word of dialogue so far, we now know they're destined to be lovers. Here's what follows:

ROSIE: Maryland's a beautiful state.

MARCO: (Looking away) This is Delaware.

ROSIE: I know. I was one of the original Chinese workmen who laid the track on this stretch. But nonetheless, Maryland is a beautiful state. So is Ohio, for that matter. (She lights her own cigarette.)

MARCO: I guess so. Columbus is a tremendous football town. You in the railroad business?

ROSIE: Not anymore. However, if you will permit me to point out, when you ask that question you really should say, "Are you in the railroad *line*?" Where's your home?

MARCO: I'm in the Army. I'm a major. I've been in the Army most of my life. We move a good deal. I was born in New Hampshire.

ROSIE: I went to a girls' camp once on Lake Francis.

MARCO: That's pretty far north.

ROSIE: Yeah.

MARCO: What's your name?

ROSIE: Eugenie.

MARCO: (He finally looks at her) Pardon?

ROSIE: No kidding, I really mean it. Crazy French pronunciation and all.

MARCO: (He looks away) It's pretty.

ROSIE: Well, thank you.

MARCO: I guess your friends call you Jenny.

ROSIE: Not yet they haven't, for which I am deeply grateful. But you may call me Jenny.

MARCO: What do your friends call you?

ROSIE: Rosie.

MARCO: (He looks at her) Why?

ROSIE: My full name is Eugenie Rose. (He looks away) Of the two names, I've always favored Rosie because it smells of brown soap and beer. Eugenie is somehow more fragile.

MARCO: Still, when I asked you what your name was, you said it was Eugenie.

ROSIE: It's quite possible I was feeling more or less fragile at that instant.

MARCO: I could never figure out what that phrase meant: more or less. (He looks at her) You Arabic?

ROSIE: No.

MARCO: (He reaches to shake her hand) My name is Ben, really Bennett. Named after Arnold Bennett.

ROSIE: The writer?

MARCO: No, a lieutenant colonel who was my father's commanding officer at the time.

ROSIE: What's your last name?

MARCO: Marco.

ROSIE: Major Marco. Are you Arabic?

MARCO: No, no.

ROSIE: Let me put it another way. Are you married?

MARCO: No. You?

ROSIE: No.

MARCO: What's your last name?

ROSIE: Chaney. I'm a production assistant for a man named Justin, who had two hits last season. I live on 54th Street, a few doors from the modern museum of art, of which I'm a tea-privileges member, no cream. I live at 53 West 54th Street, Apartment 3B. Can you remember that?

MARCO: Yes.

ROSIE: ELdorado 5-9970. Can you remember that?

MARCO: Yes.

ROSIE: Are you stationed in New York? Or is stationed the right word?

MARCO: I'm not exactly stationed in New York. I was stationed in Washington, but I got sick, and now I'm on leave, and I'm going to spend it in New York.

ROSIE: ELdorado 5-9970.

MARCO: I'm gonna look up an old friend of mine who's a newspaper man. We were in Korea together.

And that's it—the least on-the-nose love scene in movie history. On the surface—on the *nose*—it makes no sense. Taken at face value, it could perhaps be a black, post-modern comedy. But in the context of the mother of all paranoid thrillers, it's a deadly serious cat-and-mouse game between the male and female leads, as Eugenie, with increasing boldness, offers herself to Major Marco. She's his object of desire—just check out her phone exchange—the only person he can trust precisely because she's a complete stranger, and his salvation from the madness of the Korean War POW camp, where he's been programmed into believing that Raymond Shaw, the cordially loathed member of the platoon, is in fact, "the kindest, bravest, warmest, most wonderful human being I've ever known in my life."

In this movie nothing is as at seems—"Yak dung!...hope tastes good—like a cigarette should!" exclaims the sinister Oriental, Dr. Yen Lo, as he watches a brainwashed American prisoner happily smoking dried yak excrement; making the American prisoners literally smoke shit is exactly the purpose of the camp. It's precisely the emotional situation in which Marco finds himself. Eugenie, on the other hand, is exactly what she does *not* seem: a warm, sympathetic girl who's the only sane character in the movie.

As human beings who have seen something of life know, the best course may often be the least instinctive. "Turn in the direction of the skid" may be counter-intuitive when losing control of your car on sheet ice, but it's the only way you can prevent the vehicle from going into what might prove to be a terminal tailspin. "Don't tell the girl you love her," may be the fastest route to her heart.

Dramatic situations, whether in poetry, literature, plays, or screenwriting, often turn on precisely these reversals and misdirections, which—in order to keep the story rolling—are often misinterpreted by one of more of the characters, thus driving the lovers farther apart, or the antagonists even closer together. In romantic comedies, the initial distaste of the lovers for each other will be reversed by the end of the story; in tragedies, the things the two antagonists initially avoid are the things that will force the final confrontation.

Often even the characters themselves don't know what it is they really want, or even what they are saying. "Take me away from all this death," exclaims Mina Harker (Winona Ryder) in *Bram Stoker's Dracula* as, in a sexual paroxysm that is as close as a mainstream movie gets to on-screen fellatio, she drinks Dracula's blood from an incision on his breast, near his nipple—the very thing that will nearly condemn her to the eternal living hell of the Undead, and from which she is ultimately rescued by the love of her faithful husband. One is reminded of Baudelaire's poem "Sin," from *The Flowers of Evil* (translation by Wilfrid Thorley):

For me the most foul demon still doth plot;
About me like the imponderable air
He flows. I drink him, and straightaway am hot
With shameful lusts the tongue may not declare.

Or, as Dr. van Helsing observes near the climax of James V. Hart's film script: "We've all become God's madmen, all of us."

The lovers in Edith Wharton's *The Age of Innocence* can never quite get together, no matter how ardent their desire for each other; convention and their own inhibitions constantly trip them up. David Copperfield believes he's in love with—and marries—the pretty airhead, Dora Spenlow, but after her premature death from a miscarriage he realizes that the long-suffering Agnes Wickfield, who's loved him all along (something obvious to everyone but David), is the right girl for him.

The sole point of erotic contact between Bill Murray and Scarlett Johansson in Sofia Coppola's splendid little movie *Lost in Translation* is Murray's brief caress of Scarlett's bare foot as they lie chastely together, fully clothed, falling asleep on top of the bedsheets in a far-off Tokyo hotel room—and this in a movie whose arresting opening shot is of Johansson, lying on her side, her back to the camera, which is focused intently on her lush, translucently-pantied behind and bare legs as the titles roll.

That the promised sex never occurs is precisely the point. The whole point of subtext—even the in-your-face subtext of Scarlett's appetizing bottom—is for it never to happen. Or to happen serendipitously, in ways that the viewer (and perhaps the writer, in the act of creation) never expected, and only barely suspected was even possible. And yet the audience both suspects and, on some level, expects it—or, at least, expects some resolution of its expectation. As the screenwriting maxim goes: always give them what they want, never give them what they expect.

That is the moral of the story; is that not also, in essence, the moral of life? Dennis Prager, a national talk-show host and observant Jew, once said to me that "petitionary prayer" is the source of much of the atheism in the world. That when we ask—no, demand—something of God, and don't get it, we take it personally, and turn against him. But God does not promise us that, nor does Jesus. The famous, widely misinterpreted verses in Luke 11:9–13 speak to that issue:

And I say unto you, Ask, and it shall be given you; seek, and ye shall find; knock, and it shall be opened unto you / 10 For every one that asketh receiveth; and he that seeketh findeth; and to him that knock-eth it shall be opened. / 11 If a son shall ask bread of any of you that is a father, will he give him a stone? or if he ask a fish, will he for a fish give him a serpent? / 12 Or if he shall ask an egg, will he offer him a scorpion? / 13 If ye then, being evil, know how to give good gifts unto your children: how much more shall your heavenly Father give the Holy Spirit to them that ask him?

Does this mean that God—or fate, or the Furies, or the lares and penates, or Mother Gaia—will give us anything we want? No more than Santa Claus does on Christmas. No more than a screenwriter does in a motion picture. And why?

Because we don't always really want what we've asked for.

We know the bromide: be careful what you wish for; you might get it. And yet, on some level, we don't believe it. As human beings, we experience our lives in the temporal here and now—the quotidian. But, as we know from history, we are not temporal beings; irrespective of religion, or even of atheism, we are *historical beings*, shades who pass through this vale of tears—the suffering brought on by our wish, by Mother Eve's curiosity and desire, to become fully human. Like Van Helsing, on the trail of Vlad Dracul, consecrated Host, stake and hammer in hand, we are all God's madmen. But never God's puppets. And, in the heroic West, *never* God's playthings.

If I may be on the nose about it: *we are subtext.*

The modern age, literal-minded to a fault, generally ignores subtext; the cutting-off of America and Europe from their cultural roots has resulted in a distressingly pedestrian culture that takes everything (or says it takes everything) at face value—the better, as it happens, to accuse its enemies of racism, sexism, homophobia, Islamophobia, etc. Once having established the proposition that the worst sin in the world is "bigotry," and its offspring "discrimination," everything else must fall before this shibboleth.

But twisting or altering or adopting secondary definitions of a word does not an invidious quality or action make. By adding or subtracting adjectival modifiers as circumstances dictate—"discrimination," the morally neutral ability to discern differences between better and worse, into "racial discrimination" and therefore into "bigotry" and thus something legally actionable; the mandatorily neutral term "justice" into "social justice," "environmental justice" and "economic justice," thus corrupting the noun into oblivion—the Marxist Left destroys the meanings of words in its pursuit of political power.

As Susanne K. Langer, in her introduction to the English-language translation of the philosopher Ernst Cassirer's *Sprache und Mythos* (Language and Myth), perceptively notes:

> [Cassirer] was originally struck with the fact that the "theory of knowledge," as philosophers had developed it since the Middle Ages, concerned itself solely with the appreciation of "facts" and the development of orderly thought about facts. The inveterate belief of all mankind in myth, sometimes crystallized into dogmas, sometimes degraded into vulgar superstition, was always excluded from the field of philosophical interest, either as divine revelation, which philosophy could not touch, or (especially in modern times) as a miscarriage of logical explanation, a product of ignorance. But the whole realm of mythical concepts is too great a phenomenon to be accounted for as a "mistake" due to the absence of logically recorded facts... it dawned on the philosopher that theory of mind might well begin not with the analysis of knowledge, but with a search for the reason and spiritual function of this particular sort of "ignorance." Here he was helped by a stroke of insight: the realization that language, man's prime instrument of reason, reflects his mythmaking tendency more than his rationalizing tendency.

In other words: in the Beginning was the Word. *Words matter.* They are not, as some "progressives" would have them be, arbitrary, accidental, or even inimical concepts that evolved out of "bigotry" or "discrimination," but culturally meaningful terms that describe a reality known to our most ancient ancestors—that, in fact, communicate its essence. As every literate polyglot knows, there is no such thing as a perfect translation; that the act of speaking in a second or third language activates an alternative sense of meaning and a new neural pathway to expression. The more languages one speaks, the more one is in direct communication with the wellsprings of human understanding.

The German-born, neo-Kantian philosopher Cassirer—who, like members of the Frankfurt School, became a member of the faculty at Columbia University after the war—explicitly links the names of things with their essences, returning as far back in time as the ancient Egyptians to prove his point. Discussing the ritual transference of potent names to a new pharaoh, he observes that "The essential identity between the word and what it denotes becomes even more patently evident if we look at it not from the objective standpoint, but from a subjective angle. For even a person's ego, his very self and personality, is indissolubly linked, in mythic thinking, with his name. Here, the name is never a more symbol, but is part of the personal property of its bearer . . ." The talismanic power of words antedates everything; "language never denotes simply objects, things as such, but always conceptions arising from the autonomous activity of the mind."

Since the advent of the Frankfurt School, however, the objective of the post-modern assault on language has been precisely to change, dilute, or modify the meaning of our language—which is to say: to make it conform to the imaginary and generally culturally inimical needs of contemporary politics rather to preserve it as part of our heritage.

The struggle over the control of subtext, therefore, is at once a part of the larger political struggle over control of the language and at the same time an attempt to restore the original meanings of words to a general populace no longer educated in the development of modern languages, their roots and origins—in short, their essences. And yet, even "progressives" cannot beat real meaning out of the language, nor transform it into something antithetical to its original sense, unless they convince the majority of its speakers that there is something inherently immoral about it; coming from a group that believes only in a "higher" morality, but certainly nothing doctrinal or pre-Marx, this is rich.

Nor can it whale the cultural resonance out of the culture, unless it first destroys that culture—which was the whole point of Lukács's *cri de coeur*. By cutting off modern Western culture from its roots, the Leftist establishment has rendered meaningless a whole swath of our patrimony.

By demonizing Christianity on the grounds of imaginary "bigotry" (the very antithesis of Jesus's message), and thereby justifying its own atheist, anti-clerical stance, the Left has severed the great works of Western art from their modern audiences.

How can one walk through the *Kunsthistorisches Museum* in Vienna or the *Rijksmuseum* in Amsterdam and appreciate much if not most of the collection lacking knowledge of the Judeo-Christian biblical stories that underpin the works of every artist from Giotto through the early twentieth century? What do the skull and lion signify in portrayals of St. Jerome? Why is Daniel in the lion's den? What is the meaning of the large wheel in any depictions of St. Catherine? (For that matter, what does the title of Twyla Tharp's 1981 ballet *The Catherine Wheel* mean?) With the term "martyrdom" now stripped of its Christian meaning—someone who dies at the hands of others to remain true to the faith—and supplanted by its Islamic meaning: someone who kills himself and others for the advancement of the "faith," the language, and hence the world, has been turned upside down in the face of Christendom's most ancient enemy and most implacable foe.

So: subtext. In 1897, the composer Edward Elgar, 40, fell in love with Miss Dora Penny, the daughter of friends, and thirteen years his junior. Hoping to conceal his infatuation, Elgar communicated something to her in what has become known as the "Dorabella" Cipher—a cryptogram that has remained uncracked to this day, although many have offered solutions. (The cipher is reproduced at the beginning of this chapter.)

Talk about subtext—this entire episode is fraught with it. For the "Dorabella" cipher mystery not only subsumes the cipher itself, consisting of eighty-seven variations on the Greek letter ε (as in "Elgar," obviously) arranged in three hand-written rows, but also includes a panoply of extra-linguistic reference, which is why, I believe, it has not been satisfactorily solved. Let us list the resonances:

- "ε" is for Elgar.
- "Dorabella" is for Dora Penny.
- "Dorabella" means, in Italian, Dora the Beautiful.
- "Dorabella" is the name of the second sister in Mozart's opera *Così fan tutte*, a sexual puzzle-plot opera to a libretto by the libidinous and notoriously cynical Lorenzo da Ponte.

- In the opera, Dorabella is the first to succumb to the romantic attention of the switched lovers—her conquest by the disguised Guglielmo is accomplished swiftly, whereas Ferrando's wooing of the harder-to-fall Fiordiligi takes up most of the opera.
- The title, *Così fan tutte*, is notoriously hard to translate into English. For years, it was rendered as "Thus do they all," which is accurate enough, as far as it goes, but leaves out the most crucial element of the opera: that it is about the fickleness of women, and their weakness in the face of men's amorous advances. A better, more politically incorrect, version might be "All women are like that."
- The subtitle of the Mozart-da Ponte opera is "*La scuola degli amanti*," which means: "the School for Lovers." Surprise: like the other Mozart-da Ponte operas (*Le nozze di Figaro, Don Giovanni*), it's about sex. If *The Marriage of Figaro* (more precisely translated as "Figaro's Wedding") is about the putative *droit du seigneur* of the nobility, which gives the Count the right to sleep with the bride, Susanna, on her wedding night; and *Don Giovanni* concerns the doings—and constant frustrations—of the famous seducer; *Così* goes them one better into the realm of nuance (*subtext*): the Battle of the Sexes. It's the most politically incorrect opera in the repertory, and it's a wonder that the harpies and the *Erinyes* (Furies) of the *Oresteia* have not yet descended upon it.
- "Dorabella" is the name of the tenth variation in Elgar's first major international success, the *"Enigma" Variations* for orchestra, premiered in 1899, two years after he sent Dora the secret note. It comes immediately after the most famous variation in the work, "Nimrod, the Hunter," and therefore is often overlooked, when in fact it's hiding in plain sight.
- The "Dorabella" variation is a frank portrayal of Miss Penny, right down to her characteristic stutter.[1]

The key to understanding the *"Enigma" Variations* lies in the title itself. Throughout his life, Elgar, like his fictional contemporary, Sherlock Holmes, was fond of codes, secret writing, puzzles, mysteries, and conundrums. He said that the main theme of the work—the tune upon

---

1 We should not ungallantly suspect Elgar of playing on the obsolete English word, "dorbellist," a synonym for fool, indirectly derived from the thirteenth-century Scottish philosopher, Duns Scotus, from whom we also get our word, "dunce."

which all fourteen variations were based—was never actually heard; that what appears to be the main theme, stated at the outset of the work, was in fact a counterpoint to the unheard "real" musical theme. Scholars and fans have been trying to guess the real tune ever since.

This is what we hear:

In the second of my "Devlin" novels, *Early Warning* (published in Britain under its original title, *Black Widow*), I offered a possible solution to the cipher: that it was not about the Greek letters, not a substitution cipher, not even really a code; the key was the shape of the long phrase—a shape that when rendered in musical notation revealed the famous "hidden theme" of the piece, unheard but present in contrary motion.

> What if the central enigma of the Enigma Variations wasn't so enigmatic after all, but hiding right there in plain sight? There, hidden away in one of the lesser variations—not the magisterial "Nimrod," which had come, like the Pomp and Circumstance March No. 1, to symbolize the very spirit of Victorian Britain itself, but the one that immediately followed it.
>
> The squiggly, ornamented melodic line of the "Dorabella" Variation, supposedly meant to express the girl's slight hesitancy in her speech patterns. But listen closer: the variation does not simply depict one person, but two. The strings twitter, but the woodwinds answer.
>
> Dora. Bella. Dora the Beautiful. And she is having a conversation with the composer.
>
> It wasn't about a code at all.
>
> It was about Love.

That's one theory; there are others. An especially persuasive one, musically speaking, is that the "hidden theme" of the *"Enigma" Variations* is the majestic Bach chorale *"Ein Feste Burg ist unser Gott."* We'll probably never know, and neither Elgar nor Dorabella is saying.

Codes are codes for a reason: they're meant to convey information to a small circle of initiates, perhaps as few as one; the rest of the world is deliberately shut out. Was Elgar, married to an older woman, in love with a much younger girl? As we've seen, the Victorian and Edwardian eras were marked by public prudery, inventive pornography, and private sexual flamboyance, as memorably described in the anonymous classic *A Man with a Maid*. In America, Stanford White lured the young beauty Evelyn Nesbit (she was fourteen when they met, White forty-seven), into his West Twenty-Fourth Street "snuggery," whence she emerged as his mistress and later became notorious as the "Girl on the Red Velvet Swing." White was spectacularly murdered in 1906 while sitting in the roof garden of the original Madison Square Garden, which he designed, by Harry K. Thaw, by then Nesbit's husband, and irate at White for stealing the girl's virginity.

One last fun fact: in World War II, the Germans dubbed their "un-breakable" encoding machine "Enigma" after Elgar's great work. It was eventually broken by Alan Turing, whose exploits were chronicled in 2014's *The Imitation Game*, which won the Oscar that season for best adapted screenplay.

The resonances keep resounding, leading us back to the way we came.

The point is that the "Dorabella" cipher is the perfect metaphor for how much of art—and thus life, since they exist in a reciprocal and reflective relationship—functions. Which is not to say that everything is Dan Brown's *The Da Vinci Code*, but that any great work of art, whether it's the *"Eroica" Symphony* or Talleyrand and Metternich carving up the map of Europe in order to keep the peace for at least one more generation, admits to multiple interpretations and reveals hidden meanings (emotional, not necessarily literal). And those meanings and interpretations are often concealed by the simplest means possible: transparency. Naked, as Sofia Coppola so graphically illustrated with the opening shot of her heroine's derrière in *Lost in Translation*, really is often the best disguise of the artist's intentions.

We demand of our politicians "transparency" and honesty, but only a child would actually believe that to be possible, or even desirable. Election campaigns are subtextual fictions, all white papers and fifty-seven-point programs that have no chance of being implemented, but which are served up pro forma, like Roman offerings to the household gods of the media, in order to show intellectual bona fides and "gravitas." At the same time, the candidates are busily engaged in semaphoring what they really want to communicate to their followers and the undecideds: "I'm one of you," though manifestly they are not. It is up to the electorate to sort out the man from the myth; the voting public reacts and votes emotionally, not cerebrally—much to the frustration of the Ivy League–educated press corps; since their beloved Adlai Stevenson—the original egghead—twice ran against and lost to a real war hero, General Dwight D. Eisenhower, the media has sought to portray every American presidential election as a battle between the Brainiac and the Moron. But the voters can smell a fraud, know when they're being peddled something, which is why the Moron often wins.

As any reader of those twin alpha-male masterpieces, Caesar's *Commentaries* and Ulysses S. Grant's *Personal Memoirs* grasps, leadership, like art, is not a rational process. By all accounts, General George B. McClellan was a brilliant trainer of the Army of the Potomac, but he was temperamentally incapable of applying its force to Richmond during the Peninsula Campaign and the Seven Days of 1862, thus prolonging the Civil War for another three bloody years. When the Roman Civil War broke out between Caesar and Pompey, Caesar moved swiftly to secure the provinces in Spain, Gaul, and the Cisalpine region, then launched his attack on the rival general from the seaport of Brundisium (Brindisi) and across the Adriatic to Macedonia (Greece), and crushed Pompey, who was almost always on the run, at Pharsalus in 48 B.C.

A common thread weaving through both memoirs is the importance of audacity, steadiness, and supreme self-confidence. Caesar rarely fails to point out that, in crucial moments, when a fight could be lost, his appearance on the battlefield heartened his legions and propelled them to victory. In fact, he made a point of it: "The enemy knew he was coming by the scarlet cloak which he always wore in action to mark his identity," he writes in Book Seven of *The Gallic War.* By contrast, Grant, who rose to the rank of General of the Army of the United States, wore a private's blouse in the field—in part for his personal safety and in part because pomp and circumstance held no appeal for him—and showed up to accept the elegant Lee's surrender at Appomattox wearing a mud-spattered uniform and boots.

In their writings—Caesar's were composed while he was in the field in Gaul and as the war against Pompey unfolded, Grant's as he was dying of throat cancer in 1884—both men exhibited confident command of their stories by letting the facts speak for themselves, and allowing the subtext do the real talking. Caesar's lapidary style and Grant's pointed, matter-of-factness (interspersed with some riveting diversions and personal confidences) rarely betray any self-doubt or second-guessing; when the day is lost, they take their lumps and fight again on the morrow.

They were, however, very different in their reaction to setbacks. Caesar is always ready to take credit for a victory, but shifts the blame to his troops in the wake of a defeat. Here he is, addressing the legions after their bitter defeat in 48 B.C. at Dyrrachium by Pompey near the end of the Civil War [throughout the *Commentaries*, Caesar speaks of himself in the third person]:

He then mustered all his army in one place and addressed the troops. He urged them not to be disheartened of afraid at what had happened, but to balance against this one setback, and not a serious one at that, all the many successful engagements they had had. "Thank fortune," he said, "that we took Italy without bloodshed; we pacified the two Spanish provinces, where there were the most warlike of men under experienced and practiced generals; we have brought into our control the neighboring provinces, which supply us with corn. [A supply of corn—i.e. grain—was critical to the functioning of the Roman legions in the field.]

"Finally, consider how lucky were have been in that, when all the harbors and the whole as well were infested with enemy fleets, we were conveyed across safely right through the midst of them. If everything does not turn out favorably, we must help fortune by some efforts of our own. The setback we have sustained is anyone's fault rather than my own. I gave an opportunity for battle on favorable ground; I took possession of the enemy camp; I drove them out and overcame them in fighting. But, whether through your own agitation, or from some mistake, or by some stroke of fate, the victory that was a good as in our grasp was lost; so you must all make an effort to repair the damage by your valor. If you do, you will turn our loss to gain, as happened at Gergovia, and those who were afraid to fight before will actually offer themselves for battle."[2]

The speech must have worked. Caesar and his men went on to win the decisive victory at Pharsalus a month later; Pompey fled to Alexandria, where he was assassinated on the orders of the Hellenistic pharaoh, Ptolemy XIII; and Caesar took Alexander's old imperial city, installing the youthful Cleopatra on the throne of the pharaohs, mopping up the last pockets of resistance in what was then known as "Africa" (modern Tunisia).

By contrast, the famous exchange between Grant and his indispensable right-hand man, William Tecumseh Sherman, after the first day of Shiloh on April 6–7, 1862, is one of the most illuminating stories of the war, and of the man's character:

During the night rain fell in torrents and our troops were exposed to the storm without shelter. I made my headquarters under a tree a few hundred yards back from the river bank. My ankle was so much swollen from the fall of my horse the Friday night preceding, and the bruise was so painful, that I could get no rest. The drenching rain would have precluded the possibility of sleep without this additional cause. Some time after midnight, growing restive under the storm and the continuous pain, I moved back to the loghouse under the bank. This had been taken as a hospital, and all night wounded men were being brought in, their wounds dressed, a leg or an arm amputated as the case might require, and everything being done to save life or alleviate suffering. The sight was more unendurable than encountering the enemy's fire, and I returned to my tree in the rain.

The historian Bruce Catton picks up the tale from there:

Late that night tough Sherman came to see him. Sherman had found himself, in the heat of the enemy's fire that day, but now he was licked; as far as he could see, the important next step was "to

2 *The Civil War*, Book Three, 73, translation by S. A. Handford and Jane F. Gardner.

put the river between us and the enemy, and recuperate," and he hunted up Grant to see when and how the retreat could be arranged. He came on Grant, at last, at midnight or later, standing under the tree in the heavy rain, hat slouched down over his face, coat-collar up around his ears, a dimly-glowing lantern in his hand, cigar clenched between his teeth. Sherman looked at him; then, "moved," as he put it later, "by some wise and sudden instinct" not to talk about retreat, he said: "Well, Grant, we've had the devil's own day, haven't we?"

Grant said "Yes," and his cigar glowed in the darkness as he gave a quick, hard puff at it, "Yes. Lick 'em tomorrow, though."

Shiloh was when and where Grant first realized that the War Between the States was going to be far worse, and last far longer, and be far bloodier, than anyone had expected. The Federals (as Grant often refers to the Union side) were pinned with their backs against the Tennessee River. But the Confederal general, Albert Sidney Johnston, had been killed in combat, the Union lines held, and the next day General Don Carlos Buell arrived with reinforcements. Grant and Sherman counterattacked the exhausted Southern forces, and the battle was won. Despite the human cost, Grant never complained, never looked back; he had a rendezvous with destiny back east, and he knew it.

Call it heroism, call it courage. Both Caesar and Grant were able tacticians but, more important, they were superb strategists, who always kept their eye on the objective: total victory. Caesar may have invented Caesarism as he went along, but as the *Commentaries* make clear, his mission was to save what was left of the Republic from a corrupt Senate, even if he had to destroy it to do so. Grant, perhaps surprisingly, was a cultured man who loved to read novels and attend the theater; he and his wife, Julia, were both invited by the president and Mrs. Lincoln to attend *Our American Cousin* that fateful night, three years after Shiloh, but begged off. Heedless of his place in history, Grant pulled on his muddy boots, wrote out his crystalline orders, and got on with it.

From the founding father of imperial Rome to the man who saved the Union, there's a lesson there for us, should we care to relearn it. Caesar made no public pretensions to a Roman throne; Grant had declared no burning ambition to become President of the United States, although he served two terms and tried to get the nomination for a third. Neither lived on the nose, understanding that an undeclared love—their own private Dorabellas—was stronger than any direct dispatch or military order, and they left it to others to figure it out.

CHAPTER SIX

"Alexander and Aristotle Pointing at the Sky," from the *Secretum Secretorum*, 1326–27

The Birth of Tragedy

How the West was won

Who would want to live in Plato's *Republic*? It's not a frivo-lous question. Western civilization traces its origins to the ancient Greeks and, among them, the philosopher Plato is regarded as essential. Student of Socrates, teacher of Aristotle, founder of the Academy, Plato is philosophically paramount, and his works have come down to us over thousands of years remarkably intact, however filtered through the lenses of Hellenistic culture, early Christian thinkers, the educated Arabs of twelfth-century Andalusia, and the Byzantines. As the British philosopher Alfred North Whitehead has observed, "the safest general characterization of the European philosophical tradition is that it consists of a series of footnotes to Plato."

And yet, and yet . . . it is not Plato's somewhat saturnine philosophy that came to determine the course of the West, although he was much beloved by the early Church fathers. Instead, it was the work of his most famous pupil and leading philosophical antagonist, Aristotle. Let Plato keep his gloomy Cave and his proto-fascist Republic run by philosopher-kings; Aristotle, tutor of Alexander the Great, both negated and fulfilled his master's work, through the medium of constant questioning, testing, and trying, and in so doing created the basis not only for Rome, both pagan and Christian, but for the Holy Roman Empire and modern Europe as well. Sometimes footnotes can be for refutation as well as for annotation.

Curiously, Aristotle's works emerged fully in the West in part thanks to the brief flowering of Islamic scholarship, when the texts and commentaries of Averroës of Cordoba were translated into Latin and widely dispersed across the Continent; Avicenna (Ibn Sīnā) and Averroës (Ibn Rushd) were among the most significant thinkers of the period. Although they had been largely lost to the West for centuries, Aristotle's writings had survived in the East, and been preserved in Arabic translations, and the rediscovery of his work led to Aristotle's rise to philosophical prominence in Christendom. Whereas Peter Abelard, one of the first great champions of Aristotle in Paris in the twelfth century, had based his own radical philosophy on relatively fragmentary knowledge of the Greek philosopher, by the time Aquinas arrived on the scene a little more than a century later, Aristotle was well known throughout medieval Europe.

Aristotle's importance in Western thought is not due solely to his philosophy, but to its practical application. In addition to the indispensable treatises on *Ethics*, *Metaphysics*, and *Politics*, he is also the author of the *Poetics* (one of the works preserved for the West by Averroës), and it is that work in particular that concerns us here. As I argued in *The Devil's Pleasure Palace*, the story of the West is inextricably tied with up storytelling, and running throughout Western literature, from Homer to Hollywood, is the moral necessity of what I have termed the Heroic Narrative. Any major religion makes liberal use of the Heroic Narrative, and the story of the Bible is nothing if not the story of heroes. Further, I noted that the impulse toward heroism either antedates organized religions (e.g., Christianity and Islam) or is roughly contemporaneous with them, and is found in almost every culture and civilization, regardless of faith.

The *Poetics* appeared in the fourth century B.C. (it is usually dated *ca*. 355 B.C.), and its influence continues to be felt in almost every work of narrative art since, right down to what audiences watch at the movie theater, on television, or via their streaming services. Aristotle laid out what we know today as the three-act structure (beginning, middle, and end) and no doubt the modern screenplay's Pythagorean proportions—a thirty page first act, a sixty page second, and a thirty-page third; 1:2:1— owes something to the Greeks as well. There is even a useful book for beginning screenwriters called *Aristotle's Poetics for Screenwriters: Storytelling Secrets from the Greatest Mind in Western Civilization* by Michael Tierno.

Aristotle argues that the arts—poetry, music, dancing, painting, and sculpture—are imitations of real life, or *mimesis*. He further establishes the two forms of what would become the novel—the first-person and third-person narrators—and how it differs from plays; of course, the ancient Greeks did not have novels, but have a look at Aristotle's definition in Chapter Three (in the translation by S. H. Butcher):

> ... *the poet may imitate by narration—in which case he can either take another personality, as Homer does, or speak in his own person, unchanged—or he may present all his characters as living and moving before us.*

In Chapter Four, Aristotle gets right to the heart of the matter:

> *Poetry in general seems to have sprung from two causes, each of them lying deep in our nature. First, the instinct of imitation is implanted in man from childhood, one difference between him and other animals being that he is the most imitative of living creatures, and through imitation learns his earliest lessons; and no less universal is*

the pleasure felt in things imitated. We have evidence of this in the facts of experience. Objects which in themselves we view with pain, we delight to contemplate when reproduced with minute fidelity: such as the forms of the most ignoble animals and of dead bodies. The cause of this again is, that to learn gives the liveliest pleasure, not only to philosophers but to men in general; whose capacity, how-ever, of learning is more limited.

Aristotle, wise man that he was, also defines the difference between Story and Plot, something that often confuses beginning novelists and screenwriters, not to mention lay audiences. Plot is fungible; Story is not. Any story can be set among the early hominids, in dissolute boudoirs of the French aristocracy, or on Mars: it's easy to imagine, say, a version of *Les liaisons dangereuses* in any of those settings—not directly trans-posed, of course, but with the spine of the story recognizably intact. Any competent screenwriter could do it, and the trick is, but for the original French version, the audience would likely never know it. We've seen *High Noon* in outer space (*Outland*), *The Taming of the Shrew* rebooted as *Ten Things I Hate About You*, and Joseph Conrad's novel *Heart of Darkness* plopped down in the jungles of Vietnam in *Apocalypse Now*. And what would the thriller business be without *Die Hard*, which has itself become a pitch template at the studios: "It's *Die Hard* on a train! On a boat! In an elevator! In a phone booth! In a mayonnaise jar!"

Again, Tragedy is the imitation of an action; and an action implies personal agents, who necessarily possess certain distinctive quali-ties both of character and thought; for it is by these that we qualify actions themselves, and these—thought and character—are the two natural causes from which actions spring, and on actions again all success or failure depends. Hence, the Plot is the imitation of action— for by plot I here mean the arrangement of the incidents. By Charac-ter I mean that in virtue of which we ascribe certain qualities to the agents.... But most important of all is the structure of the incidents. For Tragedy is an imitation, not of men, but of an action and of life, and life consists in action, and its end is a mode of action, not a quality. Now character determines men's qualities, but it is by their actions that they are happy or the reverse.

Reading on, Aristotle seemingly gives more weight to Plot than to Character, but then his definition of "character" is slightly different from ours. As the theories of the *Poetics* developed in practice, we discovered that character dictated plot, and not vice-versa; that the ending of our Story was not determined by the resolution of the Plot, but by the revelation of Character. Still, we arrive at the same place: in the end, it is the *actions* of our characters—not their words—that determine both Plot and Story. This is why silent movies can still be followed and enjoyed: they are all about actions.

Another observation from Aristotle, which holds true to this day:

> *Of all plots and actions the episodic are the worst. I call a plot "episodic" in which the episodes or acts succeed one another without probable or necessary sequence. Bad poets compose such pieces by their own fault, good poets, to please the players; for, as they write show pieces for competitions, they stretch the plot beyond its capacity, and are often forced to break the natural continuity.*

There you have the explanation for every bad television show or movie you've ever watched. One last, crucial point from the *Poetics*:

> *A perfect Tragedy should . . . imitate actions which excite* pity *and* fear, *this being the distinctive mark of tragic imitation. It follows plainly, in the first place, that the change of fortune presented must not be the spectacle of a virtuous man brought from prosperity to adversity: for this moves neither pity nor fear; it merely shocks us.*

Let us pause here to recall Alfred Hitchcock's famous distinction between suspense and surprise:

> We are now having a very innocent little chat. Let's suppose that there is a bomb underneath this table between us. Nothing happens, and then all of a sudden, "Boom!" There is an explosion. The public is surprised, but prior to this surprise, it has seen an absolutely ordinary scene, of no special consequence. Now, let us take a suspense situation. The bomb is underneath the table and the public knows it, probably because they have seen the anarchist place it there.

The public is aware the bomb is going to explode at one o'clock and there is a clock in the decor. The public can see that it is a quarter to one. In these conditions, the same innocuous conversation becomes fascinating because the public is participating in the scene. The audience is longing to warn the characters on the screen: "You shouldn't be talking about such trivial matters. There is a bomb beneath you and it is about to explode!"

In the first case we have given the public fifteen seconds of surprise at the moment of the explosion. In the second we have provided them with fifteen minutes of suspense. The conclusion is that whenever possible the public must be informed. Except when the surprise is a twist, that is, when the unexpected ending is, in itself, the highlight of the story.

Back to Aristotle:

A well-constructed plot should, therefore, be single in its issue [unity of time and place] ...*the change of fortune should be not from bad to good but, reversely, from good to bad. It should come about as the result not of vice, but of some great error or frailty...*

In constructing the plot and working it out with the proper diction, the poet should place the scene, as far as possible, before his eyes. In this way, seeing everything with the utmost vividness, as if he were a spectator of the action, he will discover what is in keeping with it, and be most unlikely to overlook inconsistencies.

Aristotle also anticipates our modern distinction between original and adapted material—"As the for the story, whether the poet takes it ready-made or constructs it for himself"—and goes on to list the four principal attributes of character in the tragic hero: it must be good; it must have propriety ("There is a type of manly valor; but valor in a woman, or unscrupulous cleverness, is inappropriate."); it must be true to life; and it must be consistent.

In *The Godfather, Parts I and II*, Vito Corleone's character never changes—he is a man who loves his family. Neither, for that matter, does Sonny's, Fredo's, or Tom Hagen's. Only the saga's principal character, Michael, seemingly undergoes a change, from clean-cut Marine war hero to brooding, murderous mafia don—but does he, really? The only character in the movies who has always known his true self is his wife, Kay; from her first appearance in the films, she urges him to escape the criminal ways of the Corleones, something she knows, deep down, he can never and will never do. Kay is the tragic heroine of the cycle because, like Cassandra, she's annoyingly right all along. Except that, unlike Cassandra, she doesn't fully believe it herself, until it's too late—and by then one of her two children is dead.

A contemporary objection: who says women cannot be heroic? Of course they can; history is full of examples. To give Aristotle his due, it was neither a quality expected nor suspected of women, at least as the Greeks defined it. (And yet, *Lysistrata* . . .) In the *Oresteia*, Cassandra goes to her foreordained death not willingly but resignedly (she is, after all, Cassandra) and without a struggle; is that heroic or non-heroic? Closer to our own time, Beethoven's heroine Leonore, in the opera *Fidelio*, disguises herself as a man in order to rescue her imprisoned husband from the darkest recesses of Don Pizarro's dungeons, pulling a gun on the wicked governor and holding him at bay until help can arrive.

So, unlike the latter-day incarnations of the Harpies or the Furies, let us allow Aristotle's skull and bones to rest in peace and instead, like the philosopher in Rembrandt's famous painting, contemplate the bust of Homer instead. Better still, let us contemplate the illustration above, a depiction of Aristotle and his prize pupil, Alexander, as the image has come down to us from the early sixteenth century.

It's part of an illustrated manuscript, a codex currently in the possession of the British Library known as the *Secretum Secretorum of Pseudo-Aristotle* (The Secret of Secrets), a Latin translation of the Arabic *Kitab al-siyasah fi tadbir al-ri'asat al-ma'ruf bi Sirr al-Asrar*: "The Book of the Politics on the Directing of Leadership, known as 'The Secret of Secrets.'"

As we have seen, one of the contributions Arabic-Islamic scholarship made to the West (including *al-Andalus*, or modern-day Spain) was its preservation of the Hellenistic culture it derived from, and, to some extent, continued from Byzantium, whose capital was Justinian's imperial city of Constantinople. The repository of Roman culture had been under siege from various barbarians for centuries—the Bulgars, the Persians, the Crusaders (who sacked it in the early thirteenth century, during the Fourth

Crusade, in a squabble over money)—until it finally fell to the Ottomans, who conquered its millennium-stalwart defenses through clever tactics and the early adoption of gunpowder weaponry.

The Sirr al-Asrar, like all of the cultural interfaces between high-water-mark Islam and reconquering Christianity—the Spanish finally expelled the Muslims, along with the Jews in 1492, the same year that Columbus landed in the Americas—is a fascinating document. To cite the British Library's commentary on the codex:

> The origins of the treatise are uncertain. No Greek original exists, though there are claims in the Arabic treatise that it was translated from the Greek into Syriac and from Syriac into Arabic by a well-known 9th century translator, Yahya ibn al-Bitriq. It appears, however, that the treatise was actually composed originally in Arabic. The treatise also contains supposed letters from Aristotle to Alexander the Great, and this may be related to Alexander the Great in the Qur'an and the wider range of Middle Eastern Alexander romance literature. The Arabic version was translated into Persian (at least twice), Ottoman-Turkish (twice), Hebrew (and from Hebrew into Russian), Castilian and Latin. There are two Latin translations from the Arabic, the first one dating from around 1120 by John of Seville for the Portuguese queen (preserved today in some 150 copies), the second one from circa 1232 by Philippus Tripolitanus (preserved in more than 350 copies), made in the Near East (Antiochia). It is this second Latin version that was translated into English by Robert Copland and printed in 1528.

So, even as late as the early sixteenth century, Islamic intellectual influences were still being felt in Europe. It is fashionable today to cite the Islamic "golden age"—a direct result of its contact with Christian Europe, we should keep in mind—as a model, not just for what Islam could one day again become (unlikely, since militant Islam explicitly wishes to return to its seventh-century purity), but also as an apologia for Islam's many and violent sins against the international order. But until Islam casts off Saudi-fueled Wahhabism and Iranian Shi'a millenarianism, gives up its supremacist designs, and becomes willing to accommodate peaceful co-existence contact with the West—beyond its oil-driven importation of Mercedes-Benz and Maserati automobiles and Western firearms—this is unlikely.

Observe the portrait of Alexander and Aristotle at the top of this chapter, a Western interpolation into an Arabic manuscript purporting to be of Greek, indeed Aristotelian (hence the designation *Pseudo-Aristotle*) origin. The two men are attired as Europeans of the period, potentate and counselor. Alexander, the monarch, gazes thoughtfully at the sky as Aristotle illustrates some philosophical truth. His extended right hand uncertainly strokes his chin (a gesture reflected by his still-submissive pupil) while his left hand points confidently at the heavens.

Can there be a more apt illustration of the essence of Western philosophy and ethos than Aristotle's contradictory body language? The king expects answers; the tutor cannot quite provide them. The heavens are appealed to. The clouds lower. There are no right answers. Neither God nor Allah nor Yahweh is heard from. Man alone—as is his duty in the Western heroic-narrative tradition—must provide the solution through the power of his reason, his instinct, his courage, and his faith.

In the end, this is Aristotle's appeal, and his genius. Plato has come down to us as the master of the Socratic dialogue—the teacher who asks questions and expects his pupils to provide the answers—but in the *Republic*, Plato provides answers; and those answers have been tried over several millennia and been found wanting. You can argue rather persuasively—as Karl Popper does in *The Open Society and Its Enemies* (1945)—that Plato, who abhorred democracy, was a harbinger of totalitarianism, and every bit as dangerous as Marx, in part because his fantasy of Utopia was at first blush much less threatening:

> The idealization of the great idealist permeates not only the interpretations of Plato's writings, but also the translations. Drastic remarks of Plato's which do not fit the translator's views of what a humanitarian should say are frequently either toned down or misunderstood. This tendency begins with the translation of the very title of Plato's so-called "Republic." What comes first to our mind when hearing this title is that the author must be a liberal, if not a revolutionary. But the title "Republic" is, quite simply, the English form of the Latin rendering of a Greek word that had no associations of this kind, and whose proper English translation

would be "The Constitution" or "The City State" or "The State." The traditional translation "The Republic" has undoubtedly contributed to the general conviction that Plato could not have been a reactionary.

Not so Aristotle, who learned all the right lessons from the Socratic dialogues, and imparted them to more important historical figures, starting with Alexander, than any other man in history. His critical influence on the great Western thinkers is inarguable, from Marcus Aurelius to Saint Augustine to Averroës to Aquinas to Samuel Richardson (author of *Pamela*, commonly regarded as the first novel in the English language) to Dickens to Thomas Mann; from Shakespeare to David Belasco to Tom Stoppard and David Mamet; from George Axelrod to Ben Hecht to Ernest Lehman to Billy Wilder.

In his very insistence on questioning, trying to determine the nature of things as they really are, to free humanity from the iron shackles of Plato's Cave and lead us into the sunny uplands of reason, in demonstrating that the essence of philosophy and drama *were one and the same*, Aristotle made possible not only the triumph of reason but that of faith as well, establishing the need for the extra-rational that distinguishes man. Without Aristotle, as channeled through Aquinas, the Christian doctrine of, for example, transubstantiation, would have remained solely in the realm of superstition.

In so doing, Aristotle defined the Western conundrum, the uncrackable great mystery that lies at the heart of the human experience: the realization that even reason can only take us so far, and that the active—not passive, as in Hinduism or Buddhism; not submissive, as in Islam; but *defiant*—leap of faith is, at some point, necessary to complete our journey toward understanding. It's Eve's bite of the apple, but this time the fruit of both reason and faith:

> *He knows that in the day/ Ye eat thereof your eyes, that seem so clear/ Yet are but dim, shall perfectly be then/ Opened and cleared, and ye shall be as Gods,/ Knowing both good and evil, as they know.*[1]

---

1 *Paradise Lost*, Book IX.

In the West, we bite into the apple, and then take the consequences, come what may. Not only are there worlds—universes—to win, but there is always the thrill of the game. The irrational desire, or confidence, to wager everything in pursuit of the better is one of the hallmarks of the Western Heroic Narrative: the hero may go down, tragically, but it will never be for nothing. Our republics are for free men; serfs or slaves need not apply.

CHAPTER SEVEN

Jean Marais and Josette Day in Jean Cocteau's *La Belle et la Bête*, 1946

La Belle et la Bête
For each Beauty, a Beast

The story is familiar—so familiar it has moved beyond its ancient, fairy-tale origins to take a beloved place in the popular culture of the day as an art film, a Disney animated cartoon, a Broadway show, and even an opera: "Beauty and the Beast." Of very old provenance—some form of it might have its roots in pre-history—it found its way into European folklore in mid-eighteenth-century France, and took root in the Anglophonic imagination in 1889, with the publication of the prolific Scottish writer Andrew Lang's seminal *Blue Fairy Book*, the first of what became a series of twenty-five collections that cemented some of the best-loved stories firmly in Western literature. What the Brothers Grimm did for German folklore, Lang did on an international scale, and rare was the child growing up in the first half of the twentieth century who did not read at least several of the volumes.

Lang based his version on the French original of 1740 by Gabrielle-Suzanne Barbot de Villeneuve. The opening is classic—not only in its "Once upon a time," strum of the lyre, but in the way it immediately illustrates, in two paragraphs, the Aristotelian dramatic principle of the reversal of fortune, from good to very, very bad:

> Once upon a time, in a very far-off country, there lived a merchant who had been so fortunate in all his undertakings that he was enormously rich. As he had, however, six sons and six daughters, he found that his money was not too much to let them all have every-thing they fancied, as they were accustomed to do.
>
> But one day a most unexpected misfortune befell them. Their house caught fire and was speedily burnt to the ground, with all the splendid furniture, the books, pictures, gold, silver, and pre-cious goods it contained; and this was only the beginning of their troubles. Their father, who had until this moment prospered in all ways, suddenly lost every ship he had upon the sea, either by dint of pirates, shipwreck, or fire. Then he heard that his clerks in distant countries, whom he trusted entirely, had proved unfaithful; and at last from great wealth he fell into the direst poverty.

The symbolism is rich: the twelve children, evenly divided between male and female—for Europeans prized their daughters as well as their sons. The great wealth, which has led the children to unreasonable ex-pectations about life. An unexpected misfortune: a devastating fire, the collapse of the father's business empire through shipwreck and piracy, and the faithlessness of faceless clerks, in whom he had deposited his complete trust.

Another reversal of fortune then occurs—one of his ships has come home safely after all! The children immediately hand him a wish list of trinkets and treasures, but when he asks his youngest child, Beauty, what she wants, she replies: only a single red rose. When the merchant journeys into town on business, however, it turns out that his old partners, thinking him dead after his two-year absence, have already divvied up the proceeds, leaving him with just enough for sustenance.

And then our story really begins. The merchant, caught in a sudden snowstorm, stumbles upon an enchanted palace in the woods, where food magically appears and untold riches lie within his grasp. When he leaves the next day, he takes nothing with him except a red rose, which he plucks from the garden—and is immediately accosted by an irate Beast, a ferocious-looking creature (never physically described) who demands that one of the merchant's daughters come to live with him in the palace forever, as the cost of his freedom. Of course, it is Beauty who agrees to go, saving her father's life at the price of never seeing her family again.

She is duly delivered of her own free will to the Beast in his enchanted castle and, after getting over her initial fright, gradually becomes accustomed to life in the palace, where everything she could wish for—including a room filled with musical instruments of every description and a library, where "she saw everything she had ever wanted to read, as well as everything she had read, and it seemed to her that a whole lifetime would not be enough to even read the names of the books, there were so many." She falls asleep each night, dreaming of an impossibly handsome Prince, who seems to be trying to communicate with her:

> "What can I do, Prince, to make you happy?" said Beauty.
> "Only be grateful," he answered, "and do not trust too much to your eyes. And, above all, do not desert me until you have saved me from my cruel misery."

Each evening, the Beast asks her to marry him; each night, she says no. It takes her a while to get the message: that the Beast and the Prince are one and the same and that she can only find happiness by listening to her heart, not her eyes, and finally saying *Yes*. Of course, it takes a near-death experience by the Beast for Beauty to realize what's going on, but as soon as she agrees to wed him, the creature is magically transformed into her Prince.

> As she spoke a blaze of light sprang up before the windows of the palace; fireworks crackled and guns banged, and across the avenue of orange trees, in letters all made of fire-flies, was written: "Long live the Prince and his Bride."
> "Now," said the Fairy to Beauty, "I suppose you would like me to

send for all your brothers and sisters to dance at your wedding?"
And so she did, and the marriage was celebrated the very next day
with the utmost splendor, and Beauty and the Prince lived happily
ever after.

From "once upon a time" to "happily ever after"—it's the Platonic
Form of the fairy tale, complete with numerical symbolism, a supernatural occurrence, a magic castle, a curse (the Prince's off-stage, pre-existing
condition, for which we never get an explanation), and a self-sacrifice by
the pulchritudinous leading lady that frees the Beast's inner Prince, at
the point of his demise, from his curse and restores balance to the world.
Beauty is one of the templates for a certain type of female heroine in
Western culture, the woman who risks, and in some cases, gives up, her
life in order to free her man. She is Wagner's Senta in *The Flying Dutchman*, who dies, but liberates the Dutchman and his wandering ghost ship
from their unholy curse; Mina Harker in *Dracula*, who survives her close
encounter with the Count, just barely, to save her husband; Vesper Lynd
in Ian Fleming's *Casino Royale*, whose suicide shatters James Bond, but
frees him to return to his first love, the British Secret Service.

Vesper's reward? "The bitch is dead," says Bond at the novel's conclusion. But then, Bond always was a beast.

Is the story then "anti-feminist," as some surely will have it? Impossible
to see how it is, except if you accede to the Left's premise that unless men
and women can be imagined to be exactly the same (except when women
are different, i.e., better) in matters of biology, intellect, and their natural
roles in society as evolved over millennia, there must therefore be some
sort of plot afoot by the "patriarchy," occasioned by "white male privilege"
to keep women down.

In any case, how can a story that has enchanted legions and generations of little girls be anti-female? Modern "feminists," with nowhere left
to go and no worlds to conquer after their mothers' successes in the 1970s
can now only rage against Mother Nature, and Nature's God, for what they
perceive to be an unfairness directed by a cruel Fate against them. Hence
their obsessions with transvestism, transsexuality, non-gender-specific
personal pronouns multiplying like rabbits in heat, all of which has the
paradoxical effect of making them seem less like women. It diminishes
them, it reduces them to external symbols and secondary sex character-

istics; it demeans them. What could be more satanic than to deny the essential, unique, and historically validated attributes of femininity? Not even the worst misogynist could have thought this up. Meanwhile, the "feminists" wait impatiently for masculine science to free them from the imprisonment of their hormones, their cycles, their reproductive systems, and finally, their bodies. It is a sexual-cultural death wish the likes of which we've never seen.

No matter how you pin poor Belle under the post-modern micro-scope, she is an archetype for a reason. She is the embodiment of "tradi-tional" femininity—which is to say, real femininity—not because of her beauty, or her sense of filial duty, or her empathy, but because she is *the exact opposite of the Beast*. Without her, he must remain trapped in the body of a monster forever, and there is nothing his mother, the Queen, can do about it. But it's more complicated than that; in fact, worse: the merchant's blundering upon the Beast's pleasure palace, and his plucking of a single red rose for his daughter, infuriates the Beast but also offers him a way out of his predicament: the merchant's freedom for the life of his most beloved child (we never hear the names of the other kids nor, for that matter, of the father himself). But once he has Belle in his castle, and asks her to marry him, on their first date, he sets the clock ticking on his own death. Only in dreams can he reveal to her the truth of his own imprisonment and hope that the message finally gets through in time; if it doesn't, he dies—killed by Belle's unwitting rejection of the Prince with whom she has fallen in love in her dream, and of the Beast she has come to love in reality as well.

La Belle and her *Bête* might have ended up like a pair of Wharton's ever-frustrated lovers had Beauty succumbed fully to reason, as a man might have. Instead, she ultimately puts her faith in what we used to call her woman's intuition, and follows her heart instead of her fear or her head. The result is happy-ever-after.

The sneers such a phrase elicits now, in our un-wonderful age! In its prolonged siege of Western civilization, the satanic Left always prefers to wield the weapons of ugliness against beauty, going so far as to deny the very possibility of happiness, ever-after or otherwise. It prizes debunking, demystifying, de-mythologizing; it insists all saints have feet of clay, and that beneath the virginal white of Belle's costume throbs the cunt of a trollop. It delights in what it considers the Big Reveal: that a disemboweled

human gives the lie to the very notion of beauty, since we are all blood
and guts and offal under the skin.

They wish the same for our culture, which, in true Marxist fashion,
must always be shown to be a sham. Look at those hypocritical Victorians, upholding the standards of moral rectitude while in the snuggeries
they're busy buggering both the mother and the daughter—not to mention
the vicar, the altar boy, and the St. Bernard. You can practically hear the
cackles of fiendish delight as they voyeuristically yank back the curtains
on a cultural enemy's private life and expose it to an audience they hope
will be shocked, appalled, and then driven to... what? What do they hope
to accomplish?

That they somehow see "hypocrisy" as an indictment of Western
Christian civilization is a puzzlement, since nobody denies it. La Roche-
foucauld's famous aphorism—"hypocrisy is the tribute vice pays to virtue"—comes to mind, but perhaps another of the seventeenth-century
Prince de Marcillac's sayings is more apt: "If we had no faults, we would
not take so much pleasure in noticing those of others." Hypocrisy the
modern Left has in spades—or would have, if they admitted to any limits
to or limitations upon their own exotic sexual proclivities. But in the
black-is-white, up-is-down Bizarro moral universe in which they dwell,
tradition is the aberration and their own inverted "higher" moral code
the new norm.

In its effort to elevate (as "progressives" see it) the female to the level
of the male, the anti-family Left discovered that it was not quite as easy as
they had supposed, and that therefore they needed to diminish the male
in order to bring him a little closer to the level of the female. The madness
of this scheme can be instantly grasped, but these are their terms, not
ours. In the same way that the experiment of Soviet Communism solved
the problem of equality of the classes by destroying the upper classes and
making nearly everyone equally dependent upon—and afraid of—the
government, so did the cultural Marxists seek to rectify the perceived
disparity—and hence "inequality"—between the sexes by bringing both
toward the middle. They did not entirely give up on their sexual-makeover
project, as we see today in the transgender movement, with its pregnant
"males" and mustachioed former females. But any weapon to hand with
which to bludgeon the patriarchy...

The feminized, "sensitive" man was epitomized in the late 1970s by the actor Alan Alda, who in his screen appearances (*Same Time Next Year; California Suite*) often played the antithesis of the macho hunks like Robert Mitchum who had preceded him. Incredibly, in this Hollywood version of the feminist Zeitgeist, women actually seemed to prefer him. And so a new media-endorsed paradigm of masculinity was established, one in which Woody Allen was plausible dating material.

But not only can you not fool Mother Nature but you can't even keep her down for long. The Left's obsession with sexual dysfunction and transgressivism has come to dominate its politics in a pathological way. Sex, it often seems, is the only thing that really matters to them, but it is sex with a couple of corollaries—that it should be "transgressive," that it should come with absolutely no consequences. Not AIDS or any other sexually transmitted diseases that cannot be cured by the timely application of medication, not children, not even a fleeting twinge of morning-after regret or, for the female-type partner, the perp walk out of the scene of the crime.

For a segment of the population that sees childlessness as not only one possible lifestyle (made conceivable, of course, by modern science) but a positively desirable one and, in extreme cases, the only moral and ethical path for a citizen of the world and guardian of Mother Gaia, this is an attractive "philosophy." It's an echo of the whingeing query that first began to be publicly voiced in the Sixties: "How can you bring a child into this terrible world?" Which now has been transformed—as was inevitable—into "Kill it before both the child and the world suffer."

This is no exaggeration. In fact, it's exactly the sort of anti-human philosophy-cum-political-program we've come to expect from the Frankfurt School Left. That it's been so widely, if passively, accepted as even remotely reasonable by the larger culture might at first seem surprising—what could be more essential to the survival of Western civilization than procreation?—until one realizes that that is *precisely the point*. By killing the future, the Left ensures not only the termination of the present, but the eradication of the past well. It is as ruthless an extermination program as ever the National Socialists or the Stalinist Communists ever thought up, or put into practice.

Hence, the need to eliminate the Beast. The Beast—linguistically interesting that the word for "Beast" (*la Bête*) in French is feminine in gender (but not in sex)—in whichever form of hyper-masculinity he takes, is in Western culture the dominant creature in any time or place he inhabits. The marauding Viking, pillaging the Celtic settlements of Ireland. Nietzsche's "Blond Beast," tramping his way across Poland and Transylvania—he's the werewolf in every horror movie, the outlaw biker in every comedy, the hero of every Mel Gibson movie. Physically strong, impossibly brave, able to endure almost infinite amounts of suffering, he has only one objective: to kill his enemies and save the woman—or women—in his life. Call him Conan, or Dr. Morbius's Monster from Id in *Forbidden Planet*, or the Incredible Hulk, he stalks about to this day, despite the best efforts of the "feminist"/cultural-Marxist Left to emasculate him.

This exchange from the movie *Conan the Barbarian* (written and directed by John Milius and starring Arnold Schwarzenneger in his first major film role) is classic:

MONGOL GENERAL: What is best in life?
CONAN: To crush your enemies, to see them driven before you, and to hear the lamentations of their women.

Those kind of men—"big sweaty mens," as the mock-gay film critics of the now-politically incorrect television show *In Living Color,* might have put it—swept down from Scandinavia, charged west across the steppes of Central Asia, sailed across the unknown Atlantic, and walked on the Moon. To denigrate them is not an act of transgressive "bravery," but an admission of jealousy and fear. No real man thinks himself worthy of his father; no real culture denigrates its own fathers.

Which brings us back to Lang's Beast, and Cocteau's Beast, and even Disney's Beast. Look at him: big, possibly sweaty, assuredly hairy and stinky. He is the opposite, the antithesis, of the feminine, which is why Belle is at first repelled by him—the Other—and then, slowly attracted to him. Women can say they want Alan Alda, but in the end they're likely to run off with Marlon Brando in *The Wild One* for the simple reason that he is *not like them.* Opposites attract. They must. If they did not, there would be no issue, in both senses of the word.

We see it everywhere in Nature. The vacuum, which Nature abhors, attracts air, light, matter—life. As magnets attract filings, real men, despite the best demonizing efforts of the modern "feminists," attract women, and alpha males—the Beasts, whether physical or intellectual—attract the best and most beautiful women. It may not be fair, but it's natural. And doesn't the atheist Left, absent any other god than Marx, profess to love Nature?

Would Belle have fallen for Beast had he first appeared to her in his true form, the Prince? The transformed Prince in Disney's cartoon version (1991), with his long, flowing hair, big feminine eyes, and fine features, hardly looks more masculine than Belle herself, and her initial reluctance to embrace him (she strokes his thick mane of hair, touches his face) speaks volumes about her true feelings for the sexually antithetical Beast. And then he kisses her, sparks fly and rise to the heavens, and we know that she has reconciled the basic duality of all men (Alan Alda meets Dolph Lundgren), and at last we have our happy ever after.

In Ravel's porcelain suite *Ma mère l'oye* (Mother Goose, 1910), in either its original four-hand piano version or its orchestral incarnation, the composer chose not to depict the transformation scene, but rather an interlocutory between the Belle and the Beast—the getting-to-know-you, falling-in-love scene of every love story, *Les entretiens de la belle et de la bête*. We clearly hear Belle's feminine whispers, responded to by the Beast's *sotto voce* masculine rumblings; stereotypical, yes, but recognizably true, both dramatically and in real life.

In every dramatic incarnation of the Beast, he is a deeply sympathetic character—a human being trapped in an animal (a werewolf's) body. Ravel's gentle waltz concludes on a harmonically ambiguous harp glissando and violin harmonics—the opposites have attracted ... now what? Only the final chord resolves the issue.

Is the Beast a hero or a villain? Our didactic, reductive age demands an answer, and it already knows what it is. Our real, *Ur*-culture does not, and rejects the Left's response. Men die younger, get killed on the job in far greater numbers, sacrifice themselves in battle, volunteer more, gamble more, wager more, dare more, than do women. By cultural-Marxist standards, this is "unfair," so they are, therefore, idiots—creatures who, biologically, refuse to play it safe; who respond to the siren song of "Ondine," the water nymph in the first movement of Ravel's *Gaspard*, or like Ulysses, strap themselves to the mast to hear the fatal song of Sirens. But they must. Because not to do so is not to be a man.

Which brings us to this simple statement: *Arma virumque cano*, the three greatest opening words in any Western epic until Melville topped

Virgil with "Call me Ishmael." I sing of arms and man. What could be more provocative, or bellicose, or masculine, than that?

Achilles is a Beast. But the gods allow him to be killed for his mistreatment of the slain Hector's body in the *Iliad*, an unnecessary end-zone dance that transgresses upon battlefield decorum—and ultimately has blowback beyond Homer's capacity to know. Because Achilles violates the sacred compact between warriors, and ignores Hector's dying plea, the Greeks may win the decade-long Trojan War, but, ultimately, Greek culture is, literarily, defeated by the more muscular—the more *masculine*—society of the Romans. And Rome, according to the same mythic culture that gave us both the *Iliad* and the *Odyssey*—was founded by none other than Aeneas, the Trojan hero, who fled the ruins of Ilium to sail the Mediterranean to Italia, and ultimately founded the Eternal City.

His journey from refugee to hero is the subject of Virgil's great epic poem; Aeneas is not an economic migrant, or a religious supremacist invading, by stealth, and under the guise of weakness, the lands of his ancient enemies; he is cast adrift and led to a new and glorious fate. But this is not, in the end, the heart of its cultural resonance.

Ask anybody who founded Rome, and the answer (should you receive one, instead of a blank stare) is likely to be "Julius Caesar," or the slightly more historically knowledgeable "Romulus and Remus," the wolf-suckled twins. Of the *Aeneid*, little has penetrated the American popular imagination. And yet the hero, Aeneas, offered up by Virgil in homage to his patron, Augustus, born Octavian, the first Emperor of Rome, is one of the most significant figures of post-Greek mythology: not only does he organize the escape of the remaining Trojans from burning Ilium (losing his wife, Creusa, in the process), but he manages the long journey across the Mediterranean, the tragic stop in Carthage, and, at last, the arrival on the shores of bounteous *Latium* near Rome—the battle for which occupies the second half of the *Aeneid*.

And yet, for all its epic battles and arresting subplots (Nisus and Euryalus, an older warrior and his younger companion, possibly, Greek-style lovers—homosexuality in the ranks was harshly punished in ancient Rome—who die fighting during an attempted breakout from the besieged Trojan camp in Latium in Book IX), what we remember most today about the *Aeneid* is not the flight from Troy but the episode in Dido's Carthage, later to become Rome's mortal enemy and its antagonist in the Punic (derived from the Latin for "Phoenician") Wars. The Aeneid's Book IV is one of the greatest tragic love stories in Western literature, and cannot fail to touch the heart of even most jaded modern reader.

In sum: Aeneas and his men (and women, and camp followers) find safe harbor on the African coast on their flight from Troy. The word "African" was not synonymous with "black" in Roman times—there were no "African-Americans" in those days, any more than there were "Italian-Americans"—and even the part of North Africa designated "Africa" on Roman maps was not what we think of today as "African." (Caesar refers to "Africa" frequently in his *Commentaries*: "Libya" and "Africa" have quite different meanings today.) And in this "Africa" he meets the Phoenician-born Carthaginian queen, the beautiful Dido.

Opposites attract. Aeneas and his armed cohort—*Arma virumque cano*—sail into her safe harbor (metaphor alert!) and seek shelter and succor. Boy quickly meets Girl. Love ensues as opposites attract. Both have lost spouses. Both are lonely, stressed. Both are horny. Sexual activity on an epic scale ensues—so epic that, together with its tragic aftermath, it has echoed down the ages, unto the operatic stage.

Book IV of the Aeneid is a handbook to the understanding of the fundamentality of heterosexual attraction. In a text brimming with Beastly activity, it is a tender moment of Beauty and repose, akin to Ulysses' sojourn with Calypso and Circe, two literally bewitching women who, however seductive, keep the hero from his appointed rounds and ultimate destiny. Ulysses must get home to Penelope and reclaim house and home from the importunate suitors; Aeneas must abandon the greatest love of his life, Dido, and get on with the voyage to Italy, and to his new wife, Lavinia (a colorless, almost anonymous character whose only function is to set off the battle for Italy). In Virgil's text, the joy Dido and Aeneas feel in each other's arms—safe harbor—is palpable. Here is Dido, the Libyan queen, confessing her love for the mysterious Trojan to her sister, Anna (in the translation by the English poet John Dryden). And what a real woman her words reveal her to be:

> *His worth, his actions, and majestic air,*
> *A man descended from the gods declare.*
> *Fear ever argues a degenerate kind;*

His birth is well asserted by his mind.
Then, what he suffer'd, when by Fate betray'd!
What brave attempts for falling Troy he made!
Such were his looks, so gracefully he spoke,
That, were I not resolv'd against the yoke
Of hapless marriage, never to be curst
With second love, so fatal was my first,
To this one error I might yield again;
For, since Sichaeus was untimely slain,
This only man is able to subvert
The fix'd foundations of my stubborn heart.

A chance storm drives Aeneas and Dido to seek shelter in a cave. Juno, who hates Aeneas (whose mother is the goddess of Love herself, Venus) has arranged it, as part of her attempt to divert Aeneas from his appointment in Rome:

The queen and prince, as love or fortune guides,
One common cavern in her bosom hides.
Then first the trembling earth the signal gave,
And flashing fires enlighten all the cave;
Hell from below, and Juno from above,
And howling nymphs, were conscious of their love.
From this ill-omen'd hour in time arose
Debate and death, and all succeeding woes.
The queen, whom sense of honor could not move,
No longer made a secret of her love,
But call'd it marriage, by that specious name
To veil the crime and sanctify the shame.

Their love is idyllic—driven by sexual desire, shared widowhood, lust, fear, desire; two strangers in a strange land—with all the elements of *amour fou*. So, naturally, it can't end well (reversal of fortune, be careful what you wish for, the impossibility of genuine communication between the sexes, the foolish, delicious pain of love). And it doesn't—because Aeneas is a Beast who cannot tarry even wrapped in the arms of a good woman, because his masculine appointment is with Destiny, not with Beauty. Aeneas must leave her, and he does. Dido must die, and she does, by her own hand, and atop her own vengeful funeral pyre (she wants to make sure Aeneas sees it as he sails away) in one of the most poignant and pathetic passages in classical literature:

> *She paus'd, and with a sigh the robes embrac'd;*
> *Then on the couch her trembling body cast,*
> *Repress'd the ready tears, and spoke her last:*
> *"Dear pledges of my love, while Heav'n so pleas'd,*
> *Receive a soul, of mortal anguish eas'd:*
> *My fatal course is finish'd; and I go,*
> *A glorious name, among the ghosts below.*
> *A lofty city by my hands is rais'd,*
> *Pygmalion punish'd, and my lord appeas'd.*
> *What could my fortune have afforded more,*
> *Had the false Trojan never touch'd my shore!"*
> *Then kiss'd the couch; and, "Must I die," she said,*
> *"And unreveng'd? 'T is doubly to be dead!*
> *Yet ev'n this death with pleasure I receive:*
> *On any terms, 't is better than to live.*
> *These flames, from far, may the false Trojan view;*
> *These boding omens his base flight pursue!"*
> *She said, and struck; deep enter'd in her side*
> *The piercing steel, with reeking purple dyed:*
> *Clogg'd in the wound the cruel weapon stands;*
> *The spouting blood came streaming on her hands.*

"*What could my fortune have afforded more/ Had the false Trojan never touch'd my shore!*" Everywoman's lament, possibly; every "feminist's," to be sure. And so the beautiful Dido dies, consumed both by love and hatred for Aeneas, her Beast.

What should we think of Aeneas today? How should we think of him? The harpies and the furies no doubt would excoriate him, should they by chance happen upon the story: the faithless male who leaves the shared bed upon an unseen venereal command and sails away, never to be seen again, driving the heroine to a violent, painful, extravagant suicide. Is he a Beast? Or merely a man, whose higher duty compels him to abandon the only woman he's ever really loved? Aeneas takes the loss of Creusa in the flaming ruins of Troy with the equanimity of combat; for Lavinia, his feelings are unknown—she is, after all, simply a political alliance of convenience to facilitate the founding of Rome. But Dido…oh, Dido…

Here we arrive at the quintessential masculine dilemma: duty or fidelity? The lustful sultans of the *Arabian Nights* invoke the name of Allah constantly, but their principal focus is on the genitals of their women, and their own; there is little sense of any issue larger than their own sexual pleasure, or their jealousy. No wonder that, in our time, the sexually libidinous Left has made common cause with Islam. Let one last example from Burton's translation of *The Arabian Nights*, chosen at random, suffice to reveal the extent of the cultural disconnect between the Christian West and the *ummah*.

A porter has been engaged by a mysterious beautiful woman to carry some items to her home. Upon arrival the lucky fellow discovers two other beautiful women are also there, who promptly pour some wine and then disport themselves. As Burton notes, there was no social drinking in Muslim lands: when the wine comes out, the object is inebriation and sexual activity, not ice-breaking.[1] And thus ensues:

The Porter and the Three Ladies of Bagdad

Then arose the provisioneress and tightening her girdle set the table by the fountain and put the flowers and sweet herbs in their jars, and strained the wine and ranged the flasks in rows and made ready every requisite. Then sat she down, she and her sisters, placing amidst them the Porter who kept deeming himself in a dream; and she took up the wine flagon, and poured out the first cup and drank it off, and likewise a second and a third. After this she filled a fourth cup which she handed to one of her sisters; and, lastly, she crowned a goblet and passed it to the Porter, saying:—

"Drink the dear draught, drink free and fain | What healeth every grief and pain."

---

1 Burton's footnote to this passage reads, "Easterns, who utterly ignore the 'social glass' of Western civilization, drink honestly to get drunk; and, when far gone, are addicted to horse-play…which leads to quarrels and bloodshed. Hence it is held highly irreverent to assert of patriarchs, prophets and saints that they 'drank wine'; and Moslems agree with our 'Teetotallers' in denying that, except in the case of Noah, inebriates are anywhere mentioned in Holy Writ."

Battle of Agincourt

And yet play, players, and playing are essential to any culture: all the world's a stage, and not only to Shakespeare. We cannot understand the nature of a people or a civilization merely by its transient politics; we must also delve into its art, myths, stories, legends, and songs.

Wanderer Above the Sea of Fog

Ah, but what narrative is contained herein? Who is this man? How did he get there? Was the ascent arduous? Did he come to find solace or release? One step farther and he must certainly plunge to his death—where does his next step take him?

The Raft of the Medusa

Here we arrive at the salient difference between art and propaganda. Géricault's masterpiece captures the horror and despair of the raft's victims just as the *Argus* heaves into view on the distant horizon. Will the ship see them? Will it arrive in time? Or will it simply sail past, oblivious?

The Visitation

The idea of the equality of the sexes in God's eyes is a fundamentally Christian concept. Today, when the meaning of the word "equality" has been enlarged and expanded in the wake of the French Revolution, and then constricted and diminished again in turn by the reductive Marxist revolution, this may not seem like much. But to the women—and men—of the time, it was everything.

Alexander and Aristotle Pointing at the Sky (*opposite*)

The king expects answers; the tutor cannot quite provide them. The heavens are appealed to. The clouds lower. Neither God nor Allah nor Yahweh is heard from. Man alone—as is his duty in the Western heroic-narrative tradition—must provide the solution through the power of his reason, his instinct, his courage, and his faith. Can there be a more apt illustration of the essence of Western philosophy and ethos?

Summa igitur prouidentia est: ut uia uisciencia coluibiter in cordibus subiectorum magis quam dilectio. De regis simultitudine

Igitur
tertiam que
re est in regno
sicitur pluuia:
tertia. Que est
der gratia. Ce
li benedictio.
Gerre uita.
Inuentium
uiuamentum.
Pluia per plu
uiam paratur
uia meratoribz. Uirtuum edificantibz. Et
tamen in pluuia diuit contraria. Cadunt ful
mina. Inundant flumina. Gordentes mu
mescunt. Fremunt maria. Et multa alia
mala eueniunt: per que iuuentia pereunt. Ce
rumptamen accidentia mala non. quin laudab
homines gloriosum deum: in sua maiestate.
Consideantes signa sue gre. bona sue miseri
cordie. Pluia per pluuiam uiuificantur nas
centia. Uegetabilia puluilant. Crecuntis uir
vorentibz   tutibz in siuidicitur benedictio. Et ideo referunt

Italia und Germania

In choosing to base his idealized portrait of trans-Alpine cultural and political
harmony on the familial ties between Judaism and Christianity, and turning it into a
mixture of sacred and profane love, Overbeck attached a literally hidden sexual and
religious subtext that was, at the same time, entirely in keeping with the principles
of the Nazarene movement.

The Tennis-Court Oath

One hears echoes of Rousseau's famous dictum, "Man is born free, and everywhere he is in chains," from *The Social Contract* of 1762, which has been the handbook of revolutionaries ever since it first appeared, opening with an epigraph from the penultimate book of Virgil's *Aeneid*: "foederis aequas Dicamus leges"—"Let us strike an equal treaty with them"—and illustrating once again the long chains of political resonance that derive from works of art.

Two Men Contemplating the Moon

Is this not one of the central questions of our existence: is the news good or bad? Are the signal fires deceptive? Are the gods playing with us, arousing our hopes only to dash them again, as their whim takes them? Is it "some cheat," framed by Heaven? Or have we finally encountered Truth?

... when the drink got the better of them, the portress stood up and
doffed her clothes till she was mother naked. However, she let down
her hair about her body by way of shift, and throwing herself into
the basin disported herself and dived like a duck and swam up and
down, and took water in her mouth, and spurted it all over the
Porter, and washed her limbs, and between her breasts, and inside
her thighs and all around her navel. Then she came up out of the
cistern and throwing herself on the Porter's lap said, "O my lord,
O my love, what callest thou this article?" pointing to her slit, her
solution of continuity. "I call that thy cleft," quoth the Porter, and she
rejoined, "Wah! wah, art thou not ashamed to use such a word?" and
she caught him by the collar and soundly cuffed him. Said he again,
"Thy womb, thy vulva;" and she struck him a second slap crying,
"O fie, O fie, this is another ugly word; is here no shame in thee?"
Quoth he, "Thy coynte;" and she cried, "O thou! Art wholly destitute
of modesty?" and thumped and bashed him. Then cried the Porter,
"Thy clitoris,[2]*" whereat the eldest lady came down upon him with a*
yet sorer beating, and said, "No;" and he said, "'Tis so," and the Porter
went on calling the same commodity by sundry other names, but
whatever he said they beat him more and more till his neck ached
and swelled with the blows he had gotten; and on this wise they made
him a butt and a laughing stock. At last he turned upon them asking,
"And what do you women call this article?" Whereto the damsel
made answer, "The basil of the bridges."

And so the tale goes on, in the same vein, until all three women have
stripped, bathed, and queried the aroused Porter as to the proper name
of their exposed quims; it is only the sudden arrival of three one-eyed
Kalendar Princes (a group of antinomian mendicant religious mystics—
always trouble), which kicks the story in another direction and which
directly inspired the second movement of Rimsky's tone poem—which
itself relates to one of the princes' stories. Indeed, the sexual frustration
of the Porter is in part the point of the story—there are few Beasts in the
Arabian Nights; the men are either hapless eunuchs or raging cuckolds;
the fact that their descendants, the September 11 hijackers, drank booze

---

2 Burton: "Arab. 'Zambúr,' whose head is amputated in female circumcision."

and patronized strip clubs and prostitutes before their rendezvous with Allah at the World Trade Center should come as no surprise. The blue balls come with the faith. Sex is only fully to be had in heaven.

As Burton notes in another footnote to this story:

> [Edward William] Lane [another translator, who Bowdlerized the text] is scandalized and naturally enough by this scene, which is the only blot in an admirable tale admirably told. Yet even here the grossness is but little more pronounced than what we find in our old dramas (e.g. Shakespeare's *King Henry V*) written for the stage, whereas tales like *The Nights* are not read or recited before both sexes. Lastly "nothing follows all this palming work"; in Europe, the orgy would end very differently. These "nuns of Theleme" are physically pure: their debauchery is of the mind, not the body.

All sizzle, no pizzle; the member, while toyed with, remains unejaculated. The tumescent Greek men of *Lysistrata*, in Beardsley's illustrations, sporting gigantic erections the size of cricket bats, were driven to conclude a peace treaty both with each other and with their women before they exploded; the puritan Muslim culture, as the world has come to learn, allows only one acceptable outlet for all this sexual energy: violence.

Western man often erupts in violence, but his ferocity generally derives less from frustration than from an excess of misguided primitive, primate ardor. John W. Hinckley, Jr. sought to impress the actress Jodie Foster by shooting Ronald Reagan. Before hitching a ride to the Texas School Book Depository, Lee Harvey Oswald left behind for his Russian-born wife, Marina, to find his own rough translation of part of Yeletsky's aria from Tchaikovsky's opera *The Queen of Spades*: "I am ready right now to perform a heroic deed of unprecedented prowess for your sake. Oh, darling, confide in me!"

This pair, however, were losers, not true Beasts. There was nothing heroic about their actions, only the bravado of cowards willing to shoot a greater man in the back, and thus hope to bask in the reflected glory of their victims. The Beast in our story, however ferocious in voice, mien, and appearance, has a tender heart; his extreme secondary sex characteristics mask not his feminine side, but his desire to achieve union with the real, eternal feminine.

Thus, in our time, the Beast must be destroyed, for he gives the lie to sexual relativism promulgated by the modern Left; by his very physical presence, he punctures the illusion that, as the Kinks sing in *Lola:* "Girls will be boys, and boys will be girls/ It's a mixed up, muddled up, shook up world/ Except for Lola." The primal appeal of the Beast—think of Tarzan of the Apes as one of his direct descendants, along with every comic-book superhero, whose origin story almost always involves a transformation—is his Aristotelian reversal of fortune from pathetic wimp or emotionally flawed creep into someone who is strong, noble, and good. (Batman, interestingly, is the exception, since he has no super powers, and is very much mortal. But he's still hell on the ladies.)

This violates Aristotle's prescription that the reversal must go from good to bad, which is why superhero stories are so profoundly unmoving: no one likes watching a fixed fight, in which the main character's setbacks are temporary (not even Kryptonite can really destroy Superman) and his ultimate triumph assured. But, well, nobody's perfect, as Joe E. Ross says to Jack Lemmon at the end of *Some Like It Hot.*

That only the Beast can destroy himself, and almost always over a woman, is his ultimate weakness. Undefeated in battle, the king of the jungle, Kong is finally brought low, and down, by his interspecies affection for the silky, slinky Ann Darrow in the classic 1933 film that bears his name. Scaling the then-brand-new Empire State Building is child's play to him; it's a suicide mission, but Kong doesn't care. He's going to take out as many of the World War I–vintage biplanes as he can before toppling into his heroic header at the intersection of Fifth Avenue and Thirty-Fourth Street. We cheer when he snatches one of the four flying machines from the sky—the same way he pulverized the pterodactyl that was trying to make off with Ann back on Skull Island—and sends it hurtling down the side of the world's tallest skyscraper. We're touched when, mortally wounded by machine-gun fire, he picks up Ann in one great hairy, sweaty paw, holding her high above Manhattan, to give her one last, tender, heroic look of farewell.

It's left to the filmmaker Carl Denham, who brought the mighty Kong to New York City, to pronounce the big ape's epitaph. "Well, Denham," says one of the cops, "the airplanes got him."

Denham demurs. "Oh, no, it wasn't the airplanes," he says. "It was Beauty killed the Beast."

Real Woman's the only thing that can ever control or defeat him. Let the men of weaker cultures quail before their women. In the West, confronted with the power of Beauty, even the most fearsome Beast must bow before She Who Must Be Obeyed[3], before heading out to rampage once more. Thus speaks Nature. Thus do they all.

---

3 *She*, by H. Rider Haggard (1886).

CHAPTER EIGHT

Johann Friedrich Overbeck, *Italia und Germania*, 1811

Deus Lo Vult

E pluribus ummah vs. the nation-states of the West

Examine the picture above. It's by the nineteenth-century German artist Johann Friedrich Overbeck, a member of the so-called "Nazarene" school of painting, which hearkened back to the art of Giotto and the other Italian artists of the late Middle Ages and early Renaissance before Raphael for inspiration. In order re-instill Christian religious values into visual art, this group of German artists moved to Rome, where they affected medieval styles of dress and tonsure, painted frescoes, and lived a semi-monastic existence, in imitation of their forebears, and of St. Francis. Although their work strikes us as sentimental today, it greatly influenced what became the pre-Raphaelite movement in England of Dante Gabriel Rossetti and Edward Burne-Jones.

There are many points of interest in this non-biblical work by Overbeck; the Italian girl on the left, her hair crowned with a laurel wreath, holding hands with her German friend; over each of their shoulders is a landscape typical of the two countries, an Italian village on the left, a German town on the right. It's a touching image of international friendship. But, of course, it's much more.

"Behind Italia and the laurel wreath in her hair, is an idealistic Italian landscape with mountains, water and a hermitage," wrote Overbeck of his work. "A Gothic fantasy town appears behind curly, blond haired Germania and her myrtle wreath. Courting Italia, her two hands hold Italia's hand. It seems that Italia gently condescends.... Italia and Germania are both somewhat elements, that on one hand, confront each other with a foreign presence, but however my mission is now to melt them into one. It is on one hand a tribute to the homeland and on the other, a charm of everything beautiful and lordly, for which I am thankful to enjoy presently."

Caesar completed the integration of Cisalpine Gaul, now northern Italy, in 49 B.C. at the end of his Gallic Wars, then crossed the Rubicon, the river forming the province's southern border, in order to march illegally on Rome with his legions, thus precipitating the Civil War with Pompey. But neither Caesar nor the Romans ever conquered Germania, and so two quite different civilizations grew up on either side of the Alps. The lure of the south[1], however, was always strong in the Anglo-Saxon imagination, its light, warmth, food, and delicious red wine becoming associated with a higher, less hectic, and altogether more pleasant quality of life than that experienced in cloudy, rainy Frankfurt, Hamburg, Berlin, or even Munich.

Italia und Germania clearly illustrates the outward cultural differences between the two nations in costume and setting. But it was based on something quite different: a chalk drawing Overbeck made depicting the eroticized Shulamite woman from the "Song of Solomon" and Mary, the mother of Christ. In choosing to base his idealized portrait of

---

1 Elgar's tone poem *In the South* (1904) is a typical musical example; in literature, Mann's *Death in Venice* (1912) is pretty much the last word on the subject.

trans-Alpine cultural and political harmony on the familial ties between Judaism and Christianity, and turning it into a mixture of sacred and profane love, Overbeck attached a literally hidden sexual and religious subtext that was, at the same time, entirely in keeping with the principles of the Nazarene movement.

The most striking thing about the picture, for our purposes, is the period of its painting, 1811–1820—because there was neither an Italy nor a Germany in existence at the time, not as the nation-states we know today. Both Italian and German unification came well into the nineteenth century—Italy in 1861, under the Sardinian king Vittorio Emanuele II, and Germany ten years later under Otto von Bismarck of Prussia. England and France had long been fairly stable political entities, but Germany and Italy had always been collections of independent duchies, principalities, and states united by a common language and shared linguistic and cultural inheritances. It's also a time that finally saw the conclusion of the Napoleonic Wars, which ended in 1815 with the emperor's defeat at Waterloo. Overbeck's idyllic vision of peace was hard won, and was something that long-suffering Europe was ready embrace.

Today, we mistake the notion of *citizenship*—which country's passport one possesses—with the concept of *nationality*. When we read in news reports about "Swedes" with Arabic names, we know the media has drawn the narrowest possible definition of what a "Swede" is, one that ignores the entire history of the Swedish nation-state up to Olof Palme, the radical Leftist prime minister who was assassinated in 1986 but whose "progressive" policies have radically changed the makeup and character of the Swedish political entity. This redefinition of national identity is largely an American idea that has been exported to the rest of the world via the American media: since there is no particular "American" race or ethnicity (one of the country's strengths, to be sure) it does not necessarily follow that that is true of other countries. In fact, it almost never is. Sweden became Sweden because Swedes lived there; the country emerged from the people, not the people from the country, as in the United States. When real Swedes no longer live there, it might still be called "Sweden" (unlikely), but it won't be, in any meaningful sense of the word, "Swedish."

That European ethnic nationalism has become exceptional today— elsewhere, nationalism is deemed part of the struggle against colonialism and repression—reflects the success of the Marxist (and Islamist) notions of larger collective entities. Both mortal antagonists of the Enlightenment West need collective enemies, so they have designated Europeans and European-Americans as "white," and thus inimical to the rest of the world. That this is racism of the basest nature does not bother them one whit.

During the heyday of the Soviet Union, American Communists dreamed of uniting with the Motherland in what they hoped would eventually be a world-wide union of Soviet socialist "republics." In Islam, an *ummah* of Believers, ruled by a single caliph, remains the ideal, and national designations—with the exceptions of Iran and Turkey—are often simply cartographic fantasies bequeathed by Sykes and Picot after World War I.

This does not, however, apply to European nation-states, no matter how much Jean Monnet and his fellow architects of the European Union wished it otherwise. European history is vastly different from, say, sub-Saharan African, and what contributed to Europe's rise to pre-eminence from the seventeenth century on was not Europe's "diversity" but its very balkanization. Skills possessed by the Portuguese, Dutch, and English during the Age of Exploration, for example, were lacking in the landlocked countries; the German talent for music was shared across the Continent, but no one would ever confuse Bach and Beethoven with Berlioz or Bellini.

Indeed, it was the collision between and among European nation-states that created the ferment in which multifarious forms of creativity thrived. Goethe spent his *Wanderjahre* in Italy; Lord Byron headed for Italy and, fatally, Greece. The Grand Tour was part of every young northern man of means' education, which often included a schooling in the arts of love in the bordellos of the Mediterranean. Civilized Europeans, then as now, were fluent in multiple languages, and not only familiar with the cultures of their neighbors but enthusiastically appropriated the most appealing bits of them, whether loan-words, sauces, or battlefield tactics. A monochrome, "white" European culture is the malignant fantasy of the cultural-Marxist Left.

We might date the beginnings of European cooperation to the First Crusade in 1096, when volunteers from the widest possible social strata responded to Pope Urban II's call for an army to assist the Byzantine emperor in his war with the Seljuk Turks, and to liberate Jerusalem and the Holy Land from Islam—which, amazingly enough, they did, taking the Holy City in 1099. In just three years, the princelings—led by the foremost Frankish and Norman nobles of Europe, including Godfrey of Bouillon, Raymond of Toulouse, Bohemond of Taranto, and his nephew Tancred—quickly mobilized, marched across Europe to Constantinople through Asia Minor and Syria, or sailed across the Mediterranean from the Italian ports, and crushed the Turkic Sunni Muslim armies at Nicaea and Antioch, and besieged the Egyptian Fatamid Shi'ites in Jerusalem. The Crusaders—known to the Turks and Arabs collectively as the "Franks" (which became the long-standing term for Latin Christians in the Islamic world)—established administrative states in the Holy Land, Antioch, Tripoli, and Edessa, in Syria, all of which lasted for a couple of centuries.

The encounter between Western Christian states and the *ummah* of expansionist Islam was not simply military. The events of the Crusades produced memoirs, histories, folklore, and illuminated manuscripts. A particularly striking example of the last is Sébastien Mamerot's *The Expeditions to Outremer*, a manuscript illustrated under the supervision of Jean Colombe and written between 1472 and 1474 for Mamerot's patron Louis de Laval-Châtillon, an intimate at the court of Louis XI of France.

Mamerot's retelling of the war for *Outremer*—French for "across the sea"—remains a classic of the genre, as much for the miniatures painted by Colombe and his assistants as for the text itself. Colombe, we should recall, was the artist who fashioned the magnificent *Très Riches Heures du Duc de Berry*, and his work on *Outremer* is no less spectacular, if considerably less devotional; this is what war, from the medieval perspective, looked like.

Mamerot was working from secondary sources, and his fidelity to them is exemplary; errors there may be, but such is the peril of every historian writing about events that occurred several hundred years earlier; moreover, his composition took place just three decades after the invention of the printing press. Further, Mamerot was writing for a specific patron, and his perspective (and sentiments) are necessarily that of a Western European Christian, distressed by the internecine squabbling between the Byzantines, the French, the Genoese, and the Venetians, which eventually resulted in the loss of Byzantium. Still, there is almost no attitudinizing, but only a tale well told, however depressingly ended; for Constantinople's fall to Islam marked not only the end of the Byzantine Greek imperial dynasty, but also the end of the Roman Empire. That it was ruled by Greeks, the very people supplanted by the Romans, is one of history's little ironies.[2]

Mamerot concludes his long chronicle:

> At the end of six months, when the foolish conduct of those who were bringing French help led to their defeat outside the city, Louis de Laval sallied out from the city with great honor, saving all his men and goods.... And in truth, the French have not made any general crusade to Outremer since the year 1326[3]....Here end the overseas crusades made by the noble French people.

The Crusades also resonated musically from the thirteenth century on, as the returning warriors brought back new instruments, meters, poems, and sounds. The Crusaders wrote songs and dances both coming and going: Estampies, sacred marching hymns, musical depictions of the exotic places and peoples they encountered. One such is Walther von der Vogelweide's "Palastinalied" (Song of Palestine), composed during the Sixth Crusade in 1228 (Walther later turns up as a Minnesinger in Wagner's opera *Tannhäuser*); another is the plaintively entitled "Chanterai por mon corage" from the Third Crusade in 1189.

The most striking and best-known work inspired by the Crusades, however, dates from 1624: Monteverdi's *Il combattimento di Tancredi e Clorinda*. The history of opera begins with Monteverdi—*The Coronation of Poppea* is still in the repertory—as he, like Wagner two centuries later, attempted to recreate the artistic ethos of Greek drama, including poetry, dance, staging, and music. *Combattimento*, however, is not an opera, but rather a single-movement *scena* for three singers and a small ensemble consisting of a quintet of viols (a six-stringed, bowed instrument of the Renaissance, held and played vertically) and a harpsichord.

Written in the new *stile rappresentativo*, the music mirrors the action, even breaking into a string *tremolando* (the first in musical history) when Tancred and Clorinda meet on the field of battle. The bulk of the singing goes to the Narrator, who relates the story of the Christian knight, Tan-

---

2 It's important to note that the concept of ethnicity wasn't as salient then as it later became, starting with the stirrings of modern nationalism in the eighteenth century, and snowballing in the nineteenth and early twentieth centuries.
3 Actually, 1328.

cred, and the Muslim female warrior, Clorinda, with whom he is in love; literarily, Clorinda is a half-sister to Virgil's Amazon princess Camilla, in the *Aeneid*. The other two performers, baritone and soprano, sing their allotted lines but also mime the action via dance; (Stravinsky later borrowed this musico-dramatic concept for *L'Histoire du soldat* in 1918).

The pair encounter each other at night outside the walls of Jerusalem, and Tancred, not recognizing his beloved in the dark and in her armor, challenges the unknown Arab fighter to a duel, in which she is mortally wounded. Removing her helmet, Tancred realizes what has happened, but the dying Clorinda forgives him and requests baptism as a Christian. Her soul saved, she dies at peace.

> *He felt his hand tremble as he revealed*
> *The yet unseen features to the light.*
> *He saw, and he knew her. And stood there dumb.*
> *Ah, dreadful knowledge! ah, unhappy sight!*
> *Yet he did not die; calling up his strength*
> *And all his virtues, then, to guard his heart,*
> *And suppressing his grief, with the water*
> *He gave life to her, slain by his sword.*

The text is taken, verbatim, from the twelfth canto of *La Gerusalemme liberata*, the influential poem by Torquato Tasso, published in 1581, which enjoyed wide currency across Europe at the time. Long after the fall of the Crusader states in *Outremer*, the Crusades played an active part in the European imagination and memory, especially since Islam would not be fully repulsed and driven out of most of Europe until the Ottoman Turks were stopped at Vienna in 1683—a battle that began, significantly enough, on September 11, when the Turks nearly breached the city's gates, only to be routed the next day by Jan III Sobieski and his Polish cavalry.

That Tancred should be the hero of this drama is instructive. Tancred, as noted, was the nephew of Bohemond, one of principal Norman commanders of the first Crusade. It is largely forgotten that the Normans—descendants of the Vikings (*Norse = Norman* = Northmen) who gave their name to Normandy in France—conquered or settled much of continental Europe, including France and Russia, sailing down the Volga River to bequeath their gene pool to the natives (*Russia = Russi =*

Swedish marauders who founded Kiev, ultimately from *roðr*, Old Norse for "rudder"). Bohemond may have been from Taranto, in Italy, but he was not "Italian" in our sense of the word. Nor was he, by virtue of his conquest of Antioch, "Turkish," as much as today's simplistic media would have made him so.

Tancred, later briefly Prince of Galilee, gained repute (disputed today) as the first Christian fighter to enter Jerusalem—where his assurances of safety to terrified residents who had taken refuge under his banner in the Temple of Solomon were ignored in the ensuing massacre. Still, his legend grew, and during the Middle Ages he became the archetype of the superhero, the original *parfit, gentil knight* of lore, fearless in battle, ardent in wooing, faithful in love, and utterly reliable in every other matter.

That the tale of Tancred and Clorinda, a story of star-crossed lovers if there ever was one, touched Renaissance audiences so deeply is indicative of the Western sensibility—not just then, but now. The cultural-Marxist paradigm would have it that everything is determined by race, creed, class, etc., but the love of Tancred for Clorinda (however fictional) easily transcends all that. And this in the midst of one of the deadliest battles ever waged between Western Christendom and militant Islam. For true love will out; Tancred engages, and kills, Clorinda on the field of battle not because she is a woman (he doesn't know that) or even a Muslim, but because she is wearing warrior garb, and she appears to him *to be a male.* His attraction to her is heterosexual; were it homosexual, he might have stayed his sword. But no: he runs her through, just as he would any other man.

The simmering conflict between the Christian West and Islam, always waxing and waning, has long stalked and informed the Western imagination. Modern Hungary's antipathy toward Islam is a result of its long experience with the Muslim yoke; 158 years of occupation by "tolerant" Islam and, later, Communism, have taught the Hungarians that even imperfect freedom is preferable to Muslim rule and Marxism-Leninism. Similarly, the Poles want no part of the "refugee" wave of able-bodied young Muslim males that has swept across Europe since 2015 in the wake of Germany's unconscionable, inexplicable welcoming of a fifth column of invaders; religion, in post-Christian Germany, may be only a daft superstition, but it is hardly that to the adherents of Islam who are now putting down roots in the historic heart of Christendom and plotting their demographic takeover of the country that gave us the word *Kinderfeindlichkeit* (hatred of children).

Were we in the West attuned to the artistic resonance of the Musselman conquests, we might be more aware of a continuing threat even more implacable than that of the cultural Marxists. But, even in Germany, where artistic and cultural literacy is higher than it is in the United States, the severing of the connection to its own indigenous culture has been pronounced and remarkable: a fitting testament to the efficacy of its own—indigenous!—Frankfurt School of social-justice founding fathers.

At the end of the seventeenth century, however, the West's reaction to Islam's incursion was first to defeat it and then to appropriate it. The spires of the mosques became the onion domes of the Catholic churches in Austria and Bavaria. Coffee became a popular beverage. The croissant conquered France. The rampaging Turk, bent on plunder and rapine, became a figure of fun: a bogeyman with which to terrify misbehaving children. In short, the Beast of a fairy tale that had ended happily ever after. One need only take in a performance of Mozart's *The Abduction from the Seraglio* (1782), or Rossini's twins, *L'italiana in Algeri* (The Italian Girl in Algiers, 1813) and *Il turco in Italia* (The Turk in Italy, 1814), to see this in action. That all three are "comedies" only underscores the point—and how long will it be before these works are condemned as politically incorrect by the new inhabitants of the lands that gave them birth?

But "appropriation" did not indicate endorsement. On the contrary. Western powers remained so leery of Islam that, in the aftermath of the Great War, they shattered the Ottoman Empire into as many harmless constituent pieces as possible, and paved the way for the secularist revolution of Mustafa Kemal Atatürk in Turkey in 1923. Turkey at that time was the locus of any potential "caliphate," and of the need for surviving European powers, fixated on Germany, to douse any fires on Europe's eastern borders. Russia had already been lost to the Marxist lie, but the Turks could be sorted out and settled down, for a while at least. The focus was on peace: between Italia and Germania, between the familial royal cousins of Germany, Russia, and England and the rest of the world, between Europe and Asia; and between the diminished Continent and its emerging geo-political masters, the Americans.

Even so, the world was still Europe, and Europe the world. The United States was a bumptious outpost, blessed in its location between two wide oceans, but bereft of a "proper" culture, a real national identity, and many of the other trappings of a civilization that had just destroyed millions of lives in a senseless, essentially civil, war.

Then again, the Americans had only recently experienced the same thing. A war that was supposed to have been over by Christmas (like all wars) had dragged on for four brutal, bloody years. New weapons had been developed, new battlefield tactics deployed, especially on defense. After years of watching men in tight columns get shredded by cannon fire and enfilades, both Confederates and Federals had learned, by the last year of the war, to dig in, entrench themselves, and let time do much of the work that formerly rank-and-file assaults had done. Battles were now no longer on a day and date, settled on a field of honor; sieges no longer lasted just a few days, until supplies ran out and water became scarce. "I propose to fight it out on this line, if it takes all summer," dispatched Grant back to Washington, D.C., in May, 1864 from Spotsylvania, Virginia; the war didn't end until eleven months later. Grit had, in part, replaced courage; cannonades had replaced cavalry charges; Grant's force of will and clarity of objective had replaced Lee's tactical brilliance and the fortitude of his troops.

Passion was no longer sufficient to win a war; bloodlessness was.

The U.S., in all its wars after World War II, partially learned that lesson, although it fought several wars to no determination, including in Korea, Vietnam, and the Middle East, thus demonstrating the limitations of technocracy over clarity of objective and the will to win. The lesson the Europeans learned, in their post-religious social democracies, was that immediate self-preservation outweighed all other considerations. It was not necessarily preferable to be better dead than Red; Red was negotiable and Communist and socialist parties could be accommodated within the framework of liberal parliamentary democracy. The most important thing in life was not your politics, but the chance to sip Cinzano after a short day of "work" under an umbrella in the piazza while discussing American racism and the folly of American foreign policy. That the real umbrella was the nuclear one, provided gratis by the Americans, mattered not.

Seen in this sultry summer light, Tancred and the men who had taken the oath of the Cross were fools, brigands, adventurers, racists; plundering lacklanders on a crusade for the main chance; ignobles, the lot of them. Urban II was delusional; Bernard of Clairvaux was a religious zealot; the

Norman princes were avaricious and venal. There was nothing "heroic" about any of them, nor about any of their successors, whether on the Crusades or back home in Europe. Leave that to the simplistic Americans, getting their noses bloodied in Korea and Southeast Asia and Iraq and Afghanistan. Better dead than red, white, and blue. Don't be a chump, like Tancred:

> It was in this same year of 1112 that the very noble and valiant prince
> Tancred was stricken with a very serious illness. Feeling his end
> approach, he called to him Roger [of Salerno, a Norman knight], the
> son of his cousin Richard, and made him the guardian of Antioch,
> on condition that he would immediately and without dispute cede
> it to the young Bohemond when the latter arrived. Having said this,
> he also summoned his wife, the natural daughter of Philip I, and
> advised her, when he was dead, to marry a young prince raised in
> his court called Pons [Poncet], son of Count Bertrand of Tripoli.
> And when he had told them both that he thought this marriage
> reasonable and that they, no less than the kingdom, would prove the
> beneficiaries, begging them to agree to it, he forthwith gave up the
> ghost. His body was buried amidst universal lamentation and tears,
> under the porch of the church of St. Peter at Antioch.
> —Mamerot, *The Expeditions to Outremer,* Chapter 38.

P.S.—Roger married somebody else, and was killed seven years later at the bloody battle of *Ager Sanguinis*, in which he and his entire army were destroyed.[4] Tancred, having fought so hard to liberate Jerusalem, died entrusting his fiefdom to someone untrustworthy, and his principality soon vanished with him.

Since the attacks of September 11, 2001, the West has been engaged in an overt, declared (by only one side) war against Islam, a war its governing elites refuse to credit for the simple reason that they no longer believe in faith, religion, higher purpose, or, indeed, much of anything at all other than their own indolent, fleeting, issueless, and thus meaningless, sexual pleasure. Fashionably atheistic opinion in the West lacks a belief in what

---

4 To finish this particular story's cultural life cycle, Verdi tackled the 1282 Sicilian revolution against their Norman rulers in his 1855 Paris grand opera, *Les vêpres siciliennes* (The Sicilian Vespers), most often encountered now in its Italian version, *I vespri siciliani*.

it regards as the superstition of the afterlife; therefore, it disdains such a belief in others.

Today, Overbeck's ideal has been realized: Italia and Germania live in harmony. They are both rudderless, childless states, with no aspirations for the future beyond tomorrow's pension payment and state-sponsored *Urlaub*. The Germans go to Italy, the Italians visit Germany. Both are intent upon visiting the Disney versions of each other before each disappears. During the Eighties, I encountered some older German tourists in northern Italy, in the German-speaking area of the *Alto Adige*, or what the Austrians still call the *Südtirol* (the South Tyrol, to reflect the province's loss after World War I), and struck up a conversation. Why were they there? One of the men replied that he had been a prisoner of war in Italy, and fell in love with the place. He and his family had been coming back ever since.

No hard feelings—the war to end all wars had actually been the war before the war to end all wars, at least as far as Europe is concerned, if by war you meant wars the Europeans actually started themselves. At the time, *bien-pensant* thinking opposed the placement of Pershing missiles on European soil during the 1980s, on the grounds that the passive acceptance of Soviet tanks rolling unopposed (except by the Americans) through the Fulda Gap and into West Germany was surely preferable to provoking the Russian bear and knocking over the Cinzano umbrella on that square in Merano or Bolzano.

Now, thirty years and more on, Europe is as heirless as Tancred, *Italia und Germania* now both elderly, barren women who spent their lives in business, on vacation, in school, or on the dole, with nothing to show for it. The Italy of *The Godfather*, in which a man did what a man had to do to take care of his family, is as dead as the Borgias. A culture that had lasted from Aeneas to the Rubicon to the toll booth on Long Island, where the hotheaded Sonny, a true descendant of Caesar and Tancred, ate hot lead, now stares into an empty future, its replacement population arriving at seaports daily on a makeshift flotilla from the old Roman province of Libya. Somewhere, Dante weeps.

And what of Germania, the simulacrum of the Virgin, the old Holy Roman Empire, whose image guided and inspired crusaders of all stripes from the time of Constantine? The German proclivity for bellicosity was suppressed in the aftermath of the deadly Thirty Years War, and became the butt of jokes in the eighteenth century, when the mercenary Hessians were routed by George Washington and his rag-tag colonial army at the battle of Trenton. Indeed, for a time, the very notion of a German soldier was something of a joke.

German militarism was not fully weaponized until the Napoleonic Wars, and came to fruition with the Franco-Prussian War of 1870–71. After two world wars, Germany was once again demilitarized in 1945, and contemporary Germans show no appetite for a fight, unless it involves copious amounts of beer and a soccer match against the Italians, who are even less disposed to combat than they are. Whether this will once again change in the future remains to be seen. All things must pass, even Nietzsche's Blond Beast.

But unless the West is prepared to become the sexually tortured Porter of the *Arabian Nights*—effectively, a eunuch, like one of Bassa Selim's harem guards in Mozart's comic opera—that time should not be now. The collapse of the Marxist experiment in the Soviet Union should have been hailed as the triumph of the West and its Heroic Narrative[5], the victory of the individual over the State; that it was mourned instead, and repurposed by the European Union so that *this* version of socialism, at least, could at least pretend to have a human face, is an indication of just how deep the hatred for the West, in the West, really is.

---

5 As it was, politically at least, in Francis Fukuyama's *The End of History and the Last Man* (1992): "What we may be witnessing is not just the end of the Cold War, or the passing of a particular period of post-war history, but the end of history as such: that is, the end point of mankind's ideological evolution and the universalization of Western liberal democracy as the final form of human government." But both the EU and Osama bin Laden had other ideas.

CHAPTER NINE

Gustave Doré, *Inferno*, 1861

La Commedia è Divina

A walk in the woods: is this the way to Heaven or Hell?

One of the most arresting and evocative—chilling, really—passages in English literature comes early in Wilkie Collins's novel of sensation *The Woman in White* (1860). It's worth quoting in full:

> I had now arrived at that particular point of my walk where four roads met—the road to Hampstead, along which I had returned, the road to Finchley, the road to West End, and the road back to London. I had mechanically turned in this latter direction, and was strolling along the lonely high-road—idly wondering, I remember,

153

what the Cumberland young ladies would look like—when, in one moment, every drop of blood in my body was brought to a stop by the touch of a hand laid lightly and suddenly on my shoulder from behind me.

I turned on the instant, with my fingers tightening round the handle of my stick.

There, in the middle of the broad bright high-road—there, as if it had that moment sprung out of the earth or dropped from the heaven—stood the figure of a solitary Woman, dressed from head to foot in white garments, her face bent in grave inquiry on mine, her hand pointing to the dark cloud over London, as I faced her.

I was far too seriously startled by the suddenness with which this extraordinary apparition stood before me, in the dead of night and in that lonely place, to ask what she wanted. The strange woman spoke first.

"Is that the road to London?" she said.

The narrator is one Walter Hartwright, teacher of drawing, relating his first encounter with the mysterious woman in white, who may or may not be a recent escapee from an insane asylum.[1] This chance meeting, naturally, leads Hartwright into the depths of a plot so clever and convoluted and mesmerizing and yet so utterly plausible as to make much of Dickens seem contrived and simplistic, and is rivaled only by Dickens's own masterpiece *Bleak House* (1853), which perhaps Collins, Dickens's friend and rival, sought deliberately to surpass. Competition, even in literature, is a good thing, with the reader the beneficiary. For which connoisseur of the Victorian novel would sacrifice either Dickens or Collins for the other?

"Her hand pointing to the dark cloud over London." How far we are from Italia now! Instead, we are in the realm of the Britons: Saxon, Celtic, and a bit Norman, descendants of Harold and William the Conqueror. In the British Isles, the clouds are ever lowering; the heaths are ever blasted (why else would Emily Brontë dub her archetypal, accursed hero "Heathcliff" in *Wuthering Heights*?), the moors ever terrifying after

---

1 The inciting incident may have been based on an episode in Collins's own life, his first meeting with the woman who became one of his two simultaneous mistresses, Caroline Graves, although this is disputed.

nightfall. It's no accident that the two clueless dudes backpacking across the moors in John Landis's *An American Werewolf in London* (1981) get bitten under a bad moon rising as they make their fearful way across darkest Yorkshire.

The blasted heaths, the haunted woods, framed against a scudding sky; the play of light, the sudden wind and rain—no wonder the Druids and the early Celts were such mystics. All nature signaled to them, engaged with them, actively challenged them to try to interpret and understand it. Indeed, the history of the British Isles is intimately connected to its weather and its light, which contributed to the development of an indoor, learning-based culture of poetry, painting, literature, theater, scientific experiment, technological advancement, and rapid improvements in transportation, both at sea and by land. Further, the weather drove ambitious Britons over the Channel and across the seas—in part to simply escape it—on their great voyages of exploration and conquest in the world's sunnier climes.

When Hartwright is suddenly tapped on the shoulder from behind by Anne Catherick, his reverie about the girls of Cumberland is suddenly replaced by something much darker and more primal. Is she a ghost? An apparition? An evil spirit? Or just an innocent in virginal white, who has somehow lost her way? At a crossroads, no less. Most important, on what fateful journey will she ultimately lead him?

Expressing a purpose sure to infuriate modern feminists, Collins opens his novel with these words: "This is the story of what a Woman's patience can endure, and what a Man's resolution can achieve." Hartwright's chance encounter opens up a new world to him, one he has never suspected even existed. Like many of the works we've been discussing, it's a world of dark secrets, of plots, of madness, and death. It is the antithesis of the optimistic face which the Victorians presented publicly to the world, and yet one in which they were passionately, erotically involved.

The plot of *The Woman in White* is masterminded by the porcine Count Fosco, an Italian "language master" (in the beginning was the Word) who manipulates Sir Percival Glyde and everybody else so that he might get his fat hands on an heiress's fortune; even a brazen switched-identity plot is not beneath his genius. Fosco is one of the great villains of Victorian literature—"He looks like a man who could tame anything. If he had married a tigress, instead of a woman, he would have tamed the tigress," notes

Marian Halcombe, the strongest and most potent of all the characters in the novel, who still cannot resist his animal attraction.

Fosco's eventual demise at the hands of an Italian secret society he had once betrayed is an apt fate, for there is nothing of sunny Italy about the Count. He's the physical and moral model for the enemy dons in *The Godfather*, a forerunner of the Mustache Petes of the Castellammarese War that roiled New York City's gangland in the early 1930s. He is, in fact, the template—how could he not be? He practically created it—of the greasy, slippery trans-Alpine foreigner, with oily hair and flippers for hands; a Bond villain.

By his very antithesis, however, he reinforces the other, positive stereotype[2] we see in the face of *Italia* in Overbeck's painting. No good without evil; no evil without good—how often we come back to Milton's dictum.

Four hundred years earlier in Western literature, another famous wanderer took a walk in the woods—and set out upon an unimaginable journey—to Hell, Purgatory, and Heaven. Except that Dante actually did imagine it, and recorded it in the greatest poem in the Italian language: *The Divine Comedy.* The opening is at once bardic and invocatory, but also somehow very modern in its literal *in medias res* opening:

> *Midway the path of life that men pursue*
> *I found me in a darkling wood astray,*
> *For the direct way had been lost to view.*
> *Ah me, how hard a thing it is to say*
> *What was the thorny wildwood intricate*
> *Whose memory renews the first dismay!*
> *Scarcely in death is bitterness more great;*
> *But as concerns the good discovered there*
> *The other thing I saw will I relate.*
> [*Inferno*, translation by Melville Best Anderson]

Almost immediately, the poet's safety is threatened by wild animals;

---

2 Properly used, the word "stereotype" is morally neutral. During the Civil Rights era, however, it acquired a modifier, "*negative* stereotype." The modifier eventually became subsumed into the meaning of the word and thus is now omitted, which is why the concept of a stereotype has been supplanted by the neutral word "template." The practice of attaching descriptive adjectives to neutral nouns—"social justice" comes to mind—is characteristic of the Left's manipulation and weaponizing of the language.

as he falls back he becomes aware of a ghostly presence, who introduces himself as the poet Virgil: "*Sub Julio* was I born, though late the day/ And under good Augustus lived at Rome/ When false and lying deities bore sway/ I was a poet: that just hero whom/ Anchises sired, I sang . . ." The way back barred by the monsters, Virgil leads Dante down a different path, straight to Hell.

Ah, the dark woods: so integral to every fairy tale, including *Beauty and the Beast*. Their terrifying interiors hold the promise of fortune or doom, of a choice to be made: this way or that? To the prince or princess, languishing in some sort of magical confinement and only awaiting succor from the one whom Fate or Destiny has designated? Or into the jaws of some ferocious Beast?

How we hate choices. They're so prescriptive, so restrictive, so ... unfair. And yet, every work of human art is based on them. Does Friedrich's solitary hiker contemplate infinity or jump to his death? Does Shostakovich's Katarina Ismailova have sex with Sergei or remain faithful to her boring husband, Zinovy? Does the title character of Janáček's *Jenůfa* have the baby or give it to the Kostelnička to dispose of by chucking the newborn into the river?

To quote Allan Bloom again:

A serious life means being fully aware of the alternatives, thinking about them with all the intensity one brings to bear on life-and-death questions, in full recognition that every choice is a great risk with necessary consequence that are hard to bear. That is what tragic literature is about. It articulates all the noble things men want and perhaps need and shows how unbearable it is when it appears that they cannot coexist harmoniously. One need only remember what the choice between believing in God or rejecting Him used to entail for those who faced it.

The idea of choice is essential to the Western psyche. Let other cultures bow to the will of Allah, to Kismet, to Fate, to the wheel of *Fortuna*:

> *O Fortuna velut luna statu variabilis,*
> *semper crescis aut decrescis; vita detestabilis*
> *nunc obdurate et tunc curat ludo mentis aciem,*
> *egestatem, potestatem dissolvit ut glaciem.*

[*O Fortune, like the moon you are changeable, ever waxing or waning; hateful life first oppresses and then soothes as fancy takes it; poverty and power it melts them like ice.*]

In the West, we have long since put that invocation, which opens Carl Orff's most famous work, the choral cantata *Carmina Burana*, past us. We no longer believe in Fate, except in the romantic sense. (Curious that we now leave to chance decisions that can change the course of our lives, and yet persist in micro-managing issues that, left alone, could take care of themselves perfectly well.) Fate still has its place in the popular culture, particularly in the romantic-comedy genre, but of the Force of Destiny, there is little to no acknowledgment.

And yet, Fate used to obsess the Western world. Wagner made a career out it. His Norns weaved, and Siegmund and Sieglinde had a child; that child, Siegfried, died at the hands of Hagen, the bastard child of the Nibelung. Only the defrocked Valkyrie, Brünnhilde, breaks the iron cycle, by grabbing a brand from her dead lover's funeral pyre and with it burning Valhalla to the ground, precipitating the mighty Rhine flood that drowns Hagen and washes clean the sins of the gods and prepares a new world for a redeemed humanity.

A sense of destiny was essential to the Heroic Narrative; dimly at first, perhaps, then gradually dawning upon the hero that he has a mission, often unwanted and undesired, to accomplish. St. Francis of Assisi's life— once considered a Christian model—follows this path, from spoiled rich kid to spartan monk, who had his Saul on the road to Damascus moment in the ruined chapel of San Damiano, where in 1205 the voice of God whispered in his ear and changed his life. In short order, he was giving away his earthly possessions, founding what became the Franciscan order, and talking to the birds and other animals. He died painfully, lying naked on the floor. His last words were: "I have done what is mine. May Christ teach you what is yours to do."

It's easy for us, in a secular and therefore cynical age, to regard Francis not as a saint, but as mentally ill, or perhaps a self-flagellating conman. Why take the hard path when the easy one lay before him? Why live a life of extreme asceticism when the pleasures of the flesh were so tempting, and so easily available? The answer is, in a word, destiny. Millions of men and women down through the ages have done likewise, seeking their own personal destinies through prayer, service, or combat. If your destiny was a heroic death on the battlefield, so be it; if it was to be King of France (assuming you were in the right military or social class), you might pursue that. The temptation, of course, was to confuse a desire with destiny, but the hero of will and talent could also try to power through. Destiny was also a matter of choice—the choice to embrace it.

This idea of choice is essential to Western drama—in the Aristotelian world of the cinema, every movie plot involves a choice. In the three-act structure, the first major crisis comes at the end of the first act, when the main character must choose between his old life and the prospect (some-times enforced, to be sure) of a new one. If he rejects the choice, there's no movie. If he does not answer the call of destiny—even if, or especially when, he's not sure he can trust it—he forfeits his role as Hero. The hero must always take chances and make choices: in *The Godfather, Part II*, the youthful Vito Corleone's decision to murder the neighborhood mafia boss, Don Fanucci, cements his choice of a life of crime; it frees him to return to Sicily and brazenly stab to death the now-elderly boss, Don Ciccio, who had killed his family and sent him fleeing to America, setting the entire story in motion.

Other examples: in *Casablanca*, Rick Blaine must abandon his phi-losophy—"I stick my neck out for nobody"—when the woman he loved and thought lost, Ilsa Lund, walks into his gin joint in French Morocco. In the Coen brothers' splendid remake of *True Grit*, young Mattie Ross's decision to track down her father's killer is symbolized by the moment when, refused service by the ferryman (metaphor alert!), she impulsively drives her horse across a raging river, leaving the safety of Arkansas for the unknown dangers of Indian Territory in order to catch up with mar-shal Rooster Cogburn and Mr. La Boeuf, the Texas Ranger. In Hitchcock's masterpiece *Vertigo*, the choice is Scottie Ferguson's decision to plunge into San Francisco Bay, just beneath the Golden Gate Bridge, to rescue the mysterious Madeleine Elster from her suicide attempt—and in so doing, to fall in love with her.

In *Sophie's Choice*, the narrator Stingo's choice is not to return to rural WASP Virginia from Jewish Brooklyn when he gets his first look at Na-than's schizophrenia and Sophie's staggering burden of guilt, but to stay with the doomed lovers. Sophie's choice is really three choices: to make a man of Stingo by sleeping with him the night before she dies; to return to Flatbush Avenue and Nathan's soothing cyanide; and her *Ur*-choice, made under the greatest duress, to give up her daughter at Auschwitz in a hopeless attempt to save her son.

Are these real choices or are they Fate? Are we simply captives of fate, or captains of our own ship? A religion like Islam puts everything in the hands of Allah, which in our way of looking at it, in effect means that everything is left to chance. A calm acceptance of Fate is a hallmark of the eastern religions. But the West still struggles with it. Not for nothing is Verdi's middle-period opera *La forza del destino* often jocularly referred to as *The Force of Coincidence.* How do we tell them apart?

Which is it? Are we free to choose, to believe in destiny when it suits our needs, wishes, wants, and desires? Shakespeare's Romeo thinks himself "fortune's fool," but as Cassius reminds in *Julius Caesar*: "The fault, dear Brutus, is not in our stars, but in ourselves."

Perhaps it's the difference between youth and age. Young people seem fatalistically inclined to believe in destiny, especially in matters of love and career advancement: some things are either meant to be, or not meant to be. Older and wiser heads know better, or at least know different: the untimely death of a child was not "meant to be," unless the universe is controlled by a blind, idiot God.

The slaughter of World War I was not "meant to be;" it was triggered in Sarajevo by a Rube Goldberg–like a series of toppling aristocratic dominoes. One of the plotters, Nedeljko Čabrinović, tossed a bomb at the Archduke's open car on the way to the nobleman's appearance at the Town Hall, but it bounced off and exploded under a trailing vehicle. The other would-be assassins fumbled their chances. When the motorcade returned *by the same route,* Gavrilo Princip was ready. As Ferdinand's car took a wrong turn, then had to back up, Princip stepped forward and fatally shot the Archduke and Duchess with a Belgian-made semi-automatic pistol.[3]

Choices, choices. As the Duke of Mantua sings in his first aria in Verdi's *Rigoletto: Questa o quella?* This one or that one? As you might suspect from the feminine word endings, he's referring to women as targets of seduction, but they're all the same to him: "This girl or that girl? Constancy is the heart's tyrant." Later, he amplifies his card-carrying

---

3 A minor historical note: one of the plotters was a Bosnian named Muhamed Mehmedbašić, who fled to Montenegro and was later killed in World War II; Islam had a small role in starting the Great War.

piggery with an even more famous ditty, "La donna è mobile" ("Woman is fickle"). The Duke is the operatic son and heir to Mozart's *Don Giovanni* and to Don Alfonso in *Così*. And while his game is slightly different, he, too, forces the object of his desire into a choice: Gilda, Rigoletto's seduced and abandoned daughter, must choose between her unrequited love for the worthless Duke and her filial love for her father; her sense of duty to both gets her killed.

To take a walk through the unknown woods or go the safer long way 'round? Not all passages through the forest end happily ever after, as the Romans discovered in the swamps and trees of the *Teutoberger Wald* in the year 9 A.D., during the reign of Augustus. Ambushed by the Roman-trained German leader, Arminius (Hermann), three legions under the command of Publius Quinctilius Varus were annihilated, and two of them—XVII and XIX—were never reconstituted. Writing decades later, Tacitus records in the *Annals*[4] the Roman reaction to their general Germanicus's victory over Arminius a few years after the Teutoberg disaster:

> Shouting, the Romans fell upon the German rear. "Here there are no woods or swamps," they jeered. "It's a fair field, and fair chance!" The enemy had been imagining the easy slaughter of a few badly armed men. The blare of trumpets, the glitter of weapons, was all the more effective because it was totally unexpected. The Germans went down—as defenseless in defeat as success had made them impetuous. Arminius got away unhurt...

Still, Tacitus and the smarter Romans evinced a healthy respect for the German commander who once was revered in Germany as the man who blocked the expansion of the Roman Empire across the Rhine and saved German culture from Romanization. Arminius's death in 21 A.D. came not in combat with the Romans, but at the hands of members of his own tribe, the Cherusci, who thought he had become too powerful. So he died like Caesar.

> He was unmistakably the liberator of Germany, Challenger of Rome—not in its infancy, like kings and commanders before him, but at the height of its power—he had fought undecided battles, and

---

4 Book One, translation by Michael Grant.

never lost a war. He had ruled for twelve of his thirty-seven years. To this day the tribes sing of him. Yet Greek historians ignore him, reserving their admiration for Greece. We Romans, too, underestimate him, since in our devotion to antiquity we neglect modern history.[5]

Varus had chosen to march through the forest, against all advice and prudence. Arminius's choice was to betray his former masters; his choice was to use his native woods as a refuge and a launching-pad for a surprise attack; his choice was to fight, and keep on fighting until the invaders had been driven from the German lands.[6] He chose wisely.

The point of choices is not to be afraid of them. We cannot eliminate the necessity of choice—of *discrimination*—any more than we can eliminate chance. But it's helpful and desirable to have a guide, although certainly a Virgil is preferable to a Madiel. Those, however, are the chances we take when sallying forth to see our adversary "where that immortal garland is to be run for, not without dust and heat," as Milton puts it.

So adversity—dust and heat—is part of the fun. But which path do we take? Which gate? Surely not the one that says, "Abandon all hope, ye who enter here?" And yet Dante fearfully but willingly follows Virgil right through it; Virgil's hero, Aeneas, trails the Cumaean Sibyl[7] into Hades; both emerge unscathed from the horrifying, cautionary, sights they witness. The tortures of the damned are described in clinical detail, especially in Dante, who gives us the imagery of the various circles of Hell, each one worse than the next, with the divine punishments exquisitely calibrated to fit the crime. And while Dante (spoiler alert) eventually makes it to *Purgatorio* and finally *Paradiso*, it's his trip to Hell we remember most vividly.

Dante and Aeneas put their personal safety at risk for a higher purpose. Dante has little choice—it's either follow his fellow poet or return to face the snarling beasts who will surely rip him to pieces. Aeneas goes to visit

---

5 *Annals*, Book Three.

6 Max Bruch wrote an oratorio about him and sent the score to Brahms. Later, as the two composers dined together, the sound of an organ-grinder came wafting through the windows. "Listen, Bruch!" shouted the habitually dyspeptic Brahms, "that fellow has got hold of your *Arminius!*"

7 In the *Aeneid*, there's even a transsexual of sorts: "Caeneus, a woman once, and once a man/ But ending in the sex she first began." Born Caenis, she had been brutally raped by Poseidon, who generously granted his victim a single wish. She chose to be transformed into a man, so she would never have to suffer such an indignity again.

the shade of his father, Anchises, and to learn the purpose of his mission to Latium. But before he does, one encounter leaves him as shaken as a mythological hero can be:

> Not far from these Phoenician Dido stood,
> Fresh from her wound, her bosom bath'd in blood;
> Whom when the Trojan hero hardly knew,
> Obscure in shades, and with a doubtful view,
> (Doubtful as he who sees, thro' dusky night,
> Or thinks he sees, the moon's uncertain light,)
> With tears he first approach'd the sullen shade;
> And, as his love inspir'd him, thus he said:
> "Unhappy queen! then is the common breath
> Of rumor true, in your reported death,
> And I, alas! the cause? By Heav'n, I vow,
> And all the pow'rs that rule the realms below,
> Unwilling I forsook your friendly state,
> Commanded by the gods, and forc'd by fate-
> Those gods, that fate, whose unresisted might
> Have sent me to these regions void of light,
> Thro' the vast empire of eternal night.
> Nor dar'd I to presume, that, press'd with grief,
> My flight should urge you to this dire relief.
> Stay, stay your steps, and listen to my vows:
> 'T is the last interview that fate allows!"
> In vain he thus attempts her mind to move
> With tears, and pray'rs, and late-repenting love.
> Disdainfully she look'd; then turning round,
> But fix'd her eyes unmov'd upon the ground,
> And what he says and swears, regards no more
> Than the deaf rocks, when the loud billows roar;
> But whirl'd away, to shun his hateful sight,
> Hid in the forest and the shades of night;
> Then sought Sichaeus thro' the shady grove,
> Who answer'd all her cares, and equal'd all her love.
> Some pious tears the pitying hero paid,
> And follow'd with his eyes the flitting shade,
> Then took the forward way, by fate ordain'd...

Part of being a hero to the ancient Romans, apparently, was having the courage to be a cad. Aeneas pays no obvious moral price for his pious tears and lack of gallantry, and yet it is impossible to read Virgil and not to think that Dido is the great lost love of his life. We wish his fate—and hers—could be otherwise, but in the pre-Christian ethos of Augustinian Rome, not only was it not meant to be, but it could not be, and thus could not ever have been meant to be.

We, however, are free—nay, compelled—to wrestle with the moral import of this heartrending episode in hell. There could be no happily ever after for Dido or Aeneas; her duty was to shelter the hero and his men on their flight from Troy; her job was to love him and then be abandoned by him, in part to impress upon Aeneas the seriousness of the fate the gods had in store for him. Would Aeneas have fought so hard to found Rome were not the woman he loved forcibly taken from him, first by the gods (including his own mother, Venus) and then by Dido herself, condemning him to sail away as her reproachful and accusatory immolation fires rose to the sky in the wake of his ships? Dido was the burnt offering to the heavens that made Aeneas's ultimate triumph possible.

How would a modern Aeneas find his way through this moral thicket? Would he put love and sexual passion over duty and filial piety? Would a modern audience want him to? Tragic love stories hurt, not because they are rare but because they are common, and nearly everyone has experienced at least one. The missed signals, the bad timing, the sliding doors ... we all, on some level, still live in the age of innocence, and find our hearts broken with regularity.

Perhaps Gibbon's theory that the arrival of Christianity fatally weakened and then destroyed the Roman Empire has something to it. Neither Aeneas nor Caesar nor Augustus was ever inclined to turn the other cheek. Fate was duty; duty was destiny. Each man saw himself as answering to a higher morality (to use the contemporary term) that superseded his own wishes and desires. Without them, there can be no Empire.

In the conduct of contemporary American and Western public and foreign policy, this is an issue with which we must still come to terms. Countries, civilizations, cultures, are no different than people in this sense: all must take a walk into the darkling woods we call the future. In the West, latterly, we have adopted humanitarian policies designed to alleviate our temporal suffering, at great expense and at untold cost for the future. The first is monetary; the United States has racked up (at this writing) more than twenty trillion dollars in national debt, exceeding its current annual gross domestic product, and is on the hook for far more than that in unfunded liabilities. Japan, a member of the West since the end of World War II, owes eleven trillion; Italy and Germany two-and-a-half trillion each, and Britain, just over two trillion.

And yet nothing continues to be too good for us. Except in Japan—whose negative birth-replacement rate is killing it—borders are effectively open to all who would take advantage of our nations' generous welfare systems. The elderly, who generally need it least, are effectively subsidized by the young, who will need it the most in an increasingly gloomy economic and socially destabilizing future. By putting a premium on the here-and-now (in other words, on voters who vote their own pocketbooks), the West has philosophically abandoned the quaint notions of duty, fidelity, and fiscal prudence, all in the name of a parody of Christian charity called "compassion."

Compassion, however, is not a fiscal virtue, any more than "tolerance" is a moral one, or "diversity" an alloyed good. Compassion is an interior feeling, which may or may not have an ameliorative component. Tolerance is suicidal when the thing being tolerated is homicidal. Diversity is merely descriptive, and says nothing about intrinsic worth or the ability to accomplish the task at hand. The great civilizations have, in the main, shown little compassion for their enemies, have practiced intolerance with a vengeance, and have had little or no essential diversity of aim, intent, or purpose. They were successful for precisely those reasons. Only in the inimical fantasy world of the cultural Marxists are any of these concepts socially beneficial.

The argument is made that it is more important to live in the present, to ignore the past (except insofar as it shows us what not to do), and to let the future fend for itself; the implicit argument is that there is no afterlife; that the future of the country-as-founded, of the nation-as-evolved might actually end is never publicly discussed. That, however, is not only a real possibility but, frankly, the intention of those who advocate it. There is no enchanted castle at the heart of the forest, only the Devil's Pleasure Palace, a chimera designed to seduce, trap, and doom the naïve, the unwary, the gullible, and the stupid.

At the root of this Leftist argument is precisely this proposition: the

West, that great and remorseless sinner, deserves to die for its transgressions. The punishment must be death, and it must be retroactive. Forget our culture's unparalleled achievements in the arts and the medical sciences; forget the improvements it has made in the qualities of lives across the world; forget its technological and philosophical advances that reach back in an unbroken skein from ancient Greece to the Moon landing and beyond.

Here, then, are the Leftist tenets one is forced to believe in order to be accepted into polite society: that millennia of recorded history are meaningless. That the history of Western art, in all its manifestations, is proof of a vast conspiracy against the present; that the emergence of cultural-Marxist "progressivism" has (like Islam to its followers) supplanted all else that came before it. To paraphrase Groucho: who are you going to believe: your lying eyes or Karl Marx? In the Left's view, the West's guardian angel has not been Michael, but Madiel.

As the Christian[8] shouts in the opening of Bunyan's *The Pilgrim's Progress*: "What shall I do?" Bunyan's great allegory, once one of the most widely read books in the English-speaking world, begins, "As I walked through the wilderness of this world," and the first man he meets raises that existential question aloud as he embarks on his journey from the City of Destruction to the Celestial City. Along the way, the Christian loses some of his traveling companions to moral weakness or the wiles of the Flatterer (Satan), climbs the Hill of Difficulty, does battle with the fearsome beast Apollyon, survives the fleshpots of Vanity Fair, crosses over the Enchanted Ground (where to fall asleep is never to awake), and comes at last to the Delectable Mountains, the Land of Beulah, and the Celestial City itself, radiant atop Mount Zion. He does this all, by the way, after abandoning his wife, Christiana, and their children in the City of Destruction—a morally dubious situation belatedly rectified with the appearance of Part Two in 1684.

The shining city on the hill, a phrase that used to be associated with the United States, is now employed more in a derisory than actual sense. America, they sneer, has not lived up to its "founding ideals"—When?

---

8 Called the Pilgrim in Ralph Vaughan Williams's 1951 opera of the same name. As with Prokofiev's *Fiery Angel*, much of the most memorable music from Vaughn Williams's *The Pilgrim's Progress* found its way into his luminous Fifth Symphony (1943) during a period in which the composer had temporarily abandoned the stage project.

Immediately? At conception? At birth? Or right this minute? This is the endless reproach of the anti-American Left, even as it continues to pay lip service to the ideal. The phrase, with its evocation of Isaiah 2:2 ("the Lord's house shall be established in the top of the mountains") derives from Matthew 5:14, during the account of the Sermon on the Mount: "Ye are the light of the world. A city that is set on an hill cannot be hid." So, naturally, it is set up as an earthly attainable ideal rather than as an aspirational goal; our failure to realize it is proof of our perfidy.

Except that the Left's version of the shining city will perforce look much different from St. Matthew's, Bunyan's, or Ronald Reagan's. And that is the point. Whose city? Which hill? Whence comes the illumination? The aping of Christianity by the cultural Marxists continues apace. Is that the road to London? Or to the Inferno?

Light is inimical to darkness, which much be total in order for it to have any integrity. Darkness—evil—is negated by the light of a single match, anywhere in the universe. "Neither do men light a candle, and put it under a bushel, but on a candlestick; and it giveth light unto all that are in the house," continues Matthew's account of Jesus's words. "Let your light so shine before men, that they may see your good works, and glorify your Father which is in heaven."

You don't have to believe in the Father—although everything from Greek mythology to the recent past would seem to indicate that he's either a universally shared delusion, a stock literary character who for some unknown reason authors have found compelling for more than two millennia, the expression of some inner knowledge, or a secret wisdom shared by humanity since its dawn—to see the use and wisdom of the light. Pascal's Wager still makes a lot of sense to most people; it's one of the few bets you can hedge and still come out ahead. Or you can curse the darkness and wait for Fate to have its way with you.

What's new today is that we now curse the light, and welcome the darkness that somehow now comes at noon.

CHAPTER TEN

Comrades: Stalin and Lenin, 1919

Miraculous Mandarins

They're from the government, and they're here to help

S tarting in 1918, the Hungarian composer Béla Bartók began work on an idea for a ballet. Not a classical ballet, not a Russian ballet, not even the kind of avant-garde ballet that had made the reputation of his great rival Igor Stravinsky, who had had three startling successes earlier in the decade, before the war, with the Ballets Russes in Paris: *The Firebird, Petrouchka*, and *The Rite of Spring*. The Russian firebrand had set European music—and Europe itself, because the arts mattered to both intellectual and political society then—on its ear with successive master-pieces. Bartók, fifteen months older than Stravinsky but nowhere near as famous, needed something startling, something…magical.

Bartók had seemed to be following Stravinsky's career trajectory. His ballet *The Wooden Prince* had been enough of a success the year before to win a staging of his one-act opera *Bluebeard's Castle*, which had been composed in 1911 but not premiered until May 1918, in a revised version for Budapest. But the political exile of his revolutionary librettist, Béla Balázs, after the four months of Béla Kun's Hungarian Soviet Republic in 1919, had put the kibosh on further performances in Hungary.[1] Not that Bartók wasn't also a youthful revolutionary: together with his fellow Hungarian composers Zoltán Kodály and Ernő Dohnányi, he had served on the short-lived state's music council. But his primary focus was always musical, never political.

In this case, the Marxists' loss was also the world's. *Bluebeard's Castle* is one of the most arresting works of the early twentieth century, a two-hander for Bluebeard and his last wife, Judith, that is a kissing cousin both to *Beauty and the Beast* in its multiple incarnations—it's also found in Lang—and to Bram Stoker's *Dracula*, in its humanizing of existential, sympathetic evil. From its brooding opening, deep in the bass strings, in the same nether region where, musically, Wagner opened *Das Rheingold*, to its quiet, resigned, tragic, and utterly hopeless close, *Bluebeard* and the thirty-seven-year old Bartók take us deeper in the depths of the authentic male and female psyches than any composer before.

That it was written around the time of the First World War should come as no surprise. As we have seen, this was a period of great artistic and political ferment—the Germans, still hoping to win the war, had put Lenin on the train to the Finland Station in 1917, in time to start the October Revolution that brought down the Czar and knocked imperial Russia out of the war. Few European artists were immune to the currents of war, whether they were politically aware and active or not.

It's a fairy tale, of course, which means we must take it seriously. Bluebeard, a man of great wealth in the sunset of his life, has married the lovely Judith and has brought her home with him, to live in his forbidding castle. At the threshold, he offers her the opportunity to change her mind; she does not.[2]

---

1 A similar effort to establish a Communist "people's state" in Bavaria in the aftermath of Germany's defeat in World War I also died a quick death.
2 "Enter freely, and of your own will," says Count Dracula to Jonathan Harker in the second chapter of Stoker's novel, inviting the English solicitor across the threshold and into his immediate peril.

And thus is her doom sealed. Insisting on allowing light to enter the gloomy abode, she tries throw open the shuttered and curtained windows and the locked interior doors. Bluebeard begs her not to: there are places (in the male human heart) that are better left unexamined and unexplored, even by lovers, intimates, spouses. And yet, she persists: unable to deny his young and beautiful wife (a symbol of the fertility that is missing from the duke's life), one by one Bluebeard hands over the keys.

The doors creak wide to reveal a series of wonders: a torture chamber, an armory, a treasure trove. And more: the fourth door opens upon a wondrous, enchanted garden, like the Beast's; the fifth, to the accompaniment of a massive explosion of mighty tonic chords in the orchestra, reveals the master's vast demesne. (This is the opera's highlight and peak emotional moment.) And then, as the wished-for light plays upon the revelations, Judith sees that all the rooms are tinged in blood ...

We've already noticed this in the music, where dissonances have crept into the Magyar-influenced score. Judith is horrified by the torture chamber, but somehow sexually excited by it. Ditto the weapons room. The sight of Bluebeard's vast wealth only increases her ardor, her curiosity, and her barely concealed passion. And the view of his empire—the world is not enough—knocks her backward in a mighty blast of C major: the most primal of musical keys.

From this moment on, the focus switches to Bluebeard who, like any older man indulging his younger lover, has been hitherto largely reactive. Very reluctantly, he hands her key to the sixth door, which opens upon a shimmering silver lake of tears; there is no blood here, only profound sorrow. Bluebeard, desperate, begs Judith to stop, but by now she's too far gone, has too much invested. She *must* know what lies behind the seventh door.

It's his first three wives, of course, regally attired and standing silently in their eternal tomb.[3] As they emerge singly, Bluebeard acknowledges each in turn, the helpmeets of his life's morning, afternoon, and evening; now, night must fall. And Judith is his last, his queen of the night. He robes her in ermine, places a crown upon her head, and condemns her to living death eternal. There is no rescue. The door closes and locks. Darkness falls, as does the curtain.

---

3 Similarly, Dracula has three "wives" lying undead with him in his castle in the Carpathians.

Read anything into you like: chances are good you'll be right. An allegory about the end of Western civilization? Check. Be careful what you wish for? Check. The peril of May–December romances? Check. A cautionary tale about female curiosity and male emotional privacy? Check and checkmate. Bluebeard, despite his marital experience, has hopes for the future; Judith has only questions about his past. She wins, and in so doing, loses.

The world that emerged from 1918 had no hopes for the future, only questions about the past—just as we do today. Europe had fought Napoleon; had fought the Prussians; and now had fought the German Kaiser and his empire—and had won all three fights. Now its new war bride had arrived, the United States of America, somehow still virginal in her white wedding dress, but stained with the blood of Belleau Wood and St.-Mihiel.

Who will save us from Western culture? The question, naturally, was posed by the Hungarian, Lukács, one of the instigators of the Hungarian Soviet Republic and its first People's Commissar for Education and Culture. The early Hungarian Communist state didn't last very long, but the cultural-battlefield prep Lukács managed resonated and extended to the Soviet client state that followed the end of World War II.

With Balázs in exile, Bartók needed another collaborator. He found him, or at least his material, in Melchior Lengyel—like Lukács and Balázs, another Hungarian Jew with an outsider's sensibility but an insider's eye—whose 1916 story (a "pantomime grotesque") Bartók chose for his scenario. As a glimpse into Europe's recent past and its unintended and mostly unwanted future, it was hard to beat.

The notion of a mandarin class was alien to revolutionary circles, who still believed in the impossible-before-breakfast idea of the dictatorship of the proletariat being promulgated by Lenin in Russia. Mandarins were the boyars, the Junkers—the old aristocracy whom Lenin and the Bolsheviks hated unconditionally.[4]

Further, in Lengyel's telling, the Mandarin of the story was a mysterious Chinaman, who's the target of a "badger game," in which three thieves use an alluring young prostitute to entice passing men upstairs into her room in order to mug them. The first two victims have no money, so they get summarily chucked out the door. The third is the Mandarin. Physically

---

4 Lengyel eventually wound up in Hollywood, where his screenplay for *Ninotchka* (1939) was nominated for an Oscar, and an original story was turned into the Jack Benny/Carole Lombard Nazi-era comedy, *To Be or Not to Be* (1942).

repulsed by his otherness, the girl rejects him. He keeps coming. Assault-ed, he fights back against his assailants, who try to suffocate him, stab him to death, and even hang him from a lamp hook. He keeps coming. He will not bleed, or die. Instead, throughout it all, the Mandarin continues to stare at the beautiful girl, absorbing all the punishment the murderous crooks can hand out, consumed by love and unwilling to let go of life until his love is either acknowledged or reciprocated.

The rope on the lamp hook won't hold; he falls from the hanging, his body beginning to glow with a strange inner light. The muggers recoil, but the girl finally understands; like Bluebeard, the Mandarin is the Outsider, in dire need of love and understanding. She wraps her arms around him, and gives him the love he has been seeking. The Mandarin's wounds ooze; released, he dies, an oriental Tristan in the arms of his trollop Isolde.

So far, so Wagnerian; the Mandarin's physical pain is nothing com-pared to his emotional distress. If a girl he is willing to pay for won't love him, or pretend to love him, even for twenty minutes, then who will? Isolde redeems Tristan with her own death, just as Senta saves the undead Dutchman from his eternal, accursed wanderings by hurling herself off a cliff. At the girl's first, unforced embrace, the Mandarin trembles, quivers, in an aurally erotic paroxysm, subtler and less explicit but every bit as apparent as Sergei's *petit mort* in *Lady Macbeth* a couple of decades later. The skein of the Norns continues unbroken: Love transfigures, then kills.

The other clear analogy is to Rasputin, whose at least subliminally erotic power over the Russian royal family ended with his death in 1916. Like the Mandarin, he did not go gentle into the dark night that Lenin had planned for the rest of the Romanovs. According to the very likely embellished tale purveyed by one of the assassins, Prince Felix Yusupov, the Mad Monk ate the poisoned cakes and drank the poisoned Madeira, survived a gunshot wound to the chest, played possum, struggled with his assassins, was shot again, and finally collapsed and died in a snow-bank, like mad Jack Torrance in Stanley Kubrick's version of Stephen King's *The Shining*.

On one level, then, *The Miraculous Mandarin* is the massacre of the boyars, staged for our edification, with the "priest" of the Czars thrown in for good measure. Certainly audiences of the time might have seen it that way. But is it? The purpose of subtext in art is to communicate that which is incommunicable. Throughout most of the ballet, and the music, we have no idea what is going through the Mandarin's mind; as a pantomime, the ballet mimics the action of Lengyel's scenario, displaying what words would have told us, were there words. The music is violent but dispassionate; Bartók never allows any sympathy for the Outsider— the *Außenseiter*—to bleed through before the Mandarin finally expires. The work is as cold and cruel as Communism itself but, one senses, in reaction to it, not in endorsement. "It will be hellish music," wrote Bartók to his wife, and it is.

The Miraculous Mandarin was premiered in 1926, in Cologne. It did not go well: "Cologne, a city of churches, monasteries and chapels...has lived to see its first true [musical] scandal," ran a notice in a German musical journal. "Catcalls, whistling, stamping, and booing...which did not subside even after the composer's personal appearance, nor even after the safety curtain went down.... The press, with the exception of the left, protests, the clergy of both denominations hold meetings, the mayor of the city intervenes dictatorially and bans the pantomime from the repertoire [only one performance was given].... Waves of moral outrage engulf the city..." Leading the chorus of invective was none other than the mayor of Cologne, the future German chancellor Konrad Adenauer, who personally told Bartók how little he thought of his music.

If Bartók had wanted a scandal on the order of Stravinsky's *Le sacre du printemps* in Paris, he came close. It's a brutal, uncompromising score, brimming with rhythmic energy and pornophany of all kinds. The instruments are employed erotically and violently, reflecting the murderous era in which it was conceived. It had all the makings of a riotous success. The problem was with the composer's timing. The tempest-tossed Bartók was born in Nagyszentmiklós, which is today Sânnicolaul-Mare, in Romania, and few of the other places he lived in his native land still remain in modern Hungary. The composer heard it only once more, in Budapest in 1928. It wasn't fully staged again until 1945, after his death in New York City, although he reworked most of the music into a concert suite, which is still widely played.[5]

In sum, Bartók wound up with the short end of the twentieth century's

---

5 The rhythmic energy of the *Mandarin* is almost instantly recognizable, even when its ghost appears elsewhere. I once asked the British film and stage director, Ken Russell, whether he had used one section in particular as temp-track music when he was cutting the hallucination sequence in his 1980 film *Altered States*. Yes, he replied, without hesitation. John Corigliano later supplied the score.

musical stick. What had once been part of the Austro-Hungarian empire wound up a rump state squeezed between what was left of Austria and Romania, which swallowed up a chunk of Hungary's eastern provinces. After the Great War, empires crumbled, dynasties vanished; the revolutions that were bruited across the Continent (but somehow mostly landed in Russia) were revenge writ large for the hash the crowned heads had made of Europe. What was needed, many felt, was a peoples' revolution, and Marxism provided a ready answer; what few Marxists admitted was that what was needed was a new mandarin class, with themselves as the mandarins.

This was the great, satanic lie of Marxism: that the people would rule. Lenin and his Bolsheviks never had any intentions of allowing the worker's paradise they preached to actually come to pass. They co-opted the legitimate revolution that had driven the Romanovs from power and purged their rival Mensheviks, among whose early leaders was Leon Trotsky, born Lev Bronstein, who switched sides in 1917, around the time of the October Revolution. A fat lot of good it did him: opposing the rise of Stalin got him exiled, first internally, then externally, and, in 1940, assassinated in Mexico City, although the "Trotskyite" wing of the movement continues to live a zombie existence to this day in a few precincts around Manhattan's Union Square.

To use the word "sides," however is misleading. In the aftermath of the First World War, there were factions on the Left, but only one side—just as, during the breakdown of the Weimar Republic a few decades later, the Communists and National Socialists were never arguing about *what* should happen to parliamentary democracy, or how quickly, but only *how* it should happen. The end of the Molotov–Ribbentrop Pact was announced by Hitler in his surprise assault on his former comrade Stalin, with Operation Barbarossa in June, 1941; the non-aggression agreement, which lasted just shy of two years, had allowed the two Socialist countries to attack and carve up Poland and the Baltics while still circling each other warily, hungrily.

Ever since, the international Left has gone to near-inordinate lengths to try to separate the two forms of socialism in the public mind. In effect, they are forced to argue that the Munich-based National Socialist German Workers Party—which had its roots in the Bavarian Socialist Republic, among other movements of the period—was lying about its commitment

to socialism, and more or less included the term in its name in order to
fool the unwary. But the Bavarian soviet's members included both Hitler's
future chauffeur and chief of his *Schutzstaffel*, Julius Schreck, and the
notorious Sepp Dietrich, later a general in the *Waffen-SS* and the head of
the Führer's personal *Leibstandarte*, his SS bodyguards. Instead of calling
the Leftist Hitler's political party by its name, today's Leftists choose to
obscure reality by exclusively using the term "Nazi," instead, counting on
the abbreviation's invidious connotations to terminate all argument; what's
never explained is that *Nazi* is simply a shortening of the first word of the
party's name, *Nationalsozialistische*. The linkage of the two concepts—
nationalism and socialism—was intentional from the start.

Mandarins everywhere, each one more ambitious and lethal than the
next. Hitler felt no compunction about liquidating his first private army,
the brown-shirted SA (the *Sturmabteilung*) and ordering the assassination of its leader, Ernst Röhm, during the Night of the Long Knives
in 1934. Röhm had outlived his usefulness, and besides, the boss had
something even more deadly in mind. In the Soviet Union, liquidation
was the favored remedy for all enemies of the state, and both Lenin and
his successor Stalin availed themselves of it liberally. Periodic purges
swept the U.S.S.R. until the day Stalin (and Prokofiev, as we have seen)
died, and you could get the chop for any reason, or no reason at all, at the
behest of the Fiery Angel. Both Hitler and, especially, Stalin, kept little
lists. There's a memorable scene in Tony Palmer's film of Shostakovich's
Testimony depicting Stalin sitting alone at his desk, crossing the names
of those to be shot off his register, which captures the workaday banality
of mass murder perfectly.

Outright treason against either the State or the Leader (the same thing)
was punishable by death, but so were such crimes as insufficient zeal
in carrying out the political program. Zeal, like rage, is another satanic
characteristic, as we know from human history: the lust to put apostasy
to death never goes out of style, whether it's the Spanish Inquisition's
penchant for the *auto-da-fé*, Savonarola (another mad monk) and his
bonfires of the vanities, or the dark crimes against humanity of the modern socialist/Communist states. Nobody likes a zealot: humorless prigs
and self-righteous scolds who, if given the chance, easily transition into
murderous thugs, convinced they are doing the Lord's work. Whether
religiously or politically motivated, they are the same the world over and

down through history. Christians have their St. Paul; others have even worse.

This notion of insufficient zeal is especially pertinent today. One of the advantages Western cultural conservatism has over its Leftist antagonists is a constancy of belief and purpose. The cultural conservative wishes to preserve the past while learning from it—both its lessons and its mistakes—and hoping to affect the future with the knowledge gleaned from a proper study of history. This is not necessarily to endorse that history in its entirety, merely to acknowledge it and accept it for what it is. One can learn little or nothing when one is convinced of the utter righteousness and rightness of his cause; that is to say, if one is a zealot. Tearing down monuments, burning books, and airbrushing (or, now, Photoshopping) historically inconvenient personages from the record of the past is definitionally non-conservative. So is insisting that the past be liquidated for the crime of contemporary wrongthink.

Seen in this light, it is immediately apparent that in its zeal to liquidate the past, the modern international Left has not only made common cause with resentful, reactionary Islam, but also why it has. Both the cultural-Marxist Left and the zealots of Islam are bent on the destruction of the West; to Lukács's question, each raises its bloody hand to volunteer. That they'll eventually turn on each other—as the National Socialists and Soviet Communists did (and the cultural Marxists will lose)—is of no moment at the moment. What matters is that the enemy of their enemy[6] is their ally of convenience, until it comes time for thieves, murderers, and cutthroats to fall out. But by then, they believe, the principal object of their animosity will have been vanquished, and thus no matter which of them loses, their side will have won. The zealots, therefore, are the shock troops of the Revolution. But they are not mandarins; they only work for the mandarins—useful idiots, as Lenin famously called the true True Believers.

A true mandarin, on the other hand, believes in nothing except himself and his own self-aggrandizement. These men do not serve the State, the State serves them: it takes care of their financial and physical needs and it helps them exterminate their enemies. In a mandarin-led society, the State is presented as a father figure, if not an actual Big Brother. He may

---

6 In the old Soviet Union, the U.S. was referred to as the "Principal Enemy."

be a boy emperor, a regent, a figment of the imagination—but he does not rule; the mandarins do. And they are opaque. In the Bartók-Lengyel ballet, the titular Miraculous Mandarin is not miraculous because he is a wizard, but because he is immune to physical pain until the girl finally takes pity on him and finds the way, mortally, to his heart. Like his real-life incarnations in bureaucracies everywhere, his intentions are obscure and his motivation well hidden. He is the Other; his attempt to fit in with the commoners is fatal.

We can always spot Mandarins, which is why their professed fealty to the welfare of the common man rings so hollow. Study the looks on the faces of Stalin and Lenin in the photograph at the top of this chapter. Lenin cockeyes the camera with, to paraphrase Mark Twain, the confidence of an atheist holding four aces in the poker game from Hell. Stalin, meanwhile, stares ahead confidently, with a look that says, "If you think the guy to my left is bad, wait 'til you get a load of me."

Taken in the pivotal year of 1919, it depicts each man as he really was. Either could be the model for Professor Woland—Satan himself—in Mikhail Bulgakov's novel *The Master and Margarita*, which was written between 1928 and 1940, and not published until 1966. (The novel also includes a cat named Behemoth, a character named Berlioz, a heroine named Margarita, and a demonic naked whore named Hella, along with Jesus, Judas, and Pontius Pilate.) This is not an idealized portrait of *Italia und Germania*, but of two devils, one junior and one senior, who took advantage of the mayhem and carnage of the Great War to leverage unto themselves to the kind of power that even Augustus never contemplated. Their black souls captured in this moment, they are as C. S. Lewis's junior devil Wormwood is to his uncle Screwtape, but they created a satanic kingdom right here on earth that lasted for three quarters of a century.

In the end, though, even their Evil Empire fell; maybe the vampire mandarins of the Soviet *nomenklatura*, who milked the system to the fullest possible extent, could not bleed, but they could, and did, die. Killing their bodies, however, was the easy part; killing their souls is another matter entirely. Like vampires, they continue to stalk us, seeking more throats into which to sink their gleaming fangs. How, then, can we stop them?

CHAPTER ELEVEN

"Enter freely. Go safely, and leave something of the happiness you bring!"

Adrift in Bistritz
Where every day is Walpurgisnacht

3 May. Bistritz.—Left Munich at 8:35 P. M., on 1st May, arriving at Vienna early next morning; should have arrived at 6:46, but train was an hour late. Buda-Pesth seems a wonderful place, from the glimpse which I got of it from the train and the little I could walk through the streets. I feared to go very far from the station, as we had arrived late and would start as near the correct time as possible. The impression I had was that we were leaving the West and entering the East; the most western of splendid bridges over the Danube, which

is here of noble width and depth, took us among the traditions of
Turkish rule.

—Bram Stoker, *Dracula*

Each generation gets the monsters it deserves. Zombies, the walking undead, have lately enjoyed a remarkable renaissance, beginning with George A. Romero's *Night of the Living Dead* (1968), which created the template—dare we say stereotype?—of the genre. The lonely farmhouse, the diverse collection of humans trapped inside, taking shelter from some sort of catastrophe whose origin is never explained, but whose results are tangible: hordes of brain-munching reanimated corpses, staggering insatiably through a formerly bucolic country landscape now transformed into a chiaroscuro nightmare.

Zombies have been used to stand in for just about any political group that needs to be feared or demonized. By the Left, they have been commonly employed to represent the mind-numbed, brain-dead citizenry of the supposedly conformist Fifties, who turn snarling in the direction of the slightest unorthodoxy. The same label is applied to cultural and social conservatives—the irony being that there is no orthodoxy like Marxism.

With the passage of time, however, the inverse interpretation can also be argued. Take, for example, *Invasion of the Body Snatchers* (1956), directed by Don Siegel and written by Daniel Mainwaring, who had a brush with the Hollywood blacklist around this time. An instant classic, it's been remade at least three times, to diminishing shock returns but almost always to good effect; although not strictly speaking a zombie movie, the result is the same. Seeds from outer space fall to earth, where they take root as pods (they look like giant watermelons) that eventually hatch perfect replicas of human beings. These replacement "humans" look and sound exactly like the person for whom they've substituted, but they're soulless aliens bent on the replacement of humanity.[1] "You're next!" shouts the lone survivor of the pod invasion of the fictional town of Santa Mira, California, as he's being examined in an emergency room and sized up for a strait jacket.

---

1 Europe is currently living through this very nightmare, as its population, hollowed out by nearly seven decades of loss of faith, birth control, and abortion, is being supplanted by religious and cultural aliens who will ape the styles of Europeans without actually becoming Europeans.

But any work of art, or even pop-pulp, B-movie cinema, as the original *Body Snatchers* was intended to be, gets reinterpreted by subsequent generations. Malevolent conformists may switch sides but, like those of the Mandarins, their characteristics remain constant, whether they're the gorgeous Dana Wynter in a cocktail dress, Muslims shooting up Paris, or a frothing, masked "Antifa" Leftist tearing down some cultural totem or inanimate object.

Another illustration of this principle comes in *High Noon* (1952), which actually was written by a card-carrying Communist, Carl Foreman, who was blacklisted for his admitted membership in the American Communist Party, but still managed to write two of the greatest films of his era, the Gary Cooper western classic and *The Bridge on the River Kwai* (1957). Surrounded by lily-livered or uncooperative townsfolk—including his own Quaker pacifist wife Amy, played by Grace Kelly—Marshal Will Kane must alone face the villains arriving on the noon train. Is Kane the lone liberal, standing up for law and order in the teeth of passive hostility? Or is he the lone conservative (he certainly acts in defense of qualities and principles we today associate with conservatism, including manliness, courage, and self-reliance), saving unworthy liberal weenies from the consequences of their own physical and moral cowardice?

The emblematic final scene, with Kane chucking his marshal's star into the dirt and riding off in a plebeian wagon with Amy, can thus be seen in two ways, but interpreted in only one: the people weren't worthy of his mettle, and now they can bloody well fend for themselves. Whether that is a liberal or conservative action is up to the viewer.

Such is the uncertainty that attends ascribing a political program to a work of art. Politicized art is really no art at all, merely a gilding of something that already exists, rather than an original creation. My argument throughout this book has been that while art acts politically, commenting on the moral dilemmas and exigencies of the past, and affecting the way we envision the future, it is not and should never be merely a reflective appendage of politics—a transposition, as it were, of a political program into another medium, for popular consumption.

The simplest explanation for the persistence of zombie metaphor is that we don't know why they're seeking sustenance from our gray matter, and we wouldn't know even if we were zombies; the only thing that matters is that, one way or the other, they're inside our heads.

This exchange is from the 1940 Bob Hope movie *The Ghost Breakers*, set on a small Caribbean island. Hope plays Larry Lawrence, asking a local doctor, Montgomery, an important question; the character of Mary Carter is played by Paulette Goddard:

LAWRENCE: "You live here?"
MONTGOMERY: "Yes."
LAWRENCE: "Then maybe you know what a zombie is…"
MONTGOMERY: "When a person dies and is buried, it seems there are certain voodoo priests who…who have the power to bring him back to life."
CARTER: "How horrible!"
MONTGOMERY: "It's worse than horrible, because a zombie has no will of his own. You see them sometimes, walking around blindly with dead eyes, following orders, not knowing what they do, not caring."
LAWRENCE: "You mean like Democrats?"

Pretty hard to top that.

An even older mythic archetype, and one far more primal, is the figure of the vampire, the undead, Nosferatu. Vampires are encountered in nearly every culture, but they found particular favor in Western literature during the eighteenth and nineteenth centuries, where they exercised a distinct fascination on the literary imagination. Fittingly, the craze began in Germany, first with Heinrich August Ossenfelder's poem *Der Vampir* (1748)—"*And as softly thou art sleeping/ To thee shall I come creeping/ And thy life's blood drain away/ And so shalt thou be trembling/ For thus shall I be kissing/ And death's threshold thou' it be crossing/ With fear, in my cold arms.*"—and later with Gottfried August Bürger's Gothic narrative poem *Lenore* (1774.)[2] In both, the idea of vampirism is intertwined with the loss and then sudden reappearance of a lover, and the physical act of love itself—for what can be more intimate than vampirism? The Bürger

---

2 Echoed by Poe in *The Raven*: "Ah, distinctly I remember it was in the bleak December;/ And each separate dying ember wrought its ghost upon the floor./Eagerly I wished the morrow;—vainly I had sought to borrow/From my books surcease of sorrow—sorrow for the lost Lenore—/For the rare and radiant maiden whom the angels name Lenore—/ Nameless here for evermore."

poem also contains the memorable phrase *die Todten reiten schnell* ("the dead travel fast").[3]

The genre really got rolling, however, during the second decade of the nineteenth century, when four young friends gathered at the Villa Diodati on Lake Geneva, in Switzerland, during the summer of 1816. Chief among them: Lord Byron, fresh off scandalous love affairs with Lady Caroline Lamb, rumored semi-incest with his half-sister, Augusta Leigh, and a quickie marriage to, and separation from, Annabella Milbanke—in Byron, the priapic, amoral life of the artistic genius was never more vividly illustrated, until the arrival of the great pianist and composer Franz Liszt in the 1830s, himself even more Byronic than Byron himself.

Also present during that memorable three-day sojourn together was Byron's personal physician, John William Polidori; and the "It couple" of early nineteenth-century poetry, Percy Bysshe Shelley and his fiancée, Mary Wollstonecraft Godwin. For good measure, Claire Clairmont— Mary's stepsister, with whom Byron had begun an affair in London—came along as well. The free-love hippies of Haight-Ashbury had nothing on the early Romantics.

The year 1816 has become known as the Year without a Summer. Long before "climate change" replaced ghosts, werewolves, and vampires as a bogeyman with whom to frighten small children, both Europe and America, particularly in New England, experienced abnormal cold, enough to cause crops to fail and even precipitate famine in parts of British Isles and Germany. It is theorized that the eruption of Mount Tambora in Indonesia the year before resulted in a worldwide lowering of average temperatures that year, but 1816 was also near the end of the Little Ice Age as well. So on several dark and stormy nights that would do Bulwer-Lytton proud, in enforced confinement with nothing else to occupy them, the group decided to scare the wits out of each other by making up ghost stories.

The culture has never been the same—because two of those ghost stories became classics of their genres.

Curiously, neither of them was written by one of the two famous poets. After a boating trip on the lake with Byron, which ended in a near-fatal accident (Shelley couldn't swim), Shelley delivered himself of the "Hymn to Intellectual Beauty," whose first stanza reads as follows:

---

3 This phrase reappears in the Coppola *Dracula* film, uttered by one of the passengers in the coach, who hands Jonathan Harker a protective rosary.

The awful shadow of some unseen Power
Floats though unseen among us; visiting
This various world with as inconstant wing
As summer winds that creep from flower to flower;
Like moonbeams that behind some piny mountain shower,
It visits with inconstant glance
Each human heart and countenance;
Like hues and harmonies of evening,
Like clouds in starlight widely spread,
Like memory of music fled,
Like aught that for its grace may be
Dear, and yet dearer for its mystery.

Then came the really spooky stuff. Mary herself germinated her novel *Frankenstein, or, the Modern Prometheus* (1818), an original story that soon enough became one of the foundational myths not only of the culture, but of Universal Studios in Hollywood, which introduced "Karloff" to the world as the creature in James Whale's *Frankenstein* (1931), and inspired a host of sequels as Universal metamorphosed into the Monster Movie Studio. *Frankenstein*, the novel, is not particularly terrifying in its telling; the title character is not the Creature but the doctor who animates a collection of dead body parts in his quest to be like God (*"Ye shall be as Gods"*). Mary was writing a cautionary tale about the limits of human power, not a horror movie, but her monster proved more dramatically compelling, and sympathetic, than her mad scientist—and, eternally Undead, he stalks us still.

Victorians did not fear stitched-together Creatures. Life created in the lab became a twentieth-century concern—H. G. Wells's *The Island of Dr. Moreau* (1896) more fully explored the subject, as did Aldous Huxley's *Brave New World* in 1932—and resonates mightily today as we ponder the ethics of babies with three parents and multiple strands of DNA. What they did fear (a fear bequeathed to us), however, were vampires.

While in Italy, Byron sketched the third canto of his epic poem *Childe Harold's Pilgrimage*, which became the inspiration for the French composer Hector Berlioz's viola concerto *Harold in Italy*. But what is of interest to us is a short story of his that has come down to us as something called "Fragment of a Novel" or "The Burial: a Fragment," later published in 1819 as an appendix to Byron's poem *Mazeppa*.[4]

Byron, who died at age thirty-six fighting the Turks for the cause of Greek independence at Missolonghi in 1824, exerted an outsized influence for a man with such a short life span. Politics, poetry, and passion were all united in this seminal figure of the Romantic period. No rules applied to him; no borders bound him. He was the living embodiment of the necessary selfishness of the artist: a cad, a bounder, but never a mountebank. Ticketed for hell in his private life, his public life sent him to the pantheon, where he's served as an inspiration and role model for creative geniuses ever since.

Politically active, sexually insatiable, heedless of public opinion, Byron gave his name to the language as an adjective, and inspired creative artists as disparate as Niccolò Paganini, Liszt, Oscar Wilde, and Pablo Picasso. He habitually slept with a pair of pistols and a dagger by his bedside, stayed up until three o'clock in the morning and arose again at two in the afternoon. He invented the entire concept of the Artist as Hero, if not actually the Artist as Vampire, preying on his friends artistically and sexually in order to create his own Heroic Narrative. He didn't care what anybody thought of him as long as they read his works, and pretty girls still flocked willingly to his bed.[5]

Byron's attitude toward his critics may be summarized in this excerpt from a letter he wrote to his publisher, John Murray, on May 15, 1819:

---

4 The impossibly handsome lady-killer Liszt, who consciously struck a "Byronic" pose during his years as the first touring piano virtuoso, also reinterpreted and immortalized *Mazeppa* in his "Transcendental Étude No. 4" in 1852 and the symphonic poem of the same name.

5 In an interview with the *Hollywood Reporter* (Feb. 27, 2018) Camille Paglia correctly noted, "To impose rigid sex codes devised for the genteel bourgeois office on the dynamic performing arts will inevitably limit rapport, spontaneity, improvisation and perhaps creativity itself. Similarly, ethical values and guidelines that should structure the social realm of business and politics do not automatically transfer to art, which occupies the contemplative realm shared by philosophy and religion. Great art has often been made by bad people. So what? Expecting the artist to be a good person was a sentimental canard of Victorian moralism, rejected by the 'art for art's sake' movement led by Charles Baudelaire and Oscar Wilde. Indeed, as I demonstrated in my first book, *Sexual Personae*, the impulse or compulsion toward art making is often grounded in ruthless aggression and combat — which is partly why there have been so few great women artists."

Mr Hobhouse is at it again about indelicacy—there is no indelicacy—
if he wants that, let him read Swift—his great Idol—but his Imagination must be a dunghill with a Viper's nest in the middle—to engen-
der such a supposition about this poem.—For my part I think you
are all crazed.—What does he mean about "G—d damn"—there is
"damn" to be sure—but no "G—d" whatever. - And as to what he calls
a "p—ss bucket"—it is nothing but simple water—as I am a Sinner…

It's hardly shocking, therefore, that Byron was interested in both the
daemonic and the demonic. The epistolary "Fragment" relates a journey
to Asia Minor the narrator undertakes with an unwell elderly man, one
Augustus Darvell. Upon arrival at a Turkish cemetery, they see a stork
alight with a snake in its beak,[6] "steadfastly regarding us." Darvell makes
the narrator promise to bury him that very evening, on the spot where
the stork is perched:

He smiled in a ghastly manner, and said, faintly, "It is not yet time!"
As he spoke, the stork flew away. My eyes followed it for a moment,
it could hardly be longer than ten might be counted. I felt Darvell's
weight, as it were, increase upon my shoulder, and, turning to look
upon his face, perceived that he was dead!

I was shocked with the sudden certainty which could not be
mistaken—his countenance in a few minutes became nearly black.
I should have attributed so rapid a change to poison, had I not been
aware that he had no opportunity of receiving it unperceived. The
day was declining, the body was rapidly altering, and nothing remained but to fulfil his request. With the aid of Suleiman's ataghan
and my own sabre, we scooped a shallow grave upon the spot which
Darvell had indicated: the earth easily gave way, having already
received some Mahometan tenant. We dug as deeply as the time
permitted us, and throwing the dry earth upon all that remained of

---

6 A similar image in the opening paragraph of Penelope Fitzgerald's splendid short novel
The Bookshop (1978): "She had once seen a heron flying across the estuary and trying, while
it was on the wing, to swallow an eel which it had caught. The eel, in turn, was struggling
to escape from the gullet of the heron and appeared a quarter, a half, or occasionally
three-quarters of the way out. The indecision expressed by both creatures was pitiable.
They had both taken on too much."

the singular being so lately departed, we cut a few sods of greener turf from the less withered soil around us, and laid them upon his sepulchre.

Between astonishment and grief, I was tearless.

Polidori is said to have told Murray in a letter that Byron envisioned an ending in which the narrator returned to England to find the man he had buried in the Anatolian Muslim cemetery alive and well and "making love to his sister." So it was left to Polidori to flesh out Byron's sketch that night, which he did in a novella, *The Vampyre*, also published in 1819, with authorship at first ascribed to Byron. As Murray informed Byron on April 27:

> Amongst an assortment of new books which I forwarded to your Lordship through the kindness of Mr Hamilton of the Foreign Office, was a Copy of a thing called the Vampire which Mr Colburn has had the temerity to publish with your Lordships name as its author—it was first printed in the New Monthly Magazine, from which l have taken the Copy wch I now inclose. The Editor of that Journal has quarrelled with the publisher & has called this morning to exculpate himself from the baseness of the transaction—He says that he received it from—Dr Polidori—for a small sum—Polidori averring that the whole plan of it was your Lordships & merely written out by him...

The error was corrected, and the work has come down to us as Polidori's, not Byron's. (Polidori died even younger than Byron, at the age of twenty-five.) As others have noted, it established the principal elements of the genre, including the vampire's status as a nobleman and his predilection for feasting on the blood of beautiful young women. Combining the craze for Gothic settings—damsels in distress—already sweeping Europe, with the notion of the vampire as Byronic hero, it was a sure formula for success, both literary and theatrical.

It was left to the private secretary of the most famous actor of his day to give the legend its definitive form. In 1897, the Dublin-born Bram Stoker, assistant to Sir Henry Irving, published his novel *Dracula*. Like *Frankenstein*, it was written in the epistolary style then still popular, but on a far higher and literarily more inventive level, composed not just of letters, but of extracts of diaries, newspapers reports, and even transcriptions of phonographic recordings made by one of the characters, Dr. Seward. And yet the device is never tiresome; instead, it gives the fantastic tale a degree of verisimilitude lacking in the didactic and hortatory *Frankenstein*.

When every day is *Walpurgisnacht*, it's tough to keep your wits about you; it's no accident that Harker's journey in *Dracula* begins on May Day, the feast day of St. Walpurga. Originally, the novel was to have contained a chapter we know as "Dracula's Guest," set in Munich the night before, on *Walpurgisnacht* itself. The eerie sounds of a wolf stalk the narrator throughout the tale, until finally the wolf materializes, bounding from a nearby cemetery and suddenly lunging at his throat. This episode was deleted from the published version of the novel, which opens with the excerpt from Harker's diary quoted above, but is often provided as a companion piece—and in any case, the vampire-as-wolf returned in the novel, with its memorable line: "Listen to them, the children of the night. What music they make!"

Dracula's first celluloid incarnation—F. W. Murnau's *Nosferatu: eine Symphonie des Grauens* appeared in 1922; the Tod Browning version, starring Béla Lugosi, followed nine years later, coming even before *Frankenstein* in the Universal pantheon. An early talkie, it was based on a stage play and thus has a static quality that the more sophisticated *Frankenstein* film abjures; what makes it still worth watching today is Lugosi's iconic portrayal of the Count.

Hundreds more sequels, imitations, and knockoffs followed, including a series of Mexican vampire films, the Hammer Films series starring Christopher Lee (Dracula) and Peter Cushing (Van Helsing), and a comedic version, *Dracula: Dead and Loving It*, directed by Mel Brooks and starring Leslie Nielsen. Also of note are twin 1979 versions directed by Werner Herzog, one in German, and the same film shot again in English, *Nosferatu: Phantom der Nacht*; the Coppola outing with Gary Oldman as the vampire; and *Shadow of the Vampire* (2000), which depicts the making of the original *Nosferatu*—only this time, Max Schreck (played by Willem Dafoe) really *is* a vampire.

Latterly, we've had Anne Rice's series of novels about the vampire Lestat—the movie version of *Interview with the Vampire* (1994) starred Tom Cruise as the neck-biter in chief—the *Twilight* saga of vampires in love and, as the ultimate spin-off, *Fifty Shades of Grey* by E. L. James, which began its life as fan fiction, taking off from the *Twilight* series, and became, along with the *Harry Potter* novels, the biggest-selling English-language novel in history.

And no short survey of vampirism in Western literature would be complete without Baudelaire's "Metamorphoses of the Vampire," one of the six poems in *Les Fleurs du mal* (1857) condemned by a French tribunal and ordered removed from the book; Baudelaire was also fined three hundred francs, later reduced to fifty after an appeal to the empress of France. In its frank depiction of the overwhelming sexuality of the vampire, both male and female, *Les Métamorphoses du vampire* remains one of the most potent images of the vampire in all Western literature:

> *Meanwhile from her red mouth the woman, in husky tones,*
> *Twisting her body like a serpent upon hot stones*
> *And straining her white breasts from their imprisonment,*
> *Let fall these words, as potent as a heavy scent:*
> *"My lips are moist and yielding, and I know the way*
> *To keep the antique demon of remorse at bay.*
> *All sorrow die upon my bosom. I can make*
> *Old men laugh happily as children for my sake.*
> *For him who sees me naked in my tresses, I*
> *Replace the sun, the moon, and all the stars of the sky!*
> *Believe me, learned sir, I am so deeply skilled*
> *That when I wind a lover in my soft arms, and yield*
> *My breasts like two ripe fruits for his devouring—both*
> *Shy and voluptuous, insatiable and loath—*
> *Upon this bed that groans and sighs luxuriously*
> *Even the impotent angels would be damned for me!"*

Who can resist such an offer? Naturally, there's a catch:

> *When she had drained me of my very marrow, and cold*
> *And weak, I turned to give her one more kiss—behold,*
> *There are my side was nothing but a hideous*
> *Putrescent thing, all faceless and exuding pus.*
> *I closed my eyes and mercifully swooned till day:*

And when I looked at morning for that beast of prey
Who seemed to have replenished her arteries from my own,
The wan, disjoined fragments of a skeleton
Wagged up and down in a lewd posture where she had lain,
Rattling with each convulsion like a weathervane
Or an old sign that creaks upon its bracket, right
Mournfully in the wind upon a winter's night.
—[translation by George Dillon]

Que sur ces matelas qui se pâment d'émoi/ Les anges impuissants se damneraient pour moi! No wonder the poet got into trouble. No wonder the sexy vampire is here to stay. It is almost impossible for us to reject the demon lover of our dreams, no matter the price we must pay the following morn.

The opening passage from Harker's diary sets the tone not only for Stoker's story but for its larger cultural and political significance. For the Europeans of the nineteenth century, Transylvania—literally, the Land Beyond the Forest—was the embodiment of the dark woods of so many fairy tales. Warred over, colonized by German merchants but never settled by them, it had long been a battleground and a buffer zone between Islam and the West. Memories of the Turk were fresh, no matter how old they were, and Christianity was present in several forms, including the Catholicism of the Hungarians and the branches of the eastern-rite Orthodox Church across Bulgaria and Romania. Whole countries and peoples had been absorbed, exterminated, or simply vanished, such as Wallachia. The source of much myth and legend, Transylvania was a place where forbidding castles thrust their ruined turrets defiantly at the sky, as if still in anticipation of the next attack in an endless war.

"*The impression I had was that we were leaving the West and entering the East...*" For Americans, the unexplored territories lay to the west, virgin and ripe for the taking, but for Western Europeans, the unknown lay to the east, in antiquity. It was to the east that Hitler looked while demanding *Lebensraum* for the Third Reich; to Germans, the Slavs were only good for slaves, and as for the peoples of the old Roman province of Dacia and the inhabitants of the Balkans, they needed to be moved aside, their natural resources seized (such as the Ploesti oil fields), and the land turned over to the Master Race.

Nothing good ever came out of the east, but plenty of bad things happened to unwary strangers who crossed into it. Entering the East meant entering the territory of the historical Dracula. Vlad Dracul or Vlad Țepeș, *Voivode* (prince) of Wallachia, was known as Vlad the Impaler for a reason: he believed in doing unto his enemies as they did unto his people, and impaled them through the throat or rectum on long pikes, then hung them upright as human scarecrows. When the Ottomans sent emissaries to him, he had them killed by nailing their turbans to their heads. The brutality on either side of these endless wars was, by modern lights, appalling; we prefer our mass annihilation to be more antiseptic and impersonal.

Dracula is rarely if ever thought of as a political novel, but it is. The underlying conflict between Islam and Christianity forms the novel's backdrop. Dracula's bloodthirsty implacability is a direct result of his battles against the sultan Mehmed II, the conqueror of Constantinople, who brought his war against Latin Christianity further into Europe with incursions into Wallachia, Bosnia (still heavily Muslim today), and Albania (ditto); his troops even briefly invaded Italy and threatened the Eternal City in 1480.

By the end of the nineteenth century, though, Islam had been beaten back. Ferdinand and Isabella had completed the *Reconquista* of Spain in 1492, and the Musselmen had largely been cleared from the eastern lands. True, an expeditionary force under General George "Chinese" Gordon had been wiped out by the forces of the Mahdi at Khartoum, in the Sudan, in 1885, and Egyptian rule was replaced by an Islamic *sharia* state, but that defeat was avenged in 1896, when British troops under General Horatio Herbert Kitchener annihilated the Muslim forces at Omdurman, with the help of the Maxim gun.[7]

The London of 1897 was the London of Queen Victoria, with Her Majesty's government's honor restored, and of Sherlock Holmes and John H. Watson, M.D.; the idea that little more than a century later English cities would be hotbeds of radical Islamic theology, Pakistani rape gangs, and culturally inimical *jihadis* fully capable of blowing themselves up in a concert hall filled with young British girls, would have been unthinkable. And yet the West's agnostic loss of faith in its institutions has resulted in exactly that; held prisoner by "tolerance," forbidden by "compassion" to

---

7 Inspiring Belloc's famous couplet: "Whatever happens, we have got/the Maxim gun, and they have not."

articulate a coherent defense, and in the thralls of the "diversity" chimera, Britain has found itself morally and politically defenseless. Like the vampire, Islam keeps coming back, as do all the enemies of the West and its civilization. Turning the Judeo-Christian world view on its head, the Leftist narrative posits that the root of all evil is not Satan but God and Christ—who are, of course, the "real" Satans.

In Victor Hugo's unfinished epic poem from 1886, *Le fin du Satan* (The Death of Satan), we read:

> *Then it was horrible, And the darkness came and the light decreased; Brilliant Lucifer, teeming with stars, disappeared, And, lo! there appeared Satan. Thus was Hell created. And pushing night before it, as one opens a door, Horror of the virgin azure and the innocent sky, This black world emerged from the darkness, howling.*

Hugo depicts "brilliant Lucifer," the Light-Bringer, expelled from Heaven, falling for four thousand years into the abyss, transformed into Satan as he falls. Good into Evil; can Evil into Good be far behind? So the idea was present, the precedent established, long before the Creation.

The men of the West today find themselves no longer passing through Bistritz but trapped in its modern incarnation as Bistriţa—in Transylvania—on the front lines of the clash of civilizations just as its enemies are leaving the East and entering the West in numbers unimaginable a decade ago, crashing into public buildings, penetrating institutions and governments, using our own institutions and weapons against us with the aim of bringing them down, just as surely as the Twin Towers were toppled by hijacked American airplanes. Indiscriminately, the invaders kill men, women, and children, without much fear of retaliation, since the West defines acts of war as those enormities perpetrated by nation-state actors, not a fifth column of cultural-Marxist sappers or a rag-tag *ummah* of Believers.

"Take us away from all this death," we cry, and then offer our necks, because the teeth are so inviting, and because the evil, like Satan, falls so fast and yet takes so long.

CHAPTER TWELVE

Jacques-Louis David, *Le Serment du Jeu de paume*, 1791

The Stone Guest

All aboard the Rights O' Man

Behold the political tenets of the French Revolution, as adopted by the National Constituent Assembly in 1789 and recorded by one of its most passionate advocates, the British-born American revolutionary Thomas Paine, in his book *Rights of Man* (1791):[1]

ARTICLE I   Men are born and remain free and equal in rights. Social distinctions can be founded only on the common good.

---

1 In Herman Melville's last work, *Billy Budd*, published posthumously in 1924, Billy is impressed into service aboard a warship during the Napoleonic Wars from a merchant vessel named the *Rights of Man*, after Paine. In Benjamin Britten's opera of the same name, set to a libretto by E. M. Forster and Eric Crozier, Billy sings out to his former mates: "Farewell, to you forever, old Rights o' Man."

Article II   The goal of any political association is the conservation of the natural and imprescriptible rights of man. These rights are liberty, property, safety and resistance against oppression.

Article III   The principle of any sovereignty resides essentially in the Nation. No body, no individual can exert authority which does not emanate expressly from it.

Article IV   Liberty consists of doing anything which does not harm others: thus, the exercise of the natural rights of each man has only those borders which assure other members of the society the enjoyment of these same rights. These borders can be determined only by the law.

Article V   The law has the right to forbid only actions harmful to society. Anything which is not forbidden by the law cannot be impeded, and no one can be constrained to do what it does not order.

Article VI   The law is the expression of the general will. All the citizens have the right of contributing personally or through their representatives to its formation. It must be the same for all, either that it protects, or that it punishes. All the citizens, being equal in its eyes, are equally admissible to all public dignities, places, and employments, according to their capacity and without distinction other than that of their virtues and of their talents.

Article VII   No man can be accused, arrested nor detained but in the cases determined by the law, and according to the forms which it has prescribed. Those who solicit, dispatch, carry out or cause to be carried out arbitrary orders, must be punished; but any citizen called or seized under the terms of the law must obey at once; he renders himself culpable by resistance.

Article VIII   The law should establish only penalties that are strictly and evidently necessary, and no one can be punished but under a law established and promulgated before the offense and legally applied.

ARTICLE IX   Any man being presumed innocent until he is declared culpable if it is judged indispensable to arrest him, any rigor which would not be necessary for the securing of his person must be severely reprimanded by the law.

ARTICLE X   No one may be disturbed for his opinions, even religious ones, provided that their manifestation does not trouble the public order established by the law.

ARTICLE XI   The free communication of thoughts and of opinions is one of the most precious rights of man: any citizen thus may speak, write, print freely, except to respond to the abuse of this liberty, in the cases determined by the law.

ARTICLE XII   The guarantee of the rights of man and of the citizen necessitates a public force: this force is thus instituted for the advantage of all and not for the particular utility of those in whom it is trusted.

ARTICLE XIII   For the maintenance of the public force and for the expenditures of administration, a common contribution is indispensable; it must be equally distributed to all the citizens, according to their ability to pay.

ARTICLE XIV   Each citizen has the right to ascertain, by himself or through his representatives, the need for a public tax, to consent to it freely, to know the uses to which it is put, and of determining the proportion, basis, collection, and duration.

ARTICLE XV   The society has the right of requesting an account from any public agent of its administration.

ARTICLE XVI   Any society in which the guarantee of rights is not assured, nor the separation of powers determined, has no Constitution.

ARTICLE XVII   Property being an inviolable and sacred right, no

one can be deprived of private usage, if it is not when the public necessity, legally noted, evidently requires it, and under the condition
of a just and prior indemnity.

These are the liberal principles that not only fueled the revolution in
France, but revolts around the world. Instantly, one hears echoes of
Rousseau's famous dictum, "Man is born free, and everywhere he is in
chains," from *The Social Contract* of 1762. That work, which has been the
handbook of revolutionaries ever since it first appeared, opens with an
epigraph from the penultimate book of Virgil's *Aeneid*: *"foederis aequas
Dicamus leges"*—"Let us strike an equal treaty with them"—illustrating
once again the long chains of political resonance that derive from works
of art.

In which of these articles does the Left still believe today? The quaint
notion of equal rights has, in the manner of Orwell's *Animal Farm*, been
transmogrified to mean that, in the name of "social justice," some groups
are more equal than others. The same goes for property rights, since the
Marxist view of property holds that it is "theft." Article III's reference to
the Nation as being the source of all sovereignty is now hopelessly out-
dated. Article IV eventually found its way into Hugh Hefner's "Playboy
Philosophy" of self-actualized hedonism, but has otherwise been abandoned. Article V has since been modified to read, "anything not expressly
allowed is forbidden."

And so on. Article VIII seems hopelessly naïve, now that not just
crimes but punishments can be retroactive. The opinions—"even religious
ones"—expressly protected in Article X have become subject to review,
since the only faith that is now acceptable in atheist circles is Islam, and
that only because it is viewed as a civil-rights issue, not a religious one.
Article XIII's quasi-Marxist notion of an "ability to pay" is null and void
when half the country pays no income taxes at all, and thus gives the lie
to the notion of a burden equally distributed. As for "property being an
inviolable and sacred right," tell that to the next masked thug who smashes
your front window or sets your car on fire in the name, not of the law, but
of a "higher moral cause."

Here we see the fundamental weakness of the Leftist argument, although they would call it a strength: the tendency of its arguments to
"switch sides," just as in their fantastic retelling of the century after the

Civil War, the violent, racist Democrats who refused to accept the election of 1860 and then fired on Fort Sumter, and the abolitionist Republicans who crushed them in 1865, somehow "switched sides" after the Civil Rights Movement, thus allowing the party of slavery, segregation, sedition, and, latterly, secularism to escape culpability for its transparently and demonstrably wicked past. A fluid attachment to every principle save one—government power and an eventual monopoly on force—has always been the hallmark of the radical Left.

Whereas, on the side of Western cultural conservatism—a genuine commitment to Western ethical, moral, religious, literary, musical, artistic, and scientific principles and accomplishments—we remain unapologetically steadfast in our allegiance to our civilization, no matter how viciously or obscenely the Marxist Left attacks it. We know this from history: their attacks will molt, shift, and change form, which means we can always wait them out in the realm of ideas. There is no one on the Left today equal in firepower to Rousseau or Marx, which is why their movement, based entirely on resentment, jealousy, frustration, impotence, and animosity, is so intellectually spent. Where would they be without (to couch it in terms they can understand) either dead, white, European male? In what would they believe? Who would guide them?

What poor, miserable lives they lead, seething with anger yet so mentally dull that they believe every word is a secret homonym or homophone for something they've been inculcated to loathe; for the dim-bulb Left, each despised person, place, or thing is Emmanuel Goldstein (based on Trotsky) from *1984*, an Enemy of the People and the proper object of their obligatory Two Minutes Hate.

Until the October Revolution in Russia, the French Revolution was the greatest Leftist uprising in modern Western history. Unlike the American Revolution, with which it is often erroneously and misleadingly compared, and despite the active presence of Tom Paine in both, the French Revolution destroyed as much as it could of the old ways, including, temporarily, the monarchy, the nobility, and the clerics. It destroyed buildings, looted treasuries, and executed thousands of people, including its own leaders. A satanic orgy of destruction, its fires raged until Napoleon gathered the reins of power, brought order to anarchy, crowned himself Emperor—and then set out to wage destructive war on his European neighbors for a decade or more in the name of *la gloire de la France*.

The fascist impulse never lies far from the satanic. Only a stable society that does not have to worry about its own survival has the time or inclination to concern itself with relatively minor injustices, but even minor injustices can be fanned until they are suddenly everyone's pre-occupation, freighted down with great moral weight until they become internal destabilizing elements. As the French Revolution shows, chaos emerges from order and, left unchecked, reigns until its destructiveness is as exhausted as the people upon whom it is inflicted. Then order, most often in the form of a strongman, re-asserts itself. A sometimes peaceful transition of power (as in the United States, when the general George Washington, gave way to the scholarly civilian John Adams, and he in turn to the Virginia aristocrat and Francophile Thomas Jefferson), sometimes violent (Napoleon) then ensues. And the cycle begins again.

Let us now consider this historic sequential arc from the period under discussion:

Beaumarchais–Mozart–the French Revolution–Beethoven–Napoleon.

The sequence of events that followed the premiere of Pierre Beaumarchais' play *La Folle Journée, ou Le Mariage de Figaro* (A Crazy Day, or, Figaro's Wedding) in 1784 is one of the most extraordinary in Western history. Within less than a decade of its premiere, which occurred despite the trepidations of crowned heads across Europe, the Bastille was stormed, King Louis XVI and his queen, Marie Antoinette, were arrested and guillotined, and the *ancien régime* fell. And all because of a play?

Well, yes. As the British drama critic Michael Billington wrote in *The Guardian* in 2006: "Louis XVI, with uncanny prophetic insight, said of *The Marriage of Figaro*: 'For this play not to be a danger, the Bastille would have to be torn down first.' Napoleon famously described it as 'the Revolution in action.' When people question, as they constantly do, the political potency of theatre, they should always remember the shining example of Beaumarchais."

Figaro was at once a sterling comedy of manners as well as a political satire; not since *The Beggar's Opera* by John Gay and Johann Pepusch debuted in London (1728) had audiences seen anything like it. *The Beggar's Opera* was a cultural double whammy, first in making fun of the aristocracy by giving audiences a play whose heroes were highwaymen, fences, cutthroats, whores, drabs, and trollops; and second, by using popular tunes of the day to parody the excesses of Italian opera in the Handelian style then the rage in London. Mr. Peachum (impeach 'em), a receiver of stolen goods and an informant against his own class when it suits his purposes, expresses the work's inverted moral universe in his opening number and first speech:

> PEACHUM: A Lawyer is an honest Employment, so is mine. Like me too he acts in a double Capacity, both against Rogues and for 'em; for 'tis but fitting that we should protect and encourage Cheats, since we live by them.

Like Paine, Beaumarchais was a passionate supporter of the American Revolution. His *Figaro*—part of a trilogy that also includes the prequel, *The Barber of Seville*, which was famously set to music by Rossini, and *La Mère coupable* (The Guilty Mother)—takes square aim at the aristocracy and its predilection for preying, in this case, sexually, on the lower classes. From the outset, Count Almaviva has his lascivious eye on the commoner Suzanne, who is set to marry the count's valet, Figaro. There are elements of French bedroom farce throughout, but with a deadly serious subtext to which Figaro gives full voice in a fifth-act speech:

> FIGARO: No. My Lord Count, you shan't have her, you shall not have her! Because you are a great nobleman you think you are a great genius—Nobility, fortune, rank, position! How proud they make a man feel! What have you done to deserve such advantages? Put yourself to the trouble of being born—nothing more! For the rest—a very ordinary man! Whereas I, lost among the obscure crowd, have had to deploy more knowledge, more calculation and skill merely to survive than has sufficed to rule all the provinces of Spain for a century. Yet you would measure yourself against me.... Could anything be stranger than a fate like mine?

Fighting words, indeed—and put into action soon enough. The King at first forbade public production, but was mollified by some changes to the text, such as moving the locale from France to Spain,[2] and the work

---

2 Why crowned heads thought audiences wouldn't see right through the disguise is a mystery. Verdi had to face such censorship twice, in *Rigoletto* (moving the action from the French court where Victor Hugo's play, *Le roi s'amuse* had been set, to ducal Mantua), and *Un ballo in maschera*, in which the assassination of King Gustavus III of Sweden was transposed to colonial Boston.

opened at the Théâtre Français in 1784; nine years later, the king was executed on the Place de la Révolution.

What really propelled *Figaro*, however, was not the play itself but the opera faithfully fashioned from it by the librettist, da Ponte, for Mozart. This is not to diminish Beaumarchais but to establish Mozart's pre-eminence not only among composers of his day, but also as a potent international cultural influence. In *The Abduction from the Seraglio* (1782), he had established the German language as a proper tongue for operatic discourse while tackling the thorny subject of "white slavery"— that is, the kidnapping of Europeans by North African Muslim raiders, their auction at slave markets, and the installation of their women into harems. While the *Singspiel* (that is, with spoken dialogue, in the manner of a Broadway show, rather than the sung recitative of Italian opera) treated the subject with humor, the reality had long been no joke: estimates are that some one million Europeans were abducted by Barbary pirates between 1530 and 1780—one of history's great crimes that goes entirely unacknowledged and remains unpunished today.[3]

For their version of *Figaro,* da Ponte and Mozart eliminated the overtly political speeches, in part to avoid problems with the censors and with the Austrian emperor, Joseph II—who just so happened to be Marie Antoinette's brother. They cut the politically incendiary content because they didn't need it: Mozart's music carries all the subtextual freight imaginable in a radiant score that remains as moving today as it was more than two centuries ago.

There's a lovely scene in Peter Schaffer's screenplay for the motion picture *Amadeus* (1984), which he adapted from his own 1979 play. In it, Mozart overcomes the imperial courtiers' objection to his use of Beaumarchais's play—that it's not "elevated" enough[4]—by explaining that it's simply a comedy, and that opera can convey information in a way impossible on the stage. It ought to be a warning to the bewigged about what's coming, but of course it sails right over their powdered heads:

MOZART: In a play, if more than one person speaks at once . . . it's

---

3 Fear of Muslim slavers was the reason most medieval European cities weren't located on the coasts, as towns were in Roman times—they were situated on hilltop citadels to be defensible against the raiders.

4 Says Mozart: "*Oh elevated! Elevated! . . . The only thing a man should elevate is his doodle!*"

just noise. No one can understand a word. But with opera, with music.... With music you can have individuals all talking at the same
time. And it's not noise. It's a perfect harmony!

Musically speaking, that's true. Dramatically speaking, it's ten times true.
What's chaos on the theatrical stage becomes, in *Figaro*, a glorious, coherent ensemble of conflicting thoughts, desires, emotions, and objectives.
The second-act finale's septet is a paean not only to the power of opera,
but a vivid representation of democracy in action—count and countess,
barber and wife, the page boy, the lawyer, and more: all individuals, yet
all united in a common purpose. As Mozart notes earlier in the scene,
"Majesty, this is just a frolic. A piece about love...and it's new!" Of such
subterfuge is great art made.

Did Mozart understand what he had wrought? Mozart died just a
month short of his thirty-sixth birthday on December 5, 1791, so Louis
XVI outlived him. But *Figaro* has far outlived them both.

Figaro got a limited run at the Burgtheater, but it really took off after
its Prague premiere in December of 1786, a success so great that Mozart
was able to report that "...they do not talk about anything else here than—
Figaro. Nothing else is being played, blown, sung or whistled than—*Figaro*,
no opera attended than—*Figaro*. And forever *Figaro*! Certainly a great
honor for me!" From that moment, Prague's love affair with Mozart was
cemented, and nowhere else in Europe did he enjoy the same kind of
success and audience affection.

Indeed, Mozart was so popular in Prague that his next collaboration
with da Ponte, *Il dissoluto punito, ossia il Don Giovanni* (The Rake Punished, or, Don Giovanni), was commissioned for that city and performed
there in the fall of 1787. Based on the Don Juan legend, so often treated
before and since, the opera had an electric effect not only on its first
audiences but on the Romantic imagination; throughout the nineteenth
century, it was the most popular of the Mozart operas, with a daemonic
subject and a harrowing penultimate scene that greatly appealed to the
emerging Romantics' neo-Gothic sensibility.[5] In fact, the comic finale,

---

5 The Romantics' rediscovery of the Middle Ages had an electrifying effect on their imaginations. "I had intended to abandon myself to a life of the utmost leisure, as is in any case
essential when undergoing the exhausting regime of a cure.... With a book under my arm I
betook myself to the seclusion of the neighboring woods, where I would lie beside a brook

in which the survivors of the Stone Guest's capture of the Don and his dragging of the rakehell to perdition cheer the Don's demise and deliver the appropriate moral, was often cut.

As the century ended, the classicism of Mozart began to transform into the early Romanticism of Beethoven and Schubert. In France, Napoleon was undergoing his own transformation. His elevation to First Consul via a *coup d'état* on November 9, 1799—the date on the revolutionary calendar was the eighteenth of Brumaire[6]—was at first welcomed by democrats and anti-monarchists, including Beethoven, Haydn's former pupil, who was even then emerging as the leading composer of Europe. Beethoven had entitled his breakthrough symphony—the Third (1805)—"Buonaparte," but upon learning of the Little Corporal's ascendency to emperor a few months before the premiere, angrily scratched out the dedication and substituted: "to the memory of a great man."[7]

Beethoven's friend Ferdinand Ries, relates the scene:

> I was the first to tell him the news that Buonaparte had declared himself Emperor, whereupon he broke into a rage and exclaimed, "So he is no more than a common mortal! Now, too, he will tread under foot all the rights of Man, indulge only his ambition; now he will think himself superior to all men, become a tyrant!" Beethoven went to the table, seized the top of the title-page, tore it in half and threw it on the floor. The page had to be recopied, and it was only now that the symphony received the title *Sinfonia eroica.*

Did Napoleon know? Did he care? Does it even matter? The Napoleon–Beethoven relationship continues to resonate into our own age, viz. Anthony Burgess's underrated novel[8] *Napoleon Symphony: A Novel in*

---

communing with Titurel and Parzival in this strange and yet so intimately appealing poem of Wolfram. But soon the longing to create something of my own from what I found here became so strong that, although I had been warned against any stimulus of this kind while taking the waters of Marienbad, I had difficulty fighting off the impulse. This soon put me into a highly overwrought state of mind.... [I] ran like a madman to my quarters to put what was obsessing me on paper. This went on for several days, until the entire dramatic plan for Lohengrin had been set down in full detail." —Richard Wagner, *Mein Leben* (1880)

6 Inspiring Marx to write his 1852 essay on the class struggle, *The Eighteenth Brumaire of Louis Napoleon*, about the need to pulverize the existing social and political order.

7 Later in life, Beethoven apparently his changed his mind about Napoleon, and even considered dedicating the Mass In C Major, Op. 86, to the Emperor in 1810.

Four Movements (1974), which is structured to mirror the *Eroica*'s musical architecture, a feat that only a writer as brilliant and as musically well-educated as Burgess—he was also a prolific composer, as well as a linguist and translator—could have pulled off. The book is dedicated to Stanley Kubrick, who had directed the cinematic adaptation of Burgess's *A Clockwork Orange.*

Beethoven, like all the residents of Vienna, had to take shelter when French batteries were shelling the city in 1809; he hid in his brother Carl's basement with a pillow over his head in order to protect what was left of his hearing, which had started to fade in 1798 and was completely gone by 1816. In any case, Napoleon's subsequent fate, which has given the English language the concepts of "Elba," "the Hundred Days," and "Waterloo," is well known. So is the history of the *Eroica*, a landmark in the evolution of the symphonic form, at the time the biggest and most ambitious piece of its kind, which blew out the classical symphony's form and harmonic structure and made possible all subsequent works, through the magisterial symphonies of Anton Bruckner and Gustav Mahler.

The unlettered and the unmusical might argue that this is all coincidental, that the creative works of Beaumarchais, da Ponte, Mozart, and Beethoven did little or nothing to influence the course of world events; that they were, after all, mere entertainments, diversions from the serious business of revolution, continental war, and the Congress of Vienna. But they would be wrong. The sequence of events from Beaumarchais to the final defeat of Napoleon and the redrawing of the map of Europe is inextricably bound up with the intellectual and artistic ferment of the era.

In his short book *In Bluebeard's Castle: Some Notes Towards the Redefinition of Culture* (1971), George Steiner perceptively noted the impact that the Napoleonic era had on Europe's political and artistic psyches, and on its very sense of time. History that had once been merely a study of the past was now being *lived*, and creative artists like Beethoven and the Romantic poets were among the first to sense it:

> Expectations of progress, of personal and social enfranchisement
> …suddenly moved very close. The great metaphor of renewal, of the

---

8 To my mind, almost all of Burgess is underrated, especially his 1980 masterpiece *Earthly Powers*, which opens: "It was the afternoon of my eighty-first birthday, and I was in bed with my catamite when Ali announced that the archbishop had come to see me."

creation, as by a second coming of secular grace, of a just, rational city for man, took on the urgent drama of concrete possibility. The eternal "tomorrow" of utopian political vision became, as it were, Monday morning. We experience something of this dizzying sense of total possibility when reading the decrees of the *Convention* and of the Jacobin régime; injustice, superstition, poverty are to be eradicated *now*, in the next glorious hour. The world is to shed its worn skin a fortnight hence. In the grammar of Saint-Juste, the future tense is never more than moments away. If we seek to trace this irruption—it was that violent—of dawn into private sensibility, we need look only to Wordsworth's *Prelude* and to the poetry of Shelley...

That we have largely forgotten the political ramifications of artistic development is our loss. Like the statue of the Commendatore that comes to life near the end of *Don Giovanni*, the arts are often our very own Stone Guests, unwelcome visitors, perhaps, but still standing to remind us of the folly of our past actions and our congenital inability to heed their warnings. We may think, like the Don, that we are made of sterner stuff, and insouciantly invite the statue to join us for supper. It's only when we take his hand, however, that we, like the Don, can realize the full extent of our peril, and exclaim with him:

> DON GIOVANNI: What strange fear now assails my soul! Where do those flames of horror come from?
> CHORUS OF DEMONS: No horror is too dreadful for you! Come, there is worse in store!
> DON GIOVANNI: Who lacerates my soul? Who torments my body? What torment, oh me, what agony! What a Hell! What a terror!

"What fresh hell is this?" we sometimes ask ourselves as a bad situation deteriorates; as the solutions we apply demand yet more, and even worse, solutions; as a demonic chain reaction unleashes Hell itself. In retrospect, we can often look back and discover where we made our first misstep, when we first chose to reject wisdom—the wisdom of our mothers, perhaps, or of the previous generation, or of our entire civilization. Is it not still the merry month of Brumaire—the seventeenth, perhaps? Have not the old gods and old ways been deposed? Is not Caesar slain in the senate? Thus ever to tyrants and enemies of the people.

But hold—what is that, dimly viewed in the corner? Is it the Stone Guest, come back to claim a soul? Or is it our Fiery Angel, Madiel—creator, destroyer, sentinel, succubus, muse—holding aloft, like the Archangel Michael, the flaming sword that is at once warning and beacon, while declaiming the same cautionary words that Shakespeare put into the mouth of Marc Antony?

> *You all did love him once, not without cause:*
> *What cause withholds you then, to mourn for him?*
> *O judgment! thou art fled to brutish beasts,*
> *And men have lost their reason. Bear with me;*
> *My heart is in the coffin there with Caesar,*
> *And I must pause till it come back to me.*

We'd better figure it out, and quickly.

CHAPTER THIRTEEN

The final page of Bach's *Die Kunst der Fuge*, left incomplete at his death in 1750

O Magnum Mysterium
Why the West won

A mong the many discoveries and inventions of the West is the most fundamental one, which often goes unremarked today, although its ramifications are all around us, from the electrical grid to the air transportation system, to the computers we use: the ability to think complexly, to hold multiple, sometimes conflicting ideas and variables in one's head, and to create something new, but ordered and effective, out of their collision in, and collusion with, our imaginations.

Primitive societies lack this characteristic, which is why they remained, and in some case still remain, primitive. Certainly, most human societies have achieved some level of complex thought, whether in ornamental design, such as the Arabs, or in rhythmic complexity, such as the drumming of sub-Saharan Africa,[1] or the intricacies of court etiquette in Mandarin China or Imperial Japan. But few human societies, prior to the West at the end of the medieval period, managed to combine a rigorously intellectual

---

1 As mentioned earlier, in Caesar's time, the word "Africa" applied to principally to what we call today the country of Tunisia; in other words, the territory around Rome's destroyed enemy, Carthage. Via subsequent colonization, much of the North African coast was Romanized and Christianized; St. Augustine's city of Hippo was located in modern Algeria. The Vandals conquered the territory in the fourth century. It was reconquered for Byzantium by General Belisarius in 533, but finally fell to Muslim invaders in 697.

and systematic approach to artistic and scientific thought that has resulted in so much advancement over so short a period of time.[2]

As we saw in Chapter Six, the re-introduction of Aristotelian thought into the West via the Spanish Moors triggered an outpouring of creative thought, and one that has not yet run its course. It was as if someone had turned on a switch in the Western brain. Suddenly, it was not enough to think linearly, as the ancients had, or superstitiously, as the early Christians and Muslims had. Muslim intellectual curiosity, such as it was, eventually devolved—occasioned in part by military defeats in the sixteenth and seventeenth centuries—into a self-referential *ummah* in which the proper study of mankind was not mankind, as it became in the West, but the study of the Koran.[3]

Until the surprise attacks on the World Trade Center and the Pentagon in 2001, Islam never again won a significant victory against the West. Even today, its thirteen-centuries-long war against both Judaism and Christianity (for it is a religious war, especially as they see it), has been largely reduced to "lone wolf" outrages using mostly Western weapons, such as firearms and motorized vehicles.

Far more disturbing, however, is Islam's more recent tactic of cultural infiltration and replacement masquerading as "immigration." As Sweden and Germany have already experienced, few of the "immigrants" have any intention of assimilating or adopting their host countries' laws and mores; the wombs of their women will give them the victory they have sought since 1683.

Islam's effect on the countries it conquered in a burst of zealotry and bloodlust has been almost wholly disruptive. The Persians may have often been at Greek throats—and lost all the battles that mattered,

---

2 S. Frederick Starr's *Lost Enlightenment* makes a strong case for the people and culture of northeastern Persia between 800 and 1000 A.D. (the major cities of which were later destroyed by the Mongols and never really came back), which is what people refer to when they speak of an "Islamic" Golden Age. Although they wrote in Arabic—the international language of Islamdom, as Latin was for Christendom—they were almost all Persians from Herat, Merv, and elsewhere. The historical Omar Khayyam, litterateur, mathematician, astronomer, is an example.

3 The enormously influential *Incoherence of the Philosophers* by al-Ghazali (d. 1111), which attacked the scientific rationalism of Avicenna, argued that God's nature is unlimited and purely arbitrary. Contrast this with the Christian notion of God as both Logos and Good, which led via Aquinas to the theological justification of scientific inquiry.

including Salamis, Plataea, and Mycale—but they possessed a high culture of great literary, military, and scientific achievement until the Arab Muslim conquest of the Sassanid Empire, and the subordination of its Zoroastrian faith, beginning in the middle of the seventh century. The Shah of Iran's attempt to de-institutionalize Islam in Iran led to the coup by the Ayatollah Khomeini in 1979, which was at least tacitly supported by the pusillanimous Jimmy Carter administration, which viewed nearly every international development as a simulacrum of the American Civil Rights Movement. It remains one of the greatest foreign-policy blunders in American history.

A sensible Western response to Islam would emulate what worked against the Soviets: containment, but one much more rigorously conceived and enforced to include a near-total ban on technological transfer and severe limitations on emigration. Until it reforms itself to eliminate *sharia* supremacism and renounces what is a de facto policy of murder in Western lands, the Muslim world has little or nothing to offer the West. Western governments should make it clear that no further Muslim expansionism will be permitted. There is no rational reason for the cultural entity formerly known as Christendom to accept a single Muslim immigrant unless he—and it is almost always a "he" of military-service age—can be shown to possess useful Western skills, not to harbor anti-Western sentiments, not to have a criminal record or any infectious diseases, and not to be a burden on the public trust. Wahhabist Islam is not an "enrichment" the West needs, nor one it should desire.

In short, to conform exactly to the qualifications and personal qualities the immigration authorities at Ellis Island used to determine the suitability of immigrants to the United States of America. That this is even controversial, or subject to discussion, shows how far the West's self-esteem and commitment to moral principles have fallen.

Of course, given the enshrinement of "civil rights" as the *ne plus ultra* of governmental goodness, a sensible immigration policy is impossible. Islam's cultural-Marxist allies have been pushing open borders, the free movement of peoples, and one-worldism for decades; in Islam, they finally found the sheer raw numbers to make their dream possible. As long as the tidal wave of "migrants" continues to lack military weapons, the mostly young men of military age will not be seen for what they are—invaders—but instead as "refugees" seeking a "better life." And who can be against that? The hard questions—"refugees" (from what?); "migrants" (to where?); and "asylum seekers" (from what?)—are never asked.

Nevertheless, should Islam, in any of its manifestations, employ against the West the nuclear capacity it already has, it won't really matter whether the West's technological superiority can protect it. Lenin famously said that the capitalists would happily sell his Communists the rope with which to hang them. American and European commercial interests in the land of the "prophet" have ensured a comfortable Western lifestyle (a fantastic combination of Mercedes-Benz and BMW automobiles and the inventive male-gratifying sexual excesses so lovingly chronicled in *The Arabian Nights*) for the metastasizing numbers of Saudi "princes" in what they called the "Kingdom." A deployed "Islamic bomb" against New York, Washington, London, or Tel Aviv, would change everything.

Although the West has always been a pluralistic society—the cultural Marxist insult of "whiteness" has no basis in historical fact, other than as an accident of evolution, and those who profess not to see skin color are in fact those who see it most—it has always been, in the neutral sense of the word, discriminatory. It has prized inquiry over dogma (the troglodytic "Christian Right" is largely a figment of the cultural Marxist imagination), creativity over conformity, inventiveness over rote. At every important juncture of Western cultural history, Wagner's famous maxim—*Kinder, schafft Neues!*—has been applied, *con mucho gusto*. There is no eminent "university" in the West like Al-Azhar in Cairo, devoted almost entirely to the study of Koranic Islamic law; that way, to Western minds, lies intellectual stupefaction, entropy, and death.

Where did we get this notion?

From Aristotle. And Aquinas. And from all the intellectuals, scientists, and artists who followed them. The West understands—or at least used to—that there is no such thing as "sustainability." Stasis is not for the West. Neither are static-state utopias, administered and guided by Communism or National Socialism, or even the putative "end of history" triumph of liberal democracy, which lasted all of a decade between the fall of the Soviet Union and Islam's renewal of its long war against the West. For us, the notion of "sustainability" is an alien concept, for just as human beings are either growing or dying, so also is our most human of societies. Either a culture is moving forward—not in the "progressive" sense, but as exemplified by the voyages of discovery that marked European cultural and political expansion starting in the fifteenth century and which should continue in the future into outer space—or it is dying. Once a culture loses its crusading instinct, it dies. The one thing that Islam can teach us—remind us—is that a culture that no longer believes in its own foundational principles is as good as dead.

And now to something controversial.

Melody (monophony), harmony, polyphony. From the time of the troubadours and the *trouveres* of the Crusades, the advances in Western thought have not only been mirrored in our music, but occasioned by it, from Guillaume de Machaut, Josquin des Prez, and Pierre de la Rue, to Obrecht and Ockegham, to Palestrina to Johann Sebastian Bach. A popular song—e.g., *L'homme armé*—could become the subject of numerous medieval masses, not because of its secular origin (although that certainly helped, as the worshippers would respond to its familiarity), but because its implicit polyphonic structure could be successfully and inventively exploited by composers across Europe, leading to ever more complex and inventive ways of using the material.

Yes, Masses. Because the development of European polyphony, was like religious dogma itself, inspired by Aristotelian ideas of free inquiry and the teleological impulses of both Judaism and Christianity. Music, like faith, has to be headed *somewhere*. Our lives may be temporally constricted, but freedom of inquiry is not. As the scholar and writer David Goldman notes:

> Music begins with respiration and pulse, the inborn rhythms of human life. We may intensify these rhythms with percussive accents and electronic amplification and, through this intensification, achieve the momentary sort of exaltation that seems to buoy the audience at rock concerts. As [Pope] Benedict has written, this is the opposite of Christian worship: "It is the expression of elemental passions, and at rock festivals it assumes a cultic character, a form of worship, in fact, in opposition to Christian worship. People are, so to speak, released from themselves by the experience of being part of a crowd and by the emotional shock of rhythm, noise, and special lighting effects. However, in the ecstasy of having all their defenses torn down, the participants sink, as it were, beneath the elemental force of the universe."

We know, no matter what we do, that the rhythms of respiration and pulse will cease at the moment of death. But we do not know what eternity is. At best we can say what it isn't, as in Psalm 90:4, through poetic hyperbole: "For a thousand years in thy sight are but as yesterday when it is past, and as a watch in the night." Eternity manifests itself to us as an irruption of the divine into the temporal world, as a singularity, a moment that interrupts the procession of years and days, of systole and diastole.[4]

At the heart of all world music, of all world rhythm, of all world art, and therefore of every human activity, is the heart. The heart, we believe, is the repository of humanity's spiritual goodness, just as the head is its storehouse of knowledge; somewhere between the two comes wisdom. Without wisdom, there can be no rational or humanitarian politics. We speak of heart-stopping events, of heartless cruelty, of aching and broken hearts—all metaphors of the human condition that express the association of our hearts with our emotional essence.

In medieval music, the fundamental beat was the *tactus*, the basic beat of the resting human heart. This was nothing new, for all music originates as folk music, and folk music is something that arises spontaneously in all cultures, aligned in spirit, intent, and expression with the nature of the people who gave it birth. Everyone has a heart; everyone expresses his emotions slightly differently.

The challenge in Western art, as in its politics, is how to combine the heart with the head. Western painting is often organized around geometric forms. As we have seen, Géricault's painting *The Raft of the Medusa* is clearly composed of two triangles, one formed by the ship's mast on the left, the other by the human pyramid on the right. Movie scripts are constructed in a 1:2:1 arch form, with the long span of the second act equal to the lengths of the first and third combined.[5] Composers employ the architecture of a suspension bridge, as Bartók does in both his Fourth and Fifth string quartets, each one in five movements, whose movements in tempo mirror each other as follows: 1=5; 2=4; 3.

The trend toward formal complexity and hidden structural subtexts

---

4 "Sacred Music, Sacred Time," *First Things*, November, 2009.
5 Screenwriters tend to dread the vast expanse of Act Two, but it's what audiences know as "the movie"; the other two acts are the set-up and the payoff.

arose during the transition from the late Middle Ages into the Renaissance, and nowhere is it more evident than in music. The development of polyphony, in which two, three, four, or more voices (whether sung or instrumental) each has an independent existence and yet works together to create a harmonious whole, was one of the signal events in Western intellectual history, a mind- and horizon-expanding advance over the old musical forms. It challenged the mind to think along multiple parallel tracks, to work with a clear goal in sight that would be satisfying both emotionally and formally. It created a demand for mastery. It was also, politically, democratizing (as we have seen in the septet from Mozart's *Figaro*), although those effects would not be felt at the level of government until the eighteenth century.

Polyphony arose in the service of Christianity, as a way of enhancing and intensifying the religious experience. The melodies developed from the plainchant of the monks, which were tricked out with a second, accompanying, more ornamental melodic line; this was called *organum*, which took root at the Cathedral of Notre-Dame de Paris near the end of the twelfth century. Over the next few centuries, the motets of Machaut (fourteenth), the masses of Tomás Luis de Victoria, and the madrigals of Giovanni Pierluigi da Palestrina (sixteenth) spread across the Continent from France, the Lowlands, and Italy, and into the German lands.

And there, in the music of J. S. Bach (1685–1750), polyphony found its grand master. Bach was the great organizer of Western tonal music, establishing in his voluminous *oeuvre* the fundamentals of harmonic progression that would last through Wagner and into the early twentieth century. Bach demanded the regulated, or "tempered" claviers and keyboard instruments of his day, so that all twelve notes of the chromatic scale could be easily transposed from one key to another. This meant that clavichords, harpsichords, and the nascent pianoforte had to have their strings tempered away from the natural overtone series of each note (which would make them dissonant with each other) into something the Western ear could hear as a unity: that, in fact, was the point of Bach's famous *Well-Tempered Klavier*, which pianists and piano students alike still play today: twenty-four preludes and fugues in each of the twelve major and minor keys.

Near the end of his life, Bach decided to pour everything he knew about polyphony into *Die Kunst der Fuge* (The Art of the Fugue) which was left unfinished at his death. It's a strange work on many levels, a series of canons and fugues for two, three, or four voices, furthered by the fact we have no idea for which instrument, or which combination of instruments, he intended it—or even whether it was ever intended for performance at all. The work can be sung *a cappella*, without any instrumental accompaniment; played on the keyboard; or performed by a string quartet, or an even larger ensemble. One of its basic building blocks are the notes B-flat-A-C-B-natural, which in German musical notation spells out the name B-A-C-H. A crabbed series of semitones adjacent to each other in the scale, those four notes provide the cornerstone for all manner of polyphonic development. In its final "Contrapunctus," the piece does not end, but breaks off abruptly in the middle of a phrase—enigmatic, unfinished,[6] as if Bach was saying to future generations: take it from here. And they did: both Mozart and Beethoven owned private copies and no doubt consulted its principles regularly, even if only to break or expand upon them.

Think of *The Art of the Fugue* as the musical equivalent of Aquinas's similarly unfinished *Summa Theologica* and you won't be far wrong. Its effect on the Western way of thinking—not just in music, but in all aspects of European and, thus, American life—are incalculable, just as Aquinas's systematic way of thinking resonated across all fields, including science and faith, and not simply philosophy. The connecting thread between them is religion—Christianity. And therein lies some of the animosity of the atheist Left against not only Western faith but against Western culture itself, since the two are, unfortunately for them, inseparable. As Goldman notes: "The aesthetic implications of tonality changed music as profoundly as, for example, perspective in painting; the new technique enabled composers to depict Christian teleology in musical time.... The plasticity of musical time made possible by tonality, and the perception of the passage of time at multiple levels, gave Western music the capacity to evoke a sense of the sacred."[7]

The invention of tonality made possible a sense of *narrative* in music— an Aristotelean story with a beginning, middle, and an end that is going

6 One of Bach's composer sons, Carl Philipp Emanuel Bach, noted on the autograph manuscript: "*Über dieser Fuge, wo der Name B A C H im Contrasubject angebracht worden, ist der Verfasser gestorben.*" ("At the point where the composer introduces the name BACH in the countersubject to this fugue, the composer died.")
7 "The Divine Mathematics of Music," *First Things*, April 2012.

somewhere, and which exists independent of any texts. A ballad tells a story, usually strophically; the music may be charming, but our attention is on the words. Bach's sacred music, written for the Lutheran church, often tells an explicit, textual story, as with the monumental *St. Matthew Passion*, as dramatic a piece of religious theater as the eighteenth century ever produced. But so also does Bach's purely instrumental music, including the mighty organ works, such as the famous *Toccata and Fugue in D Minor*, the "*Brandenburg*" concertos, and the "*Goldberg*" *Variations* for keyboard.

The importance of this development to the Western psyche cannot be overestimated. Narrative stories are the way we impart moral messages in the present by engaging human curiosity about the future, often by means of the past. We create and tell stories so people will want to know what happens next, but the actual moral is what's happening *now*. Which is to say, the process of storytelling is as important as the message; it's no accident that we know it as the Hero's Journey, for his pilgrimage is one that we share whenever we read a book, watch a film, listen to a major symphonic work, or gaze at a painting. When, for example, an audience arrives along with the conductor and the orchestra at the end of, say, Richard Strauss's tone poem *Ein Heldenleben* (A Hero's Life), there is a sense of having completed a mighty expedition. The Heroic Narrative is the source of Western strength, pride, and accomplishment.

In order for a Narrative to be fully experienced, therefore, it must unfold *over time*; which is to say that even paintings can evoke a sense of time as well as physical space. It is not enough to simply blurt out the ending, in a kind of executive-summary version: Mimi dies at the end of *La bohème*; Bruce Willis has been dead all along in *The Sixth Sense*; the Jarndyce fortune evaporates into the hands of the lawyers at the end of *Bleak House*. We want to live the story with the characters, across time. Only in this way is the proper lesson patiently imparted—"This is the story of what a Woman's patience can endure, and what a Man's resolution can achieve"—and the artist's point made.

And yet, as we often hear, there is no time. The pace of modern life, it is said, is too fast in order to give up an hour to a Bruckner symphony, a couple of hours to *Rififi* or *Rashomon*, or several weeks to *The Magic Mountain*. Bollocks. We flatter ourselves if we think we have any less time to devote to the pursuits of the mind and the spirit than did, say, the ancient Greeks. The hoplite class of Athens could rely on a deadly, nearly annual war against either their fellow Greeks or the invading Persians as surely as they could count on the seasons or the tides. Many of them would die. And yet they produced Aeschylus, Sophocles, and Aristophanes; Aeschylus's epitaph mentions that he fought at Marathon, and says nothing about his plays or poetry.[8]

The famous "labor-saving" devices advertised as the housewife's best friends in the 1950s merely displaced women enough so that, after a brief period of putting their feet up before hubby and the kids came home, they were in the official labor force two decades later. The results, for whatever personal satisfaction some women may have gained by emulating men, were an effective halving of the family's per-capita income; the incurrence of additional expenses in the realm of child care, meals, etc.; and several generations of latchkey kids. As Henry Higgins wonders in *My Fair Lady*, "Why can't a woman be more like a man?" We now have our answer.

The pace of life, in any case, is relative. No doubt future generations will think we had it easy, with nothing to do except work desultorily at a nine-to-five government job, take annual leave, enjoy weekends and holidays off, and spend the evenings in front of giant flat-screen televisions half-watching network, cable, or satellite programming while eating take-out food delivered right to our doors. Such luxury! Such indolence!

What is meant is: we have no attention span. An attention span demands several things: native intelligence, an ability to discriminate among choices, an ability to follow along, a keen anticipation of the outcome, and, most important, a willingness to learn so that the moral is earned rather than delivered. This is precisely the opposite of what cultural Marxism wishes from its audiences. In attending a performance of Henze's *Raft of the Medusa* or any other didactic work of political propaganda, there is no doubt about which side one is supposed to root for; the Left claims to prize "nuance" in art, but almost never employs it. Instead, it calls "flawed" any argument with which it does not agree; that it contains hidden dangers to the unwary; and that the pure Leftist soul might possibly be corrupted by it.

By contrast, the ending of any real work of temporal art is only its beginning. Answering the question "what happened?" is easy. Under-

8 "Aeschylus, the Athenian, Euphorion's son, is dead. This tomb in Gela's cornlands covers him. His glorious valour the hallowed field of Marathon could tell, and the longhaired Persians had knowledge of it."

standing what it meant is hard. Understanding is a process, not a punch line. Understanding is growth. Understanding is the first step to changing the way we apprehend and think about the world. It may even involve our changing our minds. No wonder it is so dangerous to the Left. That the process emerged out of Christianity, and the Judeo-Christian tradition of inquiry, only enrages the cultural Marxists, and makes them more determined than ever to stamp it out.

Hence the century-long campaign to sever the arts from politics and isolate them in an abstract entertainment ghetto. Both sides are guilty. When it does not see them as frivolous and inconsequential, the contemporary Right views the arts with deep suspicion, as a plaything and propaganda tool of the Left. The Left, meanwhile, has explicitly employed the arts for propaganda purposes and, in some quarters, continues to view them as a tool for proselytizing the masses, but would prefer that nobody noticed. Both sides are, to a large extent, stuck in the twentieth century, the century in which politics superseded everything else in the global thrashing about that followed the collapse of European cultural and political hegemony after World War I.

As I have argued above, the artistic trends of the immediate pre-war period clearly pointed with alarm at the catastrophe that was approaching. Therefore, let us now consider the second sequential arc from our Introduction.

Count Gobineau–Father Jahn–Wagner–World War I–
Communism and National Socialism–Hitler.

If anything, this is even less disputable than the *Figaro* connection. The development of race-related theories was ongoing throughout the nineteenth century, especially as Europeans began to come into contact with (to them) exotic peoples and places as a result of exploration. Europeans had been colonizing other lands since the late fifteenth century, not only in the newly discovered Americas but in Asia and on the Indian subcontinent. The Portuguese had begun trade with Japan as early as 1543, and the Dutch a few decades later (the insular Japanese, who severely restricted the traders's presence in their islands, call this the *Nanban,* or "southern barbarian," period); the Portuguese also founded a colony at Goa, on the west coast of India, in 1505, which lasted until 1961. To impute to "racism" what was largely a matter of healthy curiosity and seafaring knowhow is a contemporary canard, designed to "question the motives" of the European explorers, as if they set out with malice aforethought in order to subjugate the brown and black peoples of the world.

Where the Europeans were indeed morally culpable, though, is in the development of literally racist biological theories some of them derived from their travels. Gobineau got the ball rolling with the publication in 1853 of his *Essai sur l'inégalité des races humaines* (Essay on the Inequality of the Human Races), which extrapolated from a European perspective a theory of innate human worth—something explicitly anti-Christian, by the way. Much as the Leftists do today, Gobineau conflated "European" with "white," and deduced the inequality of the "yellow" and "black" races accordingly.

Friedrich Ludwig "Father" Jahn, while inculcating the Germans with his notions of physical fitness—his exercise movement's motto was *"frisch, fromm, fröhlich, frei"* ("fresh, pious, cheerful, free")—transplanted Gobineau's theories to Germany, where they, alas, found rich soil. In his book *Metapolitics: the Roots of the Nazi Mind*, Peter Viereck calls Jahn "the first storm trooper," and notes that it was but a short step from the eighteenth-century linguistic and political nationalism of Johann Gottfried Herder—Herder mistakenly thought that nationalism would lead to pacifism—to Jahn and thence to Hitler and National Socialism:

> The gradual stages of this downward transition should not be
> slurred over as negligible nuances. The descent inside Germany
> appears in three distinct stages: from the literary romantics down
> to the active leader Jahn; from Jahn down to the racial determinism
> and Aryan cult of Wagner and Houston Chamberlain; from the
> talkers Wagner and Chamberlain down to the rock bottom of the
> active leader Hitler.

Contra Herder, German nationalism, combined with German envy over the burgeoning empires of the British, French, Dutch, and other lesser European powers, plus a "rational" belief in alliances and ententes as inhibitors of international conflict, ended in disaster. The War to End All Wars wound up ending the monarchies of Europe, either immediately or eventually. The gods that had shepherded the European peoples from the end of the Roman Empire to the rise of the nation-states had failed, and new gods in the form of Communism and National Socialism rose up in their place.

The Communists were directly responding to the Marxist challenge of capturing an industrial society and its means of production in the name of the "people." The National Socialists and the Italian Fascists—Mussolini was expelled from the Italian Socialist Party for his radicalism—both rejected Communism in favor of a socialized military-industrial complex, of the kind president Eisenhower warned Americans against in his farewell address in January, 1961, under central governmental control. This preserved the illusion of capitalism and enriched the corporate chiefs, for a time, without the actual necessity of it. And so the two sides fought it out, first in the streets of the dying Weimar Republic, a battle the National Socialists won, and later at Stalingrad, which put paid to Hitler's dream of *Lebensraum*.

Both sides, however, believed in the most pernicious doctrine of cultural Marxism, still routinely articulated today as if it were some sort of magic incantation: a sense that "history" was on their side. This fantastic notion derives from the Hegelian-Marxist belief in history as an abstract, almost sentient, force akin to the old notion of Destiny, but with a bastardized Christian teleological impulse. Indeed, the entire Leftist notion of "progress" and its political expression, "progressivism," stems from it. An "arc" that "bends toward justice" is the next best thing to God.

The obvious derivation of this concept, from both the spirituality of Christianity and the rationalism of the Enlightenment—a Deity as the great Watchmaker in the sky, overseeing the orderly ticking of the universe—should be at once obvious. Given the Leftist fondness for Darwin's theory of natural selection and of the origin of species, this is an odd, contradictory theory for atheists to hold. But, to quote the Emperor in *Amadeus*, there it is.

And yet, men need gods, perhaps even a God. And whether He is called Zeus or Jupiter or Yahweh or Hashem or Allah or God the Father or Jesus the Christ or Dialectical Materialism, gods we shall have. In the end, especially when death comes to call, most atheists accept Pascal's Wager and get their bets down accordingly.

Mankind also hates gods. We resent them for their influences in the fortunes of men, even as we try to appease and propitiate them. From the Greeks to our own time, Western history is partly about worship and partly about the resentment that attends enforced worship. The dynamic between the two impulses is what gives us our *Schwung*—our cultural pulse, our social intensity, our societal momentum.

And so, at the end of *The Art of the Fugue*, Bach breaks off in mid-phrase. Are the contrapuntal forces he unleashed still echoing and inspiring? Or have we finally answered Lukács's question, "Who will save us from Western culture?" with Pogo's famous aphorism, "We have met the enemy and he is us"?

Caspar David Friedrich, *Two Men Contemplating the Moon*, 1819

From Erinyes to Eumenides

The way forward might just be backward

Among the first and most striking images in Western literature is the opening of Aeschylus's play *Agamemnon*: a Watchman sits, "propped up on one arm," at his post in the hour before dawn, looking eastward, faithfully awaiting, as he has for ten long years, news from the Trojan front. Suddenly, there is light in the distance, drawing ever nigher. Is it the rising sun? Or is it the long-awaited signal torches, finally fired with the thrilling news that "Troy is taken," and of the master of the House of Atreus's return?

This book opened with Robert Fagles's translation of the Chorus's resonant question. Here is another version, this one by E. D. A. Morshead:

Behold, throughout the city wide
Have the swift feet of Rumour hied
Roused by the joyful flame:
But is the news they scatter, sooth?
Or haply do they give for truth
Some cheat which heaven doth frame?

Is this not one of the central questions of our existence: is the news good or bad? Are the signal fires deceptive? Are the gods playing with us, arousing our hopes only to dash them again, as their whim takes them? Is it "some cheat," framed by Heaven? Or have we finally encountered Truth?

For thousands of years, our artists, writers, thinkers, philosophers, scientists, and politicians have grappled with these thorny issues, responding to them in a multiplicity of ways, including empirical measurement and the use of the creative imagination. Neither is necessarily better or more accurate; the duality of head and heart will continue as long as the human being does. What I have tried to do in these pages is restore something of their balance, which for decades has tipped toward scientific empiricism divorced from artistic spirituality.

Humanity cannot exist without the Light. Light allows us to see. Light brings warmth, and warmth allows us to flourish, along with every other living thing. Light brings life itself, while Satan, Sin, and Death dwell in darkness. When, in John 14:6, Jesus says "I am the Way, the Truth, and the Life," he—or the evangelist; we are always free to choose between the historical Jesus, the mythological Jesus, or the literary Jesus; what we are not free to do is ignore the resonance of the words—is employing a metaphor with meaning for all ages.

As I hope I have also shown, the interaction between the Light and the Darkness is an essential aspect of our common humanity, and one that artists are uniquely equipped to interpret. Our species's taste for the dark side, shared by no other animal, is not only not regrettable, it is vital in order for us to come to the Light; "that is to say of knowing good by evil." When our false gods come to us, they come in the dark, in the black nights of our souls, in the hope that, in bleakest despair, we will listen to them.

Mahler's titanic (there really is no other word for it) Eighth Symphony—the "Symphony of a Thousand," referring to the number of performers in the chorus and orchestra an optimal performance could require—opens with the Latin hymn *"Veni, creator spiritus."* The work was originally conceived to be about the birth of Eros, then the "Creation by Eros." (Like Elgar's "Dorabella" cipher, it is about Love.) It concludes with a setting of Goethe's *Faust*: not from Part One, which is the popular story we all know, or think we know, but with the final scene of the much-thornier and rarely performed Part Two, and concludes with the most famous, and most potent, line in Goethe's masterpiece: *"Das Ewig-Weibliche zieht uns hinan"*—The Eternal Feminine draws us ever onward. So it is about Eros as well after all, but a love that transcends the profane and becomes, in its perfection, profoundly sacred.

The history of our art reveals, and constantly revisits, the norms of Western culture. But no matter how "transgressive" we might wish to be, the fundamental things apply: the relationship of mankind to God; the physical and spiritual bond between men and women, and its absolute primacy in the world of human creation; and the need for heroes. Iconoclasm comes and goes, often literally, but it must be seen as an aberration, the yeast in the ferment of history, if we are to have faith in our culture, our civilization, and our future; it cannot be the norm. Likewise with revolutionaries, manqué and otherwise. We must learn to distinguish between those who are the fulfillment of Western foundational principles, such as the men who wrote the Declaration of Independence and the American Constitution, whose revolution was against their own, and our, imperfection; and those whose transient "truths" have ended up, like Marx himself, on the ash heap of history, no matter how many icons they smash along the way to the boneyard.

History, therefore, is neither an arc nor a plot. Neither "his story" nor "her story." It is our story.

After the *Sturm und Drang* of the *Oresteia*, after all the blood and vengeance and guilt, the trilogy ends on a pre-Christian note of forgiveness, of a world restored, with the transformation of the Furies into the Eumenides, as the Women of Athens declaim the final chorus:

> *With loyalty we lead you, proudly go,*
> *Night's childless children, to your home below!...*
> *Pass hitherward, ye powers of Dread,*
> *With all your former wrath allayed,*
> *Into the heart of this loved land...*

Let holy hands libations bear,
And torches' sacred flame.
All-seeing Zeus and Fate come down
To battle fair for Pallas' town!

All the tropes of Western civilization are there, present at its creation, in 458 B.C.: the childless children of the night (what music they make), the bravery in the face of dread and danger, the healing power of justice and forgiveness, and, above all, the light of the sacred flame, borne by the eternal feminine, to illuminate the conflict between reason and unreason that is Man's endless and unwavering lot—to provide for us a beacon, an inspiration, and a goal.

That this comes at the very beginning of Western civilization, not its end, ought to tell us something. The battle fair for Pallas's town continues. We have our guides, if only we will heed them.

BIBLIOGRAPHY

THE FIERY ANGEL BIBLIOGRAPHY

Epic of Gilgamesh, ca. 2100 B.C.

Homer, *Iliad, ca.* 8th Century B.C.

Homer, *Odyssey, ca.* 8th Century B.C.

Aeschylus, *Oresteia,* 458 B.C.

Aristophanes, *Lysistrata,* 411 B.C.

Plato, *Republic, ca.* 380 B.C.

Aristotle, *Metaphysics ca.* 4th Century B.C.

Aristotle, *Nichomachean Ethics, ca.* 4th Century B.C.

Aristotle, *Poetics, ca.* 4th Century B.C.

Aristotle, *Politics, ca.* 4th Century B.C.

Julius Caesar, *Commentaries on the Gallic War,* 58–49 B.C.

Virgil, *Aeneid,* 29–19 B.C.

Tacitus, *Annals, ca.* 14–68 A.D.

Dante, *Inferno,* 14th century A.D.

Sébastien Mamerot, *Expeditions to Outremer, ca.* 1474

William Shakespeare, *The Tragedy of Julius Caesar, ca.* 1599

John Milton, *Areopagitica,* 1644

John Milton, *Paradise Lost,* 1667–1674

Johann Sebastian Bach, *The Well-Tempered Clavier,* 1722–42

John Gay, with music by Johann Christoph Pepusch, *The Beggar's Opera,* 1728

Johann Sebastian Bach, *The Art of the Fugue, ca.* 1751

Jean-Jacques Rousseau, *The Social Contract,* 1762

Pierre Beaumarchais, *The Marriage of Figaro,* 1778

Wolfgang Amadeus Mozart, *The Abduction from the Seraglio,* 1782

Wolfgang Amadeus Mozart, *La nozze de Figaro,* 1786

Wolfgang Amadeus Mozart, *Don Giovanni,* 1787

Wolfgang Amadeus Mozart, *Così fan tutte,* 1790

Thomas Paine, *Rights of Man,* 1791

Francis Barrett, *The Magus,* 1801

Ludwig van Beethoven, Symphony No. 3, 1803–04

Ludwig van Beethoven, *Fidelio,* 1805

Johann Wolfgang von Goethe, *Faust, Part One,* 1808

Friedrich Overbeck, *Italia und Germania*, 1811–28

Lord Byron, *Childe Harold's Pilgrimage*, 1812–18

Gioachino Rossini, *L'Italiana in Algeri*, 1813

Gioachino Rossini, *Il turco in Italia*, 1814

Percy Bysshe Shelley, "The Hymn to Intellectual Beauty," 1816

Mary Shelley, *Frankenstein; or, The Modern Prometheus*, 1818

Percy Bysshe Shelley, *Ozymandias*, 1818

John Keats, "The Poet" (A Fragment), 1818

Théodore Géricault, *The Raft of the Medusa*, 1818–1819

Lord Byron, "Fragment of a Novel," 1819

Johann Wolfgang von Goethe, *Faust, Part Two*, 1832

Richard Wagner, *Faust Overture*, 1839–55

Aloysius Bertrand, *Gaspard de la Nuit*, 1842

Richard Wagner, *The Flying Dutchman*, 1843

Richard Wagner, *Tannhauser*, 1845

Richard Wagner *Lohengrin*, 1848

Giuseppe Verdi, *Rigoletto*, 1851

Franz Liszt, *A Faust Symphony in three character pictures*, 1857

Charles Baudelaire, *Les Fleurs du mal*, 1857

Charles Darwin, *On the Origin of Species*, 1859

Wilkie Collins, *The Woman in White*, 1859

Baudelaire, Le *spleen de Paris*, 1862

Matthew Arnold, "Thyrsis," 1865

Richard Wagner, *Tristan und Isolde*, 1865

Richard Wagner, *Der Ring des Niebelungen*, 1876

One Thousand and One Nights, translation by Richard Burton, 1885

Ulysses S. Grant, *The Personal Memoirs of Ulysses S. Grant*, 1885

Victor Hugo, *La Fin de Satan*, 1886

Rimbaud, "Parade," from *Illuminations*, 1886

Nikolai Rimsky-Korsakov, *Scheherazade*, 1888

Andrew Lang, *The Blue Fairy Book*, 1889

Bram Stoker, *Dracula*, 1897

Maurice Ravel, *Gaspard de la nuit*, 1908

Valery Bryusov, *The Fiery Angel*, 1908

Charles Ives, *The Unanswered Question*, 1908

Richard Strauss, *Elektra*, 1909

Igor Stravinsky, *The Firebird*, 1910

Béla Bartók, *Bluebeard's Castle*, 1911

Igor Stravinsky, *Petrouchka*, 1911

Richard Strauss, *Der Rosenkavalier*, 1911

Richard Strauss, *Die Frau ohne Schatten*, 1911–1917

Richard Strauss, *Ariadne auf Naxos*, 1912

Igor Stravinsky, *The Rite of Spring*, 1913

Gustav Holst, *The Planets*, 1914–16

Igor Stravisnky, *L'Histoire du soldat*, 1918

Béla Bartók, *The Miraculous Mandarin*, 1918–24

Edward Elgar, Cello Concerto (Op. 85), 1919

Maurice Ravel, *La valse*, 1919–20

F. W. Murnau (director), *Nosferatu*, 1922

Thomas Mann, *The Magic Mountain*, 1924

Erich Maria Remarque, *All Quiet on the Western Front*, 1928

Tod Browning (director), *Dracula*, 1931

Merian C. Cooper & Ernest B. Schoedsack (directors), *King Kong*, 1933

Dmitri Shostakovich, *Lady Macbeth of the Mtsensk District*, 1934

Johan Huizinga, *Homo Ludens*, 1939

Jacques Barzun, *Darwin, Marx, Wagner*, 1941

Michael Curtiz (director), *Casablanca*, 1942

Jean Cocteau (director), *La Belle et la Bête*, 1946

Ernst Cassirer, *Sprache und Mythos*, 1946

Sergei Prokofiev, *The Fiery Angel*, 1955

John Frankenheimer (director), *The Manchurian Candidate*, 1962

Roman Polanski (writer and director), *Rosemary's Baby*, 1968

George Steiner, *In Bluebeard's Castle: Some Notes Towards the Redefinition of Culture*, 1971

Paul Fussell, *The Great War and Modern Memory*, 1975

Peter Schaffer, *Amadeus*, 1979

William Styron, *Sophie's Choice*, 1979

Allan Bloom, *The Closing of the American Mind*, 1987

Francis Ford Coppola (director), *Bram Stoker's Dracula*, 1992

Francis Fukuyama, *The End of History and the Last Man*, 1992

Samuel Huntington, *The Clash of Civilizations*, 1996

THE DEVIL'S PLEASURE PALACE BIBLIOGRAPHY

Sophocles, *Oedipus Rex*, 429 B.C.

Marcus Aurelius, *Meditations*, 161–180 A.D.

Augustine of Hippo, *Enchiridion, ca.* 420

Boethius, *The Consolation of Philosophy, ca.* 524

The Song of Roland, ca. 1090

Christopher Marlowe, *Doctor Faustus, ca.* 1593

William Shakespeare, *Hamlet, ca.* 1599–1602

John Milton, *Areopagitica*, 1644

John Milton, *Paradise Lost*, 1667–1674

Johann Sebastian Bach, *Goldberg Variations*, 1741

Johann Wolfgang von Goethe, *The Sorrows of Young Werther*, 1774

Immanuel Kant, *Critique of Pure Reason*, 1781

Wolfgang Amadeus Mozart, *La Clemenza di Tito*, 1781

Johann Wolfgang von Goethe, "Erlkönig," 1782

Antonio Salieri, *Prima la musica e poi le parole*, 1786

Wolfgang Amadeus Mozart, *Don Giovanni*, 1787

Wolfgang Amadeus Mozart, *The Magic Flute*, 1791

Francisco Goya, Los caprichos, 1797–98

William Blake, *The Great Red Dragon and the Woman Clothed in Sun with the Sun, ca.* 1805

Johann Wolfgang von Goethe, *Faust, Part One*, 1808

Franz Schubert, "Erlkönig," 1815

Ludwig van Beethoven, *Diabelli Variations*, 1819–1823

Carl Maria von Weber, *Der Freischütz*, 1821

Lord Byron, "January 22, Missolonghi," 1824

Frédéric Chopin, Variations on "Là ci darem la mano," Op. 2, 1827

Giacomo Meyerbeer, *Robert le diable*, 1831

Johann Wolfgang von Goethe, *Faust, Part Two*, 1832

Heinrich Maschner, *Hans Heiling*, 1832

Hector Berlioz, *Symphonie Fantastique*, 1833

Richard Wagner, *The Flying Dutchman*, 1843

Karl Marx, *A Contribution to the Critique of Hegel's Philosophy of Right*, 1844

Karl Marx, *Theses on Feuerbach*, 1845

Friedrich Engels and Karl Marx, *The Communist Manifesto*, 1848

Richard Wagner, *Das Kunstwerk der Zukunft*, 1849

Karl Marx, *The Eighteenth Brumaire of Louis Napoleon*, 1851–52

Arrigo Boito, *Mefistophele*, 1868

Lewis Carroll, *Through the Looking-Glass, and What Alice Found There*, 1872

Richard Wagner, *Der Ring des Niebelungen*, 1876

Arthur Conan Doyle, *A Study in Scarlet*, 1887

Franz Schubert, "Der Teufels Lustschloß," 1879

Richard Wagner, *Parsifal*, 1882

Giacomo Puccini, *Le Villi*, 1883

Anton Bruckner, Symphony No. 8 in C Minor, 1887/1890

Nietzsche, *The Case of Wagner*, 1888

Richard Strauss, *Tod un Verklärung*, 1888–89

Pietro Mascagni, *Cavalleria rusticana*, 1889

Friedrich Nietzsche, *Nietzsche contra Wagner*, 1895

Claude Debussy, *Pelléas et Mélisande*, 1898

Richard Strauss, *Ein Heldenleben*, 1898

Arnold Schönberg, *Verklärte Nacht*, 1899

G. K. Chesterton, Father Brown stories, 1910–36

Alban Berg, *Wozzeck*, 1914–22

Franz Kafka, *The Metamorphosis*, 1915

Lytton Strachey, *Eminent Victorians*, 1918

Franz Kafka, *In the Penal Colony*, 1919

James Joyce, *Ulysses*, 1922

Sinclair Lewis, *Babbitt*, 1922

George Bernard Shaw, *Back to Methuselah*, 1922

Ferrucio Busoni, *Doktor Faust*, 1924

Giacomo Puccini, *Turandot*, 1924

Thomas Mann, *The Magic Mountain*, 1924

Franz Kafka, *The Trial*, 1925

Alban Berg, *Lyric Suite*, 1925–26

Franz Kafka, *The Castle*, 1926

Wilhelm Reich, *The Function of the Orgasm*, 1927

H. P. Lovecraft, *The Call of Cthulhu*, 1928

G. K. Chesterton, *The Thing*, 1929

Robert Graves, *Good-Bye to All That*, 1929

Arnold Schoenberg, *Lulu*, 1929–35

Arnold J. Toynbee, *A Study of History*, 1934–61

Alban Berg, *Violin Concerto*, 1935

Erich Fromm, *Escape from Freedom*, 1941

Richard Strauss, *Capricio*, 1941

Peter Viereck, *Metapolitics: The Roots of the Nazi Mind*, 1941

Michael Curtiz (director), *Casablanca*, 1942

Max Horkheimer, *Eclipse of Reason*, 1947

Thomas Mann, *Doctor Faustus*, 1947

Ludwig von Mises, *Bureaucracy*, 1948

Richard Strauss, *Four Last Songs*, 1948

Theodor Adorno, *Philosophy of New Music*, 1949

Joseph Campbell, *The Hero with a Thousand Faces*, 1949

George Orwell, *Nineteen Eighty-Four*, 1949

Theodor Adorno, *Minima Moralia: Reflections on a Damaged Life*, 1951

Fred Zinneman (director), *High Noon*, 1952

László Benedek (director), *The Wild One*, 1953

Allen Ginsberg, "Howl," 1954–55

Eric Hoffer, *The Passionate State of Mind*, 1955

Herbert Marcuse, *Eros and Civilization*, 1955

Theodor Adorno, "Music and Language," 1956

Igor Stravinsky, *Agon*, 1957

William Empson, *Milton's God*, 1961

Stanley Kubrick (director), *Dr. Strangelove*, 1964

Herbert Marcuse, *One-Dimensional Man*, 1964

Leo Strauss, *The City and Man*, 1964

Hans Werner Henze, *Der junge Lord*, 1965

Herbert Marcuse, Barrington Moore Jr., and Robert Paul Wolff, *A Critique of Pure Tolerance*, 1965

Michelangelo Antonioni (director), *Blowup*, 1966

Hannah Arendt, *Men in Dark Times*, 1968

Saul Alinsky, *Rules for Radicals*, 1971

Francis Ford Coppola (director), *The Godfather*, 1972

Herbert Marcuse, *Counterrevolution and Revolt*, 1972

Roman Polanski (director), *Chinatown*, 1974

Martin Scorcese (director), *Taxi Driver*, 1976

Tom Wolfe, *Mauve Gloves & Madmen, Clutter & Vine*, 1976

Oliver Stone (co-writer and director), *Wall Street*, 1987

Paul Johnson, *Intellectuals*, 1988

Friedrich Hayek, *The Fatal Conceit: The Errors of Socialism*, 1988

Ethan Coen and Joel Coen (writers and directors), *Miller's Crossing*, 1990

Camille Paglia, *Sexual Personae*, 1990

Stephen Sondheim, *Assassins*, 1990

P. J. O'Rourke, *Give War a Chance*, 1992

Steven Spielberg (director), *Saving Private Ryan*, 1998

Jack Miles, *Christ: A Crisis in the Life of God*, 2001

William S. Lind, *Political Correctness: A Short History of an Ideology*, 2004

Tom Wolfe, *I Am Charlotte Simmons*, 2004

James Piereson, *Camelot and the Cultural Revolution: How the Assassination of John F. Kennedy Shattered Liberalism*, 2007

ACKNOWLEDGEMENTS

The author would like to thank Bill Walsh for his perceptive reading of the manuscript, and for his invaluable suggestions, deletions, and elisions in the interest of clarity and accuracy; all errors of fact and interpretation are exclusively the author's. Also thanks to Cristina Concepcion, my agent at Don Congdon Associates, for her invaluable help with both text and illustrations; Roger Kimball, publisher of Encounter Books whose faith in the Devil has been rewarded with this Angel, and editor Ben Riley; and to all those who helped launch *The Devil's Pleasure Palace* upon publication in 2015, including Michael Finch of the David Horowitz Freedom Center, Pete Peterson and Matthew Peterson at Pepperdine University, Dr. John Lenczowski and Mackubin Owens of the Institute of World Politics, Jay Nordlinger and Kathryn Jean Lopez at *National Review*; photographer Peter Duke, David Savage, John O'Sullivan and the Danube Institute in Budapest, the late Milt Rosenberg, Mark Levin, Dennis Prager, Hugh Hewitt, and most especially Austin Ruse, whose advocacy brought the book to widespread attention in Washington, D.C., where it has been read in the White House, the Supreme Court, Congress, and at the National Security Council.

INDEX

Page numbers followed by *n* indicate notes.